P9-CAR-288

Literal Meaning

According to the dominant position among philosophers of language today, we can legitimately ascribe determinate contents (such as truth-conditions) to natural language *sentences*, independently of what the speaker actually means. This view contrasts with that held by ordinary language philosophers fifty years ago: according to them, *speech acts*, not sentences, are the primary bearers of content. François Recanati argues for the relevance of this controversy to the current debate about semantics and pragmatics. Is 'what is said' (as opposed to merely implied) determined by linguistic conventions, or is it an aspect of 'speaker's meaning'? Do we need pragmatics to fix truth-conditions? What is 'literal meaning'? To what extent is semantic composition a creative process? How pervasive is context-sensitivity? Recanati provides an original and insightful defence of 'Contextualism', and offers an informed survey of the spectrum of positions held by linguists and philosophers working at the semantics/pragmatics interface.

FRANÇOIS RECANATI is a Research Director at the Institut Jean-Nicod (CNRS, Paris). He has published many papers and several books on the philosophy of language and mind, including *Meaning and Force* (Cambridge, 1987), *Direct Reference* (Blackwell, 1993), and *Oratio Obliqua, Oratio Recta* (MIT Press, 2000). He is also co-founder and past President of the European Society for Analytic Philosophy.

Literal Meaning

François Recanati

Institut Jean-Nicod, Paris

CAMBRIDGE
UNIVERSITY PRESS

P
325
.R344
2004

PUBLISHED BY THE PRESS SYNDICATE OF THE UNIVERSITY OF CAMBRIDGE
The Pitt Building, Trumpington Street, Cambridge, United Kingdom

CAMBRIDGE UNIVERSITY PRESS
The Edinburgh Building, Cambridge, CB2 2RU, UK
40 West 20th Street, New York, NY 10011–4211, USA
477 Williamstown Road, Port Melbourne, VIC 3207, Australia
Ruiz de Alarcón 13, 28014 Madrid, Spain
Dock House, The Waterfront, Cape Town 8001, South Africa

http://www.cambridge.org

© François Recanati 2004

This book is in copyright. Subject to statutory exception and to the provisions of relevant
collective licensing agreements, no reproduction of any part may take place without the
written permission of Cambridge University Press.

First published 2004

Printed in the United Kingdom at the University Press, Cambridge

Typeface Times 10/12 pt.   *System* LATEX 2_ε [TB]

A catalogue record for this book is available from the British Library

Library of Congress cataloguing-in-publication data
Recanati, François, 1952–
Literal meaning / François Recanati.
        p.   cm.
Includes bibliographical references and index.
ISBN 0 521 79246 0 (hardback) – ISBN 0 521 53736 3 (paperback)
1. Semantics.   2. Semantics (Philosophy).   3. Pragmatics.   I. Title.
P325.R344   2003   401′.43 – dc21   2003051475

ISBN 0 521 79246 0 hardback
ISBN 0 521 53736 3 paperback

52133030

Contents

Acknowledgments

This book started its life as a series of lectures at the University of California, Berkeley, in 1994. Those who attended my graduate seminar in philosophy that year were so passionately involved in discussing the foundational issues I had raised that we all retain wonderful memories of those weeks of continuing debate. (Or at least, I do.) The most active debaters were, undoubtedly, Herman Cappelen and Josh Dever on the student side, and John Searle and Stephen Neale on the faculty side. I am greatly indebted to the four of them for those valuable and exciting discussions.

The second major step was taken when Professor Kunihiko Imai, of Gakushuin University, invited me to present my views on the semantics/pragmatics interface during a special workshop which took place in Tokyo on 30 September 2001. For that workshop I prepared a long talk which, I soon realized, could easily be expanded into a book. A couple of years earlier I had contracted with Cambridge University Press for a book on literal meaning. (The original title was 'Context and Content', but Robert Stalnaker published a collection of papers under that title in 1999, so I had to find something else.) I decided to use the Tokyo presentation as the nucleus for that book. I am grateful to Professor Imai for the invitation, and for the discussions which took place during the workshop. I also benefited from insightful comments by Yuji Nishiyama, Haruhiko Yamaguchi and Seiji Uchida.

When the book was well under way the department of philosophy of the University of Granada (Spain), in charge of the thirteenth Inter-University Workshop on Philosophy and Cognitive Science to be held in February 2003, decided to invite me as main speaker and to organize the workshop around my work. I was supposed to give three talks during the three days of the workshop. I chose to devote the three of them to the Literalism/Contextualism controversy, which is the topic of this book. This provided me with a welcome opportunity for testing my new ideas; an opportunity for which I wish to thank Maria José Frápolli, Esther Romero and Belén Soria, as well as the SEFA (Sociedad Española de Filosofía Analítica) in cooperation with which the inter-university workshops are organized.

During the past ten years, I have had many occasions for discussing those issues with the fifteen to twenty philosophers and linguists who regularly gather in conferences on the semantics/pragmatics distinction, contribute to the same issues of the same journals, and so on. For fear of forgetting someone, I will not list them individually here, but I thank them collectively; they know who they are. Two persons in that crowd deserve special thanks: Robyn Carston, who provided detailed, chapter-by-chapter comments on a first version of the book; and Jason Stanley, whose systematic defence of the positions I attack provided a helpful and timely challenge. I am also grateful to my students and colleagues in Paris for numerous discussions which shaped my thinking on those topics.

I have used materials from previously published or forthcoming articles in many chapters. The relevant papers are: 'The Pragmatics of What is Said', in *Mind and Language* 4 (1989), 295–329; 'Contextualism and Anti-Contextualism in the Philosophy of Language', in Savas Tsohatzidis (ed.), *Foundations of Speech Act Theory: Philosophical and Linguistic Perspectives* (Routledge, 1994), 156–66; 'The Alleged Priority of Literal Interpretation', in *Cognitive Science* 19 (1995), 207–32; 'Pragmatics', in *The Routledge Encyclopedia of Philosophy* (Routledge, 1998), vol. 7, 620–33; 'Situations and the Structure of Content', in Kumiko Murasugi and Rob Stainton (eds.), *Philosophy and Linguistics* (Westview Press, 1999), 113–65; 'Déstabiliser le sens', in *Revue Internationale de Philosophie* 216 (2001), 197–208; 'What is Said', in *Synthèse* 128 (2001), 75–91; 'Literal/Nonliteral', in *Midwest Studies in Philosophy* 25 (2001), 264–74; 'Unarticulated Constituents', in *Linguistics and Philosophy* 25 (2002), 299–345; 'Does Linguistic Communication Rest on Inference?', in *Mind and Language* 17 (2002), 105–26; 'Pragmatics and Semantics', in Larry Horn and Gregory Ward (eds.), *Handbook of Pragmatics* (Blackwell, forthcoming); 'The Limits of Expressibility', in Barry Smith (ed.), *John Searle* (Cambridge University Press, forthcoming); 'Descriptions and Situations', in Marga Reimer and Anne Bezuidenhout (eds.), *Descriptions and Beyond: An Interdisciplinary Collection of Essays on Definite and Indefinite Descriptions and Other Related Phenomena* (Oxford University Press, forthcoming); and 'Relativized Propositions', in Michael O'Rourke and Corey Washington (eds.), *Situating Semantics: Essays on the Philosophy of John Perry* (MIT Press, forthcoming). I wish to thank the publishers for permission to reprint or adapt various passages from those papers.

Introduction

Around the middle of the twentieth century, there were two opposing camps within the analytic philosophy of language. The first camp – IDEAL LAN-GUAGE PHILOSOPHY, as it was then called – was that of the pioneers, Frege, Russell, Carnap, Tarski, and so on. They were, first and foremost, logicians studying formal languages and, through them, 'language' in general. They were not originally concerned with natural language, which they thought defective in various ways;[1] yet, in the 1960s, some of their disciples established the relevance of their methods to the detailed study of natural language.[2] Their efforts gave rise to contemporary FORMAL SEMANTICS, a very active discipline whose stunning developments in the last quarter of the twentieth century changed the face of linguistics.

The other camp was that of so-called ORDINARY LANGUAGE PHILOSO-PHERS, who thought important features of natural language were not revealed but hidden by the logical approach initiated by Frege and Russell. They advocated a more descriptive approach and emphasized the pragmatic nature of natural language as opposed to, say, the language of *Principia Mathematica*. Their own work[3] gave rise to contemporary pragmatics, a discipline which, like formal semantics, developed successfully within linguistics in the past forty years.

Central in the ideal language tradition had been the equation of, or at least the close connection between, the meaning of a (declarative) sentence and its truth-conditions. This truth-conditional approach to meaning is perpetuated, to a large extent, in contemporary formal semantics. A language is viewed as a system of rules or conventions, in virtue of which certain assemblages of

---

[1] There are a few exceptions. The most important one is Hans Reichenbach, whose insightful 'Analysis of conversational language' was published as a chapter – the longest – in his *Elements of Symbolic Logic* (Macmillan, 1947).

[2] See Richard Montague, *Formal Philosophy: Selected Papers* (Yale University Press, 1974), and Donald Davidson, *Inquiries into Truth and Interpretation* (Clarendon Press, 1984).

[3] The most influential authors were Austin, Strawson, Grice and the later Wittgenstein. Grice is a special case, for he had, as he once said, one foot in each of the two camps (Paul Grice, 'Retrospective Epilogue', in his *Studies in the Way of Words* (Harvard University Press, 1989), p. 372).

symbols count as well-formed, meaningful sentences. The meaning of a sentence (or of any complex symbol) is determined by the meanings of its parts and the way they are put together. Meaning itself is patterned after reference. The meaning of a simple symbol is the conventional assignment of a worldly entity to that symbol: for example, names are assigned objects, monadic predicates are assigned properties or sets of objects, and so on. The meaning of a declarative sentence, determined by the meanings of its constituents and the way they are put together, is equated with its truth-conditions. For example, the subject-predicate construction is associated with a semantic rule for determining the truth-conditions of a subject-predicate sentence on the basis of the meaning assigned to the subject and that assigned to the predicate. On this picture, knowing a language is like knowing a 'theory' by means of which one can deductively establish the truth-conditions of any sentence of that language.

This truth-conditional approach to meaning is one of the things which ordinary language philosophers found quite unpalatable. According to them, reference and truth cannot be ascribed to linguistic expressions in abstraction from their use. In vacuo, words do not refer and sentences do not have truth-conditions. Words–world relations are established through, and indissociable from, the use of language. It is therefore misleading to construe the meaning of a word as some worldly entity that it represents or, more generally, as its truth-conditional contribution. The meaning of a word, insofar as there is such a thing, should rather be equated with its use-potential or its use-conditions. In any case, what must be studied primarily is speech: the activity of saying things. Then we will be in a position to understand language, the instrument we use in speech. Austin's theory of speech acts and Grice's theory of speaker's meaning were both meant to provide the foundation for a theory of language, or at least for a theory of linguistic meaning.

Despite the early antagonism I have just described, semantics (the formal study of meaning and truth-conditions) and pragmatics (the study of language in use) are now conceived of as complementary disciplines, shedding light on different aspects of language. The heated arguments between ideal language philosophers and ordinary language philosophers are almost forgotten. There are two main reasons for the new situation. On the one hand semanticists, in moving from artificial to natural languages, have given up Carnap's idea that the semantic relation between words and the world can be studied in abstraction from the context of use.[4] That the Carnapian abstraction is illegitimate given the pervasiveness of context-sensitivity in natural language is fully acknowledged by those working in formal semantics. On the other hand those

---

[4] See my 'Pragmatics and Semantics', in Larry Horn and Gregory Ward (eds.), *Handbook of Pragmatics* (Blackwell, forthcoming).

working in pragmatics no longer hold that 'meaning is use'. Instructed by Grice, they systematically draw a distinction between what a given expression means, and what *its use* means or conveys, in a particular context (or even in general).

Still, the ongoing debate about the best delimitation of the respective territories of semantics and pragmatics betrays the persistence of two recognizable currents or approaches within contemporary theorizing. According to the dominant position, which I call 'Literalism', we may legitimately ascribe truth-conditional content to natural language *sentences*, quite independently of what the speaker who utters this sentence means. Literalism contrasts with another view, reminiscent of that held by ordinary language philosophers half a century ago. That other view, which I call 'Contextualism', holds that *speech acts* are the primary bearers of content. Only in the context of a speech act does a sentence express a determinate content.

I say that Literalism is the dominant position because I believe most philosophers of language and linguists would accept the following description of the division of labour between semantics and pragmatics:

Semantics deals with the literal meaning of words and sentences as determined by the rules of the language, while pragmatics deals with what users of the language mean by their utterances of words or sentences. To determine 'what the speaker means' is to answer questions such as: Was John's utterance intended as a piece of advice or as a threat? By saying that it was late, did Mary mean that I should have left earlier? Notions such as that of illocutionary force (Austin) and conversational implicature (Grice) thus turn out to be the central pragmatic notions. In contrast, the central semantic notions turn out to be reference and truth. It is in terms of *these* notions that one can make explicit what the conventional significance of most words and expressions consists in.

The meaning of an expression may be insufficient to determine its referential content: that is so whenever the expression is indexical or otherwise context-dependent. In such cases, the meaning of the expression provides a rule which, given a context, enables the interpreter to determine the content of the expression in that context. The content thus determined in context by the conventional meanings of words is their *literal content*. The literal content of a complete declarative utterance is 'what is said', or the proposition expressed, by that utterance.

As Grice emphasized, a speaker's meaning is not a matter of rules but a matter of intentions: what someone means is what he or she overtly intends (or, as Grice says, 'M-intends') to get across through his or her utterance. Communication succeeds when the M-intentions of the speaker are recognized by the hearer. Part of the evidence used by the hearer in working out what the speaker means is provided by the literal content of the uttered sentence, to which the hearer has independent access via his knowledge of the language. In ideal cases of linguistic communication, the speaker means exactly what she says, and no more is required to understand the speech act than a correct understanding of the sentence uttered in performing it. In real life, however, what the speaker means typically goes beyond, or otherwise diverges from, what the uttered sentence literally says. In such cases the hearer must rely on background knowledge to determine what the speaker means – what her communicative intentions are.

There is much that is correct in this description, but there also is something which I think must be rejected, namely the *contrast* between literal truth-conditions and speaker's meaning. That contrast commits us to Literalism, and in this book I want to argue for Contextualism. According to Contextualism, the contrast between what the speaker means and what she literally says is illusory, and the notion of 'what the sentence says' incoherent. What is said (the truth-conditional content of the utterance) is nothing but an aspect of speaker's meaning. That is not to deny that there *is* a legitimate contrast to be drawn between what the speaker says and what he or she merely implies. Both, however, belong to the realm of 'speaker's meaning' and are pragmatic through and through.

I will not only criticize Literalism and argue for Contextualism in the following chapters. I will discuss all sorts of intermediate positions corresponding to views actually held in the current debate about the semantics/pragmatics interface. Whether or not one accepts my arguments, I hope the survey of logical space which I provide will be useful to those interested in the debate, and will contribute to shaping it in the years to come.

1 Two approaches to 'what is said'

1.1 The basic triad

Anyone who has reflected on the sentence meaning/speaker's meaning distinction knows that a simple distinction is in fact insufficient. Two equally important distinctions must be made. First, there is the distinction between the linguistic meaning of a sentence-type, and what is said (the proposition expressed) by an utterance of the sentence. For example, the English sentence 'I am French' has a certain meaning which, *qua* meaning of a sentence-type, is not affected by changes in the context of utterance. This context-independent meaning contrasts with the context-dependent propositions which the sentence expresses with respect to particular contexts. Thus 'I am French', said by me, expresses the proposition that I am French; if you utter the sentence, it expresses a different proposition, even though its linguistic meaning remains the same across contexts of use.

Second, there is a no less important distinction between what is actually said and what is merely 'conveyed' by the utterance. My utterance of 'I am French' expresses the proposition that I am French, but there are contexts in which it conveys much more. Suppose that, having been asked whether I can cook, I reply: 'I am French.' Clearly my utterance (in this context) provides an affirmative answer to the question. The meaning of the utterance in such a case includes more than what is literally said; it also includes what the utterance 'implicates'.[1]

'What is said' being a term common to both distinctions, we end up with a triad:

> sentence meaning
> vs
> what is said
> vs
> what is implicated

[1] See Paul Grice, *Studies in the Way of Words* (Harvard University Press, 1989), p. 24: 'I wish to introduce, as terms of art, the verb *implicate* and the related nouns *implicature* (cf. *implying*) and *implicatum* (cf. *what is implied*). The point of this manoeuvre is to avoid having, on each occasion, to choose beween this or that member of the family of verbs for which *implicate* is to do general duty.'

The distinguishing characteristic of sentence meaning (the linguistic meaning of the sentence type) is that it is conventional and context-independent. Moreover, in general at least, it falls short of constituting a complete proposition, that is, something truth-evaluable. In contrast, both 'what is said' and 'what is implicated' are context-dependent and propositional. The difference between 'what is said' and 'what is implicated' is that the former is constrained by sentence meaning in a way in which the implicatures aren't. What is said results from fleshing out the meaning of the sentence (which is like a semantic 'skeleton') so as to make it propositional. The propositions one can arrive at through this process of contextual enrichment or 'fleshing out' are constrained by the skeleton which serves as input to the process. Thus 'I am French' can express an indefinite number of propositions, but the propositions in question all have to be compatible with the semantic potential of the sentence; this is why the English sentence 'I am French' cannot express the proposition that kangaroos have tails. There is no such constraint on the propositions which an utterance of the sentence can communicate through the mechanism of implicature. Given enough background, an utterance of 'I am French' might implicate that kangaroos have tails. What's implicated is implicated by virtue of an inference, and the inference chain can (in principle) be as long and involve as many background assumptions as one wishes.

The basic triad can be mapped back onto the simple sentence meaning/speaker's meaning distinction by grouping together two of the three levels. There are two ways to do it, corresponding to two interpretations for the triad. The 'minimalist' interpretation stresses the close connection between sentence meaning and what is said; together, sentence meaning and what is said constitute the *literal meaning* of the utterance as opposed to what *the speaker* means:

$$\text{literal meaning} \begin{cases} \text{sentence meaning} \\ \text{what is said} \end{cases}$$
$$\text{vs}$$
$$\text{speaker's meaning}$$

The other, 'non-minimalist' interpretation of the triad stresses the commonality between what is said and what is implicated, both of which are taken to be pragmatically determined:

$$\text{sentence meaning}$$
$$\text{vs}$$
$$\text{speaker's meaning} \begin{cases} \text{what is said} \\ \text{what is implicated} \end{cases}$$

Essential to this interpretation is the claim that 'what is said', though constrained by the meaning of the sentence, is not as tightly constrained as is traditionally thought and, in particular, does not obey what I will refer to as the 'minimalist' constraint.

1.2   Minimalism

As I said above, what distinguishes 'what is said' from the implicatures is the fact that the former must be 'closely related to the conventional meaning of the words (the sentence) [one] has uttered'.[2] However, this constraint can be construed more or less strictly. What I call 'Minimalism' construes the constraint very strictly; 'what is said', in the minimalist framework, departs from the conventional meaning of the sentence (and incorporates contextual elements) *only when this is necessary to 'complete' the meaning of the sentence and make it propositional*. In other words, the distance between sentence meaning and what is said is kept to a minimum (hence the name 'Minimalism').

The crucial notion here is that of 'saturation'. Saturation is the process whereby the meaning of the sentence is completed and made propositional through the contextual assignment of semantic values to the constituents of the sentence whose interpretation is context-dependent (and, possibly, through the contextual provision of 'unarticulated' propositional constituents, if one assumes, as some philosophers do, that such constituents are sometimes needed to make the sentence fully propositional). This process takes place whenever the meaning of the sentence includes something like a 'slot' requiring completion or a 'free variable' requiring contextual instantiation.[3] Thus an indexical sentence like 'He is tall' does not express a complete proposition unless a referent has been contextually assigned to the demonstrative pronoun 'he', which acts like a free variable in need of contextual instantiation. Genitives provide another well-known example: an utterance including the phrase 'John's book' does not express a complete proposition unless a particular relation has been identified as holding between the book and John. Nominal compounds work the same way: 'burglar nightmare' means something like 'a nightmare that bears a certain relation R to burglars', which relation must be contextually identified. Other well-known examples of saturation include parametric predicates ('small', 'on the left'), definite null instantiation (that is, the case where one of the arguments in the semantic structure of a lexeme, typically a verb, is not syntactically realized and must be contextually identified, as when someone says 'I heard' or 'I noticed'), and so on and so forth.

Whenever saturation is in order, appeal to the context is necessary for the utterance to express a complete proposition: from a semantic point of view, saturation is a *mandatory* contextual process. Other contextual processes – for example, the inference process generating implicatures – are semantically

---

[2] Grice, *Way of Words*, p. 25.

[3] Even when saturation consists in contextually providing a constituent that is unarticulated in surface syntax (as the implicit argument in 'I noticed'), it is something in the sentence (here the predicate 'notice', which arguably denotes a two-place relation) which triggers the search for the contextual element and makes it obligatory. See §2.1 of my 'Unarticulated Constituents', in *Linguistics and Philosophy* 25 (2002), 299–345.

optional in the sense that the aspects of meaning they generate are dispensable; the utterance would still express a complete proposition without them. According to Minimalism, those extra constituents of meaning which are not necessary for propositionality are external to what is said. The only justification for including some pragmatically determined constituent of meaning into what is said (as opposed to what is merely conveyed) is the indispensability of such a constituent – the fact that the utterance would not express a complete proposition if the context did not provide such a constituent.

1.3   Literal truth-conditions vs actual truth-conditions

Consider examples (1)–(6), often discussed in the literature:

(1) I've had breakfast.
(2) You are not going to die.
(3) It's raining.
(4) The table is covered with books.
(5) Everybody went to Paris.
(6) John has three children.

In all such cases, as we shall see, the minimalist constraint implies that what the utterance literally says is not what intuitively seems to be said.

From a minimalist point of view, the first sentence, 'I've had breakfast', expresses the proposition that S (the speaker) has had breakfast before t* (the time of utterance). Strictly speaking this proposition would be true if the speaker had had breakfast twenty years ago and never since. This is clearly not what the speaker means (when she answers the question 'Do you want something to eat?' and replies 'I've had breakfast'); she means something much more specific, namely that she's had breakfast *on that very day* (that is, the day which includes t*). This aspect of speaker's meaning, however, has to be construed as external to what is said and as being merely conveyed, in the same way in which the utterer of 'I am French' implies, but does not say, that he is a good cook. That is so because the 'minimal' interpretation, to the effect that the speaker's life was not entirely breakfastless, is sufficient to make the utterance propositional. Nothing in the sentence itself forces us to bring in the implicit reference to a particular time span. Indeed we can easily imagine contexts in which a speaker would use the same sentence to assert the minimal proposition and nothing more.[4]

The same thing holds even more clearly for the second example. Kent Bach, to whom it is due, imagines a child crying because of a minor cut and her mother uttering (2) in response. What is meant is: 'You're not going to die from that cut.' But literally the utterance expresses the proposition that the kid will not die *tout court* – as if he or she were immortal. The extra element contextually

---

[4] Dan Sperber and Deirdre Wilson, *Relevance: Communication and Cognition* (Blackwell, 1986), pp. 189–90. For an alternative analysis of that example, see my 'Pragmatics of What is Said', in *Mind and Language* 4 (1989), pp. 305–6, and §6.2 below.

provided (the implicit reference to the cut) does not correspond to anything in the sentence itself; nor is it an unarticulated constituent whose contextual provision is necessary to make the utterance fully propositional. Again, we can easily imagine a context in which the same sentence would be used to communicate the minimal proposition and nothing more.[5]

What about (3)? John Perry and many others after him have argued as follows.[6] Even though nothing in the sentence 'It's raining' stands for a place, nevertheless it does not express a complete proposition unless a place is contextually provided. The verb 'to rain', Perry says, denotes a dyadic relation – a relation between times and places. In a given place, it doesn't just rain or not, it rains at some times while not raining at others; similarly, at a given time, it rains in some places while not raining in others. To evaluate a statement of rain as true or false, Perry says, we need both a time and a place. Since the statement 'It is raining' explicitly gives us only the two-place relation (supplied by the verb) and the temporal argument (indexically supplied by the present tense), the relevant locational argument must be contextually supplied for the utterance to express a complete proposition. If Perry is right, the contextual provision of the place concerned by the rain is an instance of saturation, like the assignment of a contextual value to the present tense: both the place and the time are constituents of what is said, even though, unlike the time, the place remains unarticulated in surface syntax.

But is Perry right? If really the contextual provision of a place was mandatory, hence an instance of saturation, *every* token of 'It's raining' would be unevaluable unless a place were contextually specified. Yet I have no difficulty imagining a counterexample, that is, a context in which 'It is raining' is evaluable even though no particular place is contextually singled out. In 'Unarticulated Constituents' I depicted an imaginary situation in which

rain has become extremely rare and important, and rain detectors have been disposed all over the territory (whatever the territory – possibly the whole Earth). In the imagined scenario, each detector triggers an alarm bell in the Monitoring Room when it detects rain. There is a single bell; the location of the triggering detector is indicated by a light on a board in the Monitoring Room. After weeks of total drought, the bell eventually rings in the Monitoring Room. Hearing it, the weatherman on duty in the adjacent room shouts: 'It's raining!' His utterance is true, iff it is raining (at the time of utterance) in some place or other.[7]

The fact that one can imagine an utterance of 'It's raining' that is true iff it is raining (at the time of utterance) in some place or other arguably establishes

---

[5] Kent Bach, 'Conversational Implicature', in *Mind and Language* 9 (1994), p. 134. For an alternative analysis of that example (in terms of domain restriction), see below § 6.2.

[6] John Perry, 'Thought Without Representation' (1986), reprinted (with a postscript) in his collection *The Problem of the Essential Indexical and Other Essays* (Oxford University Press, 1993), 205–25.

[7] Recanati, 'Unarticulated Constituents', p. 317.

the pragmatic nature of the felt necessity to single out a particular place, in the contexts in which such a necessity is indeed felt. When a particular place is contextually provided as relevant to the evaluation of the utterance, it is for pragmatic reasons, not because it is linguistically required. (Again, if it were linguistically required, in virtue of semantic properties of the sentence type, it would be required in *every* context.) If this is right, then the contextual provision of a place is not an instance of saturation after all: it's not something that's mandatory. It follows (by minimalist standards) that the place is not a constituent of what is strictly and literally said: when I say 'It is raining' (rather than something more specific like 'It's raining in Paris' or 'It's raining here'), what I *literally* say is true iff it's raining somewhere or other.[8] That is obviously not what I mean, since what I mean involves a particular place. Appearances notwithstanding, the situation is similar to the case of 'I've had breakfast', where a restricted time interval is contextually provided for pragmatic reasons, without being linguistically mandated.

Examples (4) and (5) are amenable to the same sort of treatment. According to standard Russellian analysis, a definite description conveys an implication of uniqueness: hence 'The table is covered with books' is true iff there is one and only one table and it is covered with books. To make sense of this, we need either to focus on a restricted situation in which there is indeed a single table, or to expand the predicate 'table' and enrich it into, say, 'table of the living-room' in order to satisfy the uniqueness constraint. Either way, it is arguable that the form of enrichment through which we make sense of the utterance is not linguistically mandated: it is only pragmatically required. If we don't enrich, what we get is an already complete proposition (albeit one that is pretty absurd): the proposition that the only existing table is covered with books. Similarly with example (5): without enrichment the utterance expresses a proposition that is true iff every existing person went to Paris. Such a proposition is unlikely to be true, but that does not make it incomplete. On this view the enrichment process through which, in context, we reach the proposition actually communicated (to the effect that everybody *in such and such group* went to Paris) is not linguistically but pragmatically required; hence it is not an instance of saturation, but an optional process of 'free enrichment'. It follows that, in those examples as much as in the previous ones, the proposition literally expressed is different from, and more general than, the proposition actually communicated.

1.4   A problem for Minimalism

In general, the literal truth-conditions posited as part of the minimalist analysis turn out to be very different from the intuitive truth-conditions which

---

[8] See Emma Borg, 'Saying What You Mean: Unarticulated Constituents and Communication' (forthcoming) for a defence of that claim.

untutored conversational participants would ascribe to the utterance. This divergence between the intuitive truth-conditions of an utterance and the literal truth-conditions postulated by the theorist is particularly striking in connection with examples like (6). According to a fairly standard view,[9] the proposition literally expressed by (6) is the proposition that John has at least three children, that is, no less than three but possibly more. In certain contexts this corresponds to what the speaker actually means (as when I say, 'If John has three children he can benefit from lower rates on public transport') but in other contexts what the speaker means is quite different. Suppose for example that I am asked how many children John has and that I reply by uttering (6). Clearly, in this context, I mean that John has (exactly) three children – no more and no less. This is standardly accounted for by saying that the proposition literally expressed, to the effect that John has at least three children, combines with the 'implicature' that John has no more than three children (a generalized implicature that is accounted for in terms of the maxim of quantity);[10] as a result of this combination, what is globally communicated – and what I actually mean – is the proposition that John has exactly three children. Now *this is the only proposition I am conscious of expressing by my utterance*; in particular, I am unaware of having expressed the 'minimal' proposition that John has at least three children. To account for this obvious fact, the minimalist claims that we are aware only of what is globally conveyed or 'communicated' by the utterance. Analysing this into 'what is literally said' and 'what is implied' is the linguist's task, not something that is incumbent upon the normal language user. Figure 1.1 (p. 12) illustrates this widespread conception.

The problem with this conception is that it lacks generality. Recall the example I gave earlier – the utterance 'I am French' used to convey that I am a good cook. In the relevant situation of utterance, both the speaker and the listener are aware that the speaker says he is French, and thereby implies he is a good cook. This typical case of implicature is very different from a case like (6) in which the speaker is not only (like the hearer) unaware of the proposition literally expressed, but would strongly deny having said what the minimalist claims was actually said.

It turns out that there are two sorts of case. On the one hand there are prototypical cases of implied meaning, in which the participants in the speech situation are aware both of what is said and of what is implied, and also of the inferential

[9] See Larry Horn, *The Natural History of Negation* (Chicago University Press, 1989), pp. 205–16.
[10] As Grice puts it in one of his early papers, 'one should not make a weaker statement rather than a stronger one unless there is a good reason for so doing' (Paul Grice, 'The Causal Theory of Perception', in *Proceedings of the Aristotelian Society*, Supplementary Volume 35 (1961), p. 132). Since the statement that John has (at least) three children is weaker than the statement that John has n children (for $n > 3$), the maxim is obeyed only if John has no more than three children. (If John has more than three children, the statement that he has three is too weak and violates the maxim.) The statement 'John has three children' therefore implicates that John has no more than three children, in virtue of the presumption that the maxim is obeyed.

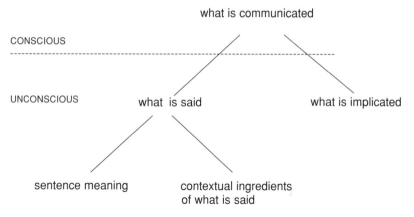

Figure 1.1 The standard approach

connection between them. On the other hand, there are the cases illustrated by (1)–(6).

Given his willingness to treat certain aspects of the intuitive meaning of (1)–(6) as conversational implicatures external to what is literally said, the minimalist must explain why those implicatures, unlike the prototypical cases (for instance the French/cook example), do not have the property of conscious 'availability'.

The only explanation I have come across in the literature makes use of Grice's distinction between 'generalized' and 'particularized' conversational implicatures, that is, between implicatures which arise 'by default', without any particular context or special scenario being necessary, and those which require such specific contexts. In contrast with the latter, the former are 'hard to distinguish from the *semantic* content of linguistic expressions, because such implicatures [are] routinely associated with linguistic expressions in all ordinary contexts'.[11] Generalized implicatures are unconsciously and automatically generated and interpreted. They belong to the 'micropragmatic' rather than to the 'macropragmatic' level, in Robin Campbell's typology:

> A macropragmatic process is one constituted by a sequence of explicit inferences governed by principles of rational cooperation. A micropragmatic process develops as a cryptic [= unconscious] and heuristic procedure which partially replaces some macropragmatic process and which defaults to it in the event of breakdown.[12]

[11] Stephen Levinson, *Pragmatics* (Cambridge University Press, 1983), p. 127. See also his *Presumptive Meanings: The Theory of Generalized Conversational Implicature* (MIT Press, 2000).

[12] Robin Campbell, 'Language Acquisition, Psychological Dualism and the Definition of Pragmatics', in Herman Parret, Marina Sbisà and Jeff Verschueren (eds.), *Possibilities and Limitations of Pragmatics* (Benjamins, 1981), p. 101.

But there are problems with this explanation. According to Horn, the generalized nature of an implicature does not entail its conscious unavailability – its 'cryptic' character.[13] In other words, it is possible for an implicature to be both 'generalized' and intuitively accessible as an implicature distinct from what is said. Thus Horn insists that the generalized scalar implicature from 'some' to 'not all' *is* consciously available (in contrast to that from 'three' to 'exactly three'). A speaker saying 'Some students came to the meeting' normally implies that not all students came, and when this is so there is no tendency on the part of the interpreter to conflate the implicature with what is said. This is actually debatable, for the 'implicature' at issue can arise at sub-sentential level (for example, 'He believes some students came'), and in such cases there are reasons to doubt that the availability condition is satisfied. Be that as it may, the 'generalization' of an implicature does not seem to be necessary for its unconscious character. Many particularized 'bridging' inferences are automatic and unconscious. To take an example from Robyn Carston, 'He went to the cliff and jumped' is readily interpreted as saying that the person referred to jumped *over the cliff*, even though this is only contextually suggested.

1.5   The availability of what is said

In earlier writings I put forward a conception diametrically opposed to that illustrated by figure 1.1 above.[14] 'What is said', I held, *is* consciously available to the participants in the speech situation (figure 1.2). 'What is communicated' is not a distinct level where 'what is said' and 'what is implied' have been merged and integrated into a unified whole; it is merely a name for the level at which we find both what is said and what is implied, which level is characterized by conscious accessibility. On this picture, there are only two basic levels: the bottom level at which we find both the meaning of the sentence and the contextual factors which combine with it to yield what is said; and the top level at which we find both what is said and what is implied, both being consciously accessible (and accessible as distinct).

The availability of what is said follows from Grice's idea that saying itself is a variety of non-natural meaning. One of the distinguishing characteristics of non-natural meaning, on Grice's analysis, is its essential overtness. Non-natural meaning works by openly letting the addressee recognize one's primary intention (for example, the intention to impart a certain piece of information, or the intention to have the addressee behave in a certain way), that is, by

---

[13] Larry Horn, 'The Said and the Unsaid', in Chris Barker and David Dowty (eds.), *SALT 2: Proceedings of the Second Conference on Semantics and Linguistic Theory* (Ohio State University Working Papers in Linguistics 40, 1992), 163–92.

[14] See 'The Pragmatics of What is Said', already cited; *Direct Reference: From Language to Thought* (Blackwell, 1993), pp. 233–74; and 'What is Said', in *Synthèse* 128 (2001), 75–91.

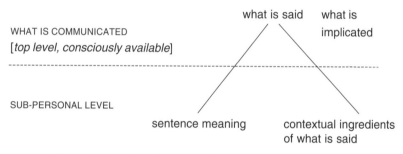

Figure 1.2 An alternative approach

(openly) expressing that intention so as to make it graspable. This can be done in all sorts of ways, verbal or non-verbal. Even if we restrict ourselves to verbal communication, there are many ways in which we can mean things by uttering words. *Saying* is one way; *implying* is another.

The view that 'saying' is a variety of non-natural meaning entails that what is said (like what is meant in general, including what is implied) *must* be available – it must be open to public view. That is so because non-natural meaning is essentially a matter of intention-recognition. On this view what is said by uttering a sentence depends upon, and can hardly be severed from, the speaker's publicly recognizable intentions. Hence my 'Availability Principle', according to which 'what is said' must be analysed in conformity to the intuitions shared by those who fully understand the utterance[15] – typically the speaker and the hearer, in a normal conversational setting.

I take the conversational participants' intuitions concerning what is said to be revealed by their views concerning the utterance's truth-conditions. I assume that whoever fully understands a declarative utterance knows which state of affairs would possibly constitute a truth-maker for that utterance, that is, knows in what sort of circumstance it would be true. The ability to pair an utterance with a type of situation in this way is more basic than, and in any case does not presuppose, the ability to *report* what is said by using indirect speech; it does not even presuppose mastery of the notion of 'saying'. Thus the proper way to elicit such intuitions is not to ask the subjects 'What do you think is said (as opposed to implied or whatever) by this sentence as uttered in that situation'?[16]

---

[15] Recanati, *Direct Reference*, p. 248.

[16] Michael Thau notes that: 'speakers almost never explicitly think about the distinction between what they've said and what they've implicated. So the question of what a speaker takes himself to have said by some utterance will have to depend upon the answer he *would* give if he *were* asked. And it's very likely that in many circumstances there won't be a single answer, that the answer will differ depending on how the question is put. It's also very likely that the answer will vary from circumstance to circumstance' (*Consciousness and Cognition* (Oxford University Press, 2002), p. 148). Contrary to what Thau thinks, however, this does not speak against the

I therefore tend to agree with Bach's criticism of the experiments through which Gibbs and Moise attempted to support the availability based approach:[17]

[They] thought they could get their data about what is said, and thereby test the validity of Recanati's Availability Principle, by asking people what is said by a given utterance, or by asking them whether something that is conveyed by a given utterance is implicated or merely said. Evidently they assume that what people *say* about what is said is strongly indicative of what *is* said. In fact, what it is indicative of is how people apply the phrase 'what is said' . . . It tells us little about what is said, much less about the cognitive processes whereby people understand utterances.[18]

However, Bach himself uses what he calls the 'IQ test' to determine what is said, that is, *he ties what is said to indirect speech reports of what is said.*[19] I find this procedure most objectionable, and that is *not* what I mean when I claim that what is said should be individuated according to the intuitions of normal interpreters. Thus I strongly disagree with Cappelen and Lepore's surprising statement:

We ourselves don't see how to elicit intuitions about what-is-said by an utterance of a sentence without appealing to intuitions about the accuracy of indirect reports of the form 'He said that . . .' or 'What he said is that . . .' or even 'What was said is that . . .'[20]

I find this statement surprising, because there obviously *is* another way of eliciting truth-conditional intuitions. One has simply to provide subjects with scenarios describing situations, or, even better, with – possibly animated – pictures of situations, and to ask them to evaluate the target utterance as true or false with respect to the situations in question.[21] That procedure has been used by several researchers to test speaker's intuitions about, for example, the truth-conditions of donkey sentences. Thus Bart Geurts describes his experimental set-up (inspired from earlier work by Yoon) as follows:

Twenty native speakers of Dutch were asked to judge whether or not donkey sentences correctly described pictured situations. Instructions urged subjects to answer either true

availability based approach. The speaker's intuitions concerning what is said need *not* involve the very notion of what is said.

[17] Raymond Gibbs and Jessica Moise, 'Pragmatics in Understanding What is Said', in *Cognition* 62 (1997), 51–74.

[18] Kent Bach, 'Seemingly Semantic Intuitions', in Joseph Keim Campbell, Michael O'Rourke and David Schier (eds.), *Meaning and Truth* (Seven Bridges Press, 2002), p. 27.

[19] 'IQ' means INDIRECT QUOTATION. On the IQ test, see Bach's papers 'Semantic Slack', in Savas Tsohatzidis (ed.), *Foundations of Speech Act Theory* (Routledge, 1994), 267–91, 'The Myth of Conventional Implicature', in *Linguistics and Philosophy* 22 (1999), 327–66, and 'You Don't Say?', in *Synthèse* 128 (2001), 15–44.

[20] Herman Cappelen and Ernie Lepore, 'On an Alleged Connection Between Indirect Speech and the Theory of Meaning', in *Mind and Language* 12 (1997), p. 280.

[21] For an implicit use of that procedure, see Saul Kripke, *Naming and Necessity* (Blackwell, 1980), p. 12 .

or false, but they were also given the option of leaving the matter open in case they couldn't make up their minds.[22]

This procedure presupposes that normal interpreters have intuitions concerning the truth-conditional content of utterances. On my view, those intuitions correspond to a certain 'level' in the comprehension process – a level that a proper theory of language understanding must capture. That is the level of 'what is said' (as opposed to, for example, what is implied).

1.6   The availability based approach

From a psychological point of view, we can draw a helpful parallel between understanding what one is told and understanding what one sees. In vision, the retinal stimuli undergo a complex (multi-stage) train of processing which ultimately outputs a conscious perception, with the dual character noted by Brentano: the subject is aware both of what he sees, and of the fact that he is seeing it. Although more complex in certain respects, the situation with language is similar. The auditory signal undergoes a multi-stage train of processing which ultimately outputs a conceptual experience: the subject understands what is said. This is very much like (high-level) perception. If I am told that it is four o'clock, I hear that it is four o'clock, just as, when I look at my watch, I see that it is four o'clock. Like the visual experience, the locutionary experience possesses a dual character: we are aware both of what is said, and of the fact that the speaker is saying it.

In calling understanding an *experience*, like perception, I want to stress its conscious character. Understanding what is said involves entertaining a mental representation of the subject-matter of the utterance that is both determinate enough (truth-evaluable) *and* consciously available to the subject. This suggests a criterion, distinct from the minimalist criterion, for demarcating what is said. Instead of looking at things from the linguistic side and equating 'what is said' with the minimal proposition one arrives at through saturation, we can take a more psychological stance and equate what is said with (the semantic content of) the conscious output of the complex train of processing which underlies comprehension.[23]

To be sure, that output itself is subject to further processing through, for example, inferential exploitation. Consider, once again, vision. Seeing John's car, I can infer that he is around. Similarly, hearing that John has had breakfast, I can infer that he is not hungry and does not need to be fed. Just as what

---

[22] Bart Geurts, 'Donkey Business', in *Linguistics and Philosophy* 25 (2002), p. 135.

[23] As Ian Rumfitt once put it, 'what is said in the course of an utterance is nothing other than what somebody who understands the utterance understands to be said' ('Content and Context: the Paratactic Theory Revisited and Revised', in *Mind* 102 (1993), p. 439).

is seen corresponds to the primary conscious output of visual processing, not to what can be secondarily derived from it, 'what is said' corresponds to the primary truth-evaluable representation made available to the subject (at the personal level)[24] as a result of processing the sentence. It is therefore minimal in a certain sense, though not (as we shall see) in the sense of Minimalism. Accordingly, I distinguish between two sorts of pragmatic process. The contextual processes which, like saturation, are (sub-personally) involved in the determination of what is said I call *primary* pragmatic processes. In contrast, *secondary* pragmatic processes are ordinary inferential processes taking us from what is said, or rather from the speaker's saying of what is said, to something that (under standard assumptions of rationality and cooperativeness) follows from the fact that the speaker has said what she has said. To the extent that the speaker overtly intends the hearer to recognize such consequences as following from her speech act, they form an integral part of what the speaker means by her utterance. That is, roughly, Grice's theory of 'conversational implicature'. An essential aspect of that theory is that the hearer must be able to recognize what is said and to work out the inferential connection between what is said and what is implied by saying it. Again, it follows that what is said must be consciously available to the interpreter. It must satisfy what I call the availability constraint.

In this framework we solve the difficulty raised in section 1.5. We no longer have two sorts of case of implicature – the prototypical cases where the interlocutors are aware of what is said, aware of what is implied, and aware of the inferential connection between them, and the cases in which there is no such awareness. Conscious awareness is now a built-in feature of both what is said and the implicatures. That is so because what is said is the conscious output of linguistic-cum-pragmatic processing, and the implicatures correspond to further conscious representations inferentially derived, at the personal rather than sub-personal level, from what is said (or, rather, from the speaker's saying what is said). The alleged cases in which the speech participants themselves are not distinctly aware of what is said and of what is implied are reclassified: they are no longer treated as cases of 'implicature', strictly speaking, but as cases in which a primary pragmatic process operates in the (sub-personal) determination of what is said.[25]

---

[24] On the contrast between the personal and sub-personal levels, see Daniel Dennett, *Content and Consciousness* (Routledge and Kegan Paul, 1969), pp. 93–6, and 'Toward a Cognitive Theory of Consciousness', in his *Brainstorms: Philosophical Essays on Mind and Psychology* (MIT Press, 1981), p. 153.

[25] This is consonant with the approach taken by some semanticists who insist that, for example, scalar 'implicatures' 'are not computed *after* truth-conditions of (root) sentences have been figured out; they are computed phrase by phrase' (Gennaro Chierchia, 'Scalar Implicatures, Polarity Phenomena, and the Syntax/Pragmatics Interface', forthcoming). In chapter 2, I will stress the fact that primary pragmatic processes operate locally, in contrast to secondary pragmatic processes, which can only operate when the truth-conditions of the sentence have been worked out.

1.7   'Saying' as a pragmatic notion

So far I have followed Grice, who construes saying as a variety of meaning. But this pragmatic approach to 'saying' is controversial. Most philosophers use the notion of 'what is said' (or 'the proposition expressed') in such a way that it is *not* a 'pragmatic' notion – having to do with what the speaker means or with what the hearer understands. What is said is supposed to be a property of the *sentence* (with respect to the context at hand) – a property which it has in virtue of the rules of the language. Minimalism is closely associated with such a non-pragmatic way of looking at what is said. In the minimalist framework, saturation is the only contextual process allowed to affect 'what is said', because it alone is a *bottom-up* process, that is, a process triggered (and made obligatory) by a linguistic expression in the sentence itself.[26] All other contextual processes determine aspects of meaning external and additional to what is said. Take, for example, 'free enrichment' – the process responsible for making the interpretation of an utterance more specific than its literal interpretation (as when 'jumped' is contextually understood as 'jumped over the cliff'). That form of enrichment is 'free' in the sense of not being linguistically controlled. Thus what triggers the contextual provision of the relevant temporal restriction in example (1) ('I've had breakfast') is not something in the sentence but simply the fact that the utterance is meant as an answer to a question about the speaker's present state of hunger (which state can be causally affected only by a breakfast taken on the same day). While saturation is a bottom-up, linguistically controlled pragmatic process, free enrichment is a top-down, pragmatically controlled pragmatic process. Insofar as it is pragmatically rather than linguistically controlled, free enrichment is taken to be irrelevant to 'what is said', on the non-pragmatic construal of what is said.

I will discuss the non-pragmatic construal of what is said in chapter 4. For the time being, I'm interested in the pragmatic construal, based on Grice's idea, and the reasons it provides for rejecting the minimalist constraint (§1.8). Before turning to that issue, however, I want to rebut a couple of objections to the pragmatic construal.

The first objection is this. If, following Grice, we construe saying as a variety of meaning, we will be prevented from acknowledging an important class of cases in which the speaker does not mean what he says. Irony is a good example of that class of cases. If I say 'John is a fine friend' ironically, in a context in which it is obvious to everybody that I think just the opposite, it is clear that I do not mean what I say: I mean the opposite. Still, I *say* that John is a fine friend. Grice's construal of saying as a variety of meaning prevents him from

---

[26] As I pointed out in footnote 3, p. 7, that is true even when saturation consists in providing a so-called 'unarticulated constituent'.

acknowledging that fact. According to Grice, when I say 'John is a fine friend' in the mentioned situation, I do not *really* say that John is a fine friend – I *pretend* to be saying it. The pragmatic construal of saying forces Grice to draw a distinction between 'saying' and 'making as if to say'.

As far as I am concerned, I find Grice's distinction (between genuine saying and making as if to say) perfectly legitimate, but I can understand the worries of those who feel that the notion of 'saying' he uses is too much on the pragmatic, illocutionary side.[27] We certainly need a notion of 'what is said' which captures *the objective content of an utterance irrespective of its pragmatic force as a serious assertion or as an ironical utterance*. Still, I find the objection superficial, for it is quite easy actually to construct the desired notion within Grice's own framework. Grice uses 'say' in a strict sense. In that sense whatever is said must be meant. But we can easily define a broader sense for 'say':

S says that *p*, in the broad sense, iff he either says that *p* (in the strict sense) or makes as if to say that *p* (again, in the strict sense of 'say').

I will henceforth use 'say' in that broad sense, which remains within the confines of the pragmatic construal.

Another objection to the pragmatic construal focuses on the loss of objectivity that allegedly goes with it. What is said is objective in the sense that it is possible both for the speaker to make a mistake and say something other than what he means, and for the hearer to misunderstand what the speaker is saying. Those mistakes are possible, the objector will argue, because what is said is an objective property of the sentence (in context). But on the pragmatic construal, it is not clear that this objectivity can be captured. Imagine the following situation: the speaker wants to say that Paul is tall, and, mistaking Tim for Paul, says 'He is tall' while pointing to Tim. The speaker thus inadvertently says that Tim is tall. Now imagine that the hearer also mistakes Tim for Paul. Thanks to this lucky mistake, he grasps what the speaker means, thinking that this is what he has said. The speaker and the hearer therefore converge on a certain interpretation, which is not objectively what was said, but which they both (mistakenly) think is what was said. How, in the framework I have sketched, will it be possible to dissociate what is actually said from the protagonists' mistaken apprehension of what is said? Have we not equated what is said with their understanding of what is said?

We have not. We have equated what is said with what a *normal interpreter* would understand as being said, in the context at hand. A normal interpreter knows which sentence was uttered, knows the meaning of that sentence, knows

[27] 'The verb "say", as Grice uses it, does not mark a (locutionary) level distinct from that marked by such illocutionary verbs as "state" and "tell", but rather functions as a generic illocutionary verb' (Bach, 'You Don't Say?', p. 41).

the relevant contextual facts (who is being pointed to, and so on).[28] Ordinary users of the language *are* normal interpreters, in most situations. They know the relevant facts and have the relevant abilities. But there are situations (as in the above example) where the actual users make mistakes and are not normal interpreters. In such situations their interpretations do not fix what is said. To determine what is said, we need to look at the interpretation that a normal interpreter would give. This is objective enough, yet remains within the confines of the pragmatic construal.

1.8   Availability vs Minimalism

In the framework I have sketched, there is a basic constraint on what is said:

Availability
What is said must be intuitively accessible to the conversational participants (unless something goes wrong and they do not count as 'normal interpreters').

This constraint leads us to give up Minimalism. That is the price to pay if we want Availability to be satisfied.

The reason why Availability is incompatible with Minimalism is simple enough. The aspects of the meaning of (1)–(6) which the minimalist construes as conversational implicatures are, one may admit, contextual ingredients in the overall meaning of the utterance. They do *not* belong to the conventional meaning of the sentence. The minimalist claims that they do not belong to 'what is said' either, because they are optional: those contextual aspects of the meaning of the utterance are not necessary for the latter to express a complete proposition. But the availability constraint pulls in the other direction. The very fact that the minimal propositions allegedly expressed are not consciously available shows that it would be a mistake to equate them to what is said; rather, the availability constraint dictates that the aspects of meaning which Minimalism construes as external to what is said (for example, the implicit reference to a place in (3), or to the cut in (2), or to a time interval in (1)) are actually *constitutive* of what is said, because *when we subtract them from the intuitive meaning of the utterance the proposition which results is no longer something accessible to the participants in the speech situation.* Thus we have two quite distinct phenomena: examples like 'I am French'/'I am a good cook' involve something which is said and whose saying implies something else; examples like (1)–(6), in contrast, do not involve the distinction between what is said and what is implied but a different distinction between the literal meaning of the sentence and contextual ingredients entering into the determination of what

---

[28] This is all tacit knowledge, not the sort of 'conscious awareness' I talk about in connection with secondary pragmatic processes.

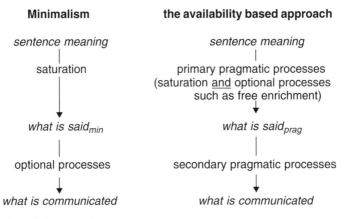

Figure 1.3 Comparing the approaches

is said. If we maintain that those ingredients are indeed 'optional' rather than necessary for propositionality, this implies that *we must give up the minimalist criterion according to which the context contributes to what is said only when this is necessary for some proposition to be expressed.*

According to the view we arrive at, truth-conditional interpretation is pragmatic to a large extent. Various pragmatic processes come into play in the very determination of what is said; not merely saturation – the contextual assignment of values to indexicals and free variables in the logical form of the utterance – but also free enrichment and other processes which are not linguistically triggered but are pragmatic through and through. Figure 1.3 summarizes the contrast between the two conceptions (Minimalism, and the availability based approach).

According to the availability based approach, the crucial distinction is not between mandatory and optional contextual processes, but between those that are 'primary' and those that are 'secondary'. Primary pragmatic processes include not only saturation, but also 'optional' processes such as free enrichment. Independent evidence for their inclusion in this category is provided by the fact that, in general, the notion of 'what is said' we need to capture the input to secondary, inferential processes already incorporates contextual elements of the optional variety. Consider examples (1)–(6) once again. In each case we may suppose that the speaker implies various things by saying what she does. Thus, by saying that she's had breakfast, the speaker implies that she is not hungry and does not want to be fed. By saying that the child is not going to die, the mother implies that the cut is not serious; and so forth. Now those implicatures can be worked out only if the speaker is recognized as expressing the (non-minimal) proposition that she's had breakfast *that morning*, or that the child won't die *from that cut*. Clearly, if the speaker had had breakfast twenty years ago (rather than that very morning), nothing would follow concerning the speaker's present state of hunger and her willingness or unwillingness to eat something. The implicature could not be derived, if what the speaker says was not given the richer, temporally restricted interpretation. If therefore we accept the Gricean picture, according to which 'what is said' serves as input to the secondary process of implicature-generation, we must, *pace* Grice himself, acknowledge the non-minimal character of what is said. This provides some support to the availability based approach, as against Minimalism.

2 Primary pragmatic processes

2.1 Enrichment, loosening and transfer

Secondary pragmatic processes are 'post-propositional'. They cannot take place unless some proposition p is considered as having been expressed, for they proceed by inferentially deriving some further proposition q (the implicature) from the fact that p has been expressed. In contrast, primary pragmatic processes are 'pre-propositional': they do not presuppose the prior identification of some proposition serving as input to the process.[1] Another difference is the fact that secondary pragmatic processes are conscious in the sense that normal interpreters are aware both of what is said and of what is implied and are capable of working out the inferential connection between them. Primary pragmatic processes are not conscious in that sense. Normal interpreters need not be aware of the context-independent meanings of the expressions used, nor of the processes through which those meanings are enriched or otherwise adjusted to fit the situation of use. Unless they are linguists or would-be linguists, they are aware only of the output of the primary processes involved in contextual adjustment.

Saturation is a primary pragmatic process. If the uttered sentence is 'She is smaller than John's sister', then in order to work out what is said I must (at least) determine to whom the speaker refers by the pronoun 'she' and what the relevant relation is between John and the mentioned sister. Were saturation a secondary pragmatic process, I would have to proceed in reverse order, that is, to identify what is said in order to determine those things.

Beside saturation, which is linguistically mandated (bottom-up), there are, I claim, other primary pragmatic processes that are optional and context-driven (top-down). The paradigm case is free enrichment, illustrated by example (1):

(1) Mary took out her key and opened the door.

In virtue of a 'bridging inference', we naturally understand the second conjunct as meaning that Mary opened the door with the key mentioned in the first

---

[1] On the distinction between 'pre-semantic' and 'post-semantic' pragmatics, see Levinson, *Presumptive Meanings*, p. 187, and Ken Taylor, 'Sex, Breakfast, and Descriptus Interruptus', in *Synthèse* 128 (2001), pp. 48–9.

conjunct; yet this is not explicitly articulated in the sentence. Insofar as the bridging inference affects the intuitive truth-conditions of the utterance, it does so as a result of free enrichment.[2]

In typical cases free enrichment consists in making the interpretation of some expression in the sentence contextually more specific. This process has sometimes been described in the literature as 'specifization'. For example the mass term 'rabbit' will be preferentially interpreted as meaning *rabbit fur* in the context of 'He wears rabbit' and as meaning *rabbit meat* in the context of 'He eats rabbit.'[3] This not a matter of selecting a particular value in a finite set; with a little imagination, one can think of dozens of possible interpretations for 'rabbit' by manipulating the stipulated context of utterance; and there is no limit to the number of interpretations one can imagine in such a way. Nor can the process of specifization be construed as linguistically mandated, that is, as involving a hidden variable. Were it linguistically mandated (bottom up), it would be mandatory, but it is not: in some contexts the mass term 'rabbit' means nothing more than R A B B I T   S T U F F ('after the accident, there was rabbit all over the highway').

Can free enrichment be equated with specifization, or are there instances of free enrichment that are not cases of specifization? The provision of (optional) unarticulated constituents is supposed to be a case of free enrichment in which it

---

[2] The term 'bridging inference' was originally introduced by Herb Clark, a pioneer of pragmatic studies, in the seventies (see e.g. 'Bridging', in Peter Johnson-Laird and John Wason (eds.), *Thinking: Readings in Cognitive Science* (Cambridge University Press, 1977), 411–20). Example (1) is discussed by Robyn Carston in 'Implicature, Explicature, and Truth-Theoretic Semantics', in Ruth Kempson (ed.), *Mental Representations: The Interface between Language and Reality* (Cambridge University Press, 1988), 155–81.

[3] This example is discussed in Geoff Nunberg and Annie Zaenen, 'Systematic Polysemy in Lexicology and Lexicography', in Hannu Tommola, Krista Varantola, Tarja Tolonen and Jürgen Schopp (eds.), *Proceedings of Euralex 2* (University of Tampere, 1992), 387–98. A number of similar examples are discussed in the cognitive science literature on 'concept combination', which parallels the semantics and pragmatics literature. Concept combination is said to require not only specifization, that is, the addition of features, but also feature cancellation or loosening (as in 'stone lion' or 'fake gun'). See Bradley Franks, 'Sense Generation: A "Quasi-Classical" Approach to Concepts and Concept Combination', in *Cognitive Science* 19 (1995), 441–505. See also Richard Gerrig and Gregory Murphy, 'Contextual Influences on the Comprehension of Complex Concepts', in *Language and Cognitive Processes,* 7 (1992), 205–30; Thomas Goschke and Dirk Koppelberg, 'Connectionist Representations, Semantic Compositionality, and the Instability of Concept Structure', in *Psychological Research* 52 (1990), 253–70; Gregory Murphy, 'Noun Phrase Interpretation and Conceptual Combination', in *Journal of Memory and Language* 29 (1990), 259–88, and 'The Comprehension of Complex Concepts', in *Cognitive Science* 12 (1988), 529–62; Douglas Medin and Edward Shoben, 'Context and Structure in Conceptual Combination', in *Cognitive Psychology* 20 (1988), 158–90; Jim Hampton, 'Inheritance of Attributes in Natural Concept Conjunctions', in *Memory and Cognition* 15 (1987), 55–71. Further references can be found in those papers. For relevant discussions, see also Paula Schwanenflugel (ed.), *The Psychology of Word Meanings* (Lawrence Erlbaum Associates, 1991), and Raymond Gibbs, *The Poetics of Mind: Figurative Thought, Language, and Understanding* (Cambridge University Press, 1994).

is not *the interpretation of some expression in the sentence* that is enriched, but more globally *the interpretation of the sentence.* In most cases, however, what can be done in terms of unarticulated constituents can also be done in terms of specifization. We can construe the implicit instrument in the second conjunct of (1) either as an unarticulated constituent (corresponding to the implicit prepositional phrase 'with the key'), or as an aspect of the interpretation of the predicate 'open' resulting from specifization (the concept contextually expressed by 'open' being the specific, ad hoc concept OPEN_WITH_KEY, rather than the generic concept OPEN).[4] The same options are presumably available for dealing with the 'rabbit fur/meat' example. In such cases, I will assume that there is a single form of free enrichment, which can be handled in different frameworks – either in terms of specifization (ad hoc concepts) or in terms of unarticulated constituents. Which framework we choose to handle such cases depends upon extraneous considerations. (For example, if we want to preserve the principle of compositionality, we'd better opt for the specifization view which spares us the postulation of syntactically unarticulated constituents.) Still, there is a type of case for which I think we need the notion of unarticulated constituent and cannot make do with specifization and ad hoc concepts: whenever the alleged unarticulated constituent is the intended 'circumstance of evaluation', we can't deal with it in terms of specifization or ad hoc concept. That type of case will be discussed in chapter 8.

Another issue regarding enrichment is whether or not it can be described as 'strengthening' or logical enrichment, as I suggested in *Direct Reference* (p. 261). A predicate has conditions of application, and strengthening consists in *restricting* the application of a predicate by contextually providing further conditions that are not linguistically encoded. Thus 'table' has such and such conditions of application packed into the concept TABLE, and through contextual strengthening the further condition IN_THE_LIVING_ROOM is provided, which results in a restricted application. Thus construed enrichment can account for the (so-called) contextual restriction of quantifiers and for the interpretation of (so-called) 'incomplete' definite descriptions. ('All the books are on the table', where a particular set of books and a particular table are in question.)[5]

---

[4] The notion of 'ad hoc concept', introduced by Larry Barsalou (see for example 'Ad hoc Categories', in *Memory and Cognition* 11 (1983), 211–27), now belongs to the toolkit of relevance theory. See Dan Sperber and Deirdre Wilson, 'The Mapping Between the Mental and the Public Lexicon', in Peter Carruthers and Jill Boucher (eds.), *Language and Thought: Interdisciplinary Themes* (Cambridge University Press, 1998), 184–200; Robyn Carston, 'Enrichment and Loosening: Complementary Processes in Deriving the Proposition Expressed?', in *Linguistische Berichte* 8 (1997), 103–27, and *Thoughts and Utterances: The Pragmatics of Explicit Communication* (Blackwell, 2002), chapter 5; Deirdre Wilson, and Dan Sperber, 'Truthfulness and Relevance', in *Mind* 111 (2002), 583–632.

[5] Stephen Neale (*This, That and the Other* (typescript), chapter 1) objects to my notion of strengthening: 'It is sometimes said that enrichment in Sperber and Wilson's sense involves *strengthening*

The converse of enrichment is loosening.[6] There is loosening whenever a condition of application packed into the concept literally expressed by a predicate is contextually dropped so that the application of the predicate is widened. An example is 'The ATM swallowed my credit card.' There can be no real swallowing on the part of an ATM, since ATMs are not living organisms with the right bodily equipment for swallowing. By relaxing the conditions of application for 'swallow', we construct an ad hoc concept with wider application.

A third type of primary pragmatic process that is not linguistically mandated (bottom up) but contextually driven is semantic transfer.[7] In transfer the output is neither an enriched nor an impoverished version of the concept literally expressed by the input expression. It's a different concept altogether, bearing a systematic relation to it. Thus 'parked out back' denotes either the property a car has when it is parked out back, or a different property, namely the property a car-owner has whenever his or her car has the former property ('I am parked out back'). Arguably, 'parked out back' literally denotes the former property, and comes to denote the latter property as a result of transfer. Similarly, the expression 'ham sandwich' in 'The ham sandwich left without paying' arguably denotes, through transfer, the derived property HAM_SANDWICH_ORDERER rather than the linguistically encoded property HAM_SANDWICH.

A number of problems arise in connection with primary pragmatic processes. Do we really need the four categories I have mentioned? It may be argued that

in that the post-enrichment statement entails the statement one might associate with the utterance prior to enrichment. That this cannot be true in general is made clear by cases involving (non-persistent) determiners like "every", "no" and "some". If, when discussing a dinner party I attended last night, I say, "everyone drank a lot of wine", I am saying only that everyone who attended the dinner party drank a lot of wine, and this does not entail that everyone (unqualified) drank a lot of wine.'
But I had already disposed of that objection in *Direct Reference* (pp. 262–3): 'Strengthening, it may be argued, can be understood as operating *locally*. For example, in the case of "Every boy came", we might say that it is the predicate "boy" that is strengthened into "boy in the class", rather than the proposition "Every boy came" into "Every boy in the class came".' (See also 'The Pragmatics of What is Said', p. 307 n.)

[6] Dan Sperber and Deirdre Wilson, 'Loose Talk', in *Proceedings of the Aristotelian Society* 86 (1986), 153–71; Carston, 'Enrichment and Loosening'. Similar notions include 'feature cancellation' (Jonathan Cohen, 'Some Remarks on Grice's Views About the Logical Particles of Natural Language', in Yehoshua Bar-Hillel (ed.), *Pragmatics of Natural Languages* (Reidel, 1971), 50–68; Franks, 'Sense Generation'), 'concept broadening' as opposed to 'concept narrowing' (Renate Bartsch, 'The Structure of Word Meanings: Polysemy, Metaphor, Metonymy', in Fred Landman and Frank Veltman (eds.), *Varieties of Formal Semantics* (Foris Publications, 1984), p. 32; see also Levinson, *Presumptive Meanings*), and 'pragmatic generalization' as opposed to 'pragmatic specialization' (Charles Ruhl, *On Monosemy: A Study in Linguistic Semantics* (State University of New York Press, 1989)). Paul Ziff speaks of 'augmenting' and 'diminishing' senses ('What is Said', in Donald Davidson and Gilbert Harman (eds.), *Semantics of Natural Language* (Reidel, 1972), p. 719).

[7] See Geoffrey Nunberg, 'The Non-Uniqueness of Semantic Solutions: Polysemy', in *Linguistics and Philosophy* 3 (1979), 143–84, and 'Transfers of Meaning', in *Journal of Semantics* 12 (1995), 109–32.

we need fewer categories, or that we need more. In particular, if we construe enrichment not as logical strengthening but as a quasi-syntactic process of 'expansion' through which a representation (or a structured content) is made more complex by the addition of further constituents, then it may be that we don't need transfer, nor even loosening, but that we can handle everything in terms of that (little constrained) notion of expansion. Be that as it may, I will not deal with those problems, internal to the theory of primary pragmatic processes, in this chapter. What I am concerned with is a more basic set of issues pertaining to the very distinction between primary and secondary pragmatic processes.

2.2   Rejecting the Gricean picture

Even though he construed saying as a variety of non-natural meaning, Grice espoused Minimalism. On his view, disambiguation and saturation suffice to give us the literal interpretation of the utterance – what is literally said. All other pragmatic processes involved in the interpretation of the utterance are secondary and presuppose the identification of what is said. Interpretation is construed as a two-step procedure: (i) The interpreter accesses the literal interpretations of all constituents in the sentence and uses them to compute the proposition literally expressed, with respect to the context at hand; (ii) on the basis of this proposition and general conversational principles he or she infers what the speaker means (which may be distinct from what is said, that is, from the proposition literally expressed).

The picture I have presented also makes interpretation a two-step procedure, but there is a major difference. The primary pragmatic processes that are involved in determining what is said include not only saturation (and disambiguation) but also optional processes such as free enrichment, loosening and semantic transfer. Those processes take us from the *literal meaning* of some constituent (the meaning that is linguistically encoded, or that which results from saturating the linguistically encoded meaning) to a *derived meaning* which may be richer, poorer, or involve some kind of transfer. I hold that, for such processes to take place, *there is no need to antecedently compute the proposition literally expressed*. That is why I take those processes to be 'primary', like saturation. What I am disputing therefore is the claim that the process of semantic composition which consists in putting together the semantic values of the parts to determine the semantic value of the whole begins by paying attention only to literal semantic values (as delivered through disambiguation and saturation), and turns to derived values only *after* the literal semantic value of the whole (the proposition literally expressed) has been computed.

There is a simple argument purporting to show that the Gricean picture must be right. Enrichment, loosening and transfer all take as input the literal meaning of some expression; hence they cannot take place unless that literal meaning has been accessed. This seems to support the Gricean picture, according to which *we process the literal interpretation first, and move on to the derived interpretation only when this is required to make sense of the speaker's utterance.*

This argument is fallacious.[8] I admit that the literal interpretation must come first, insofar as the derived interpretation is derived *from it* through enrichment, loosening or transfer. But I want to resist the conclusion that the literal interpretation must be 'processed' first, in the sense that is relevant to the debate. Or, to put it another way: what I am rejecting is not the claim that the literal interpretation *of the constituent* is accessed before the derived interpretation — that I take to be obvious — but the claim that a similar priority holds at the level of the complete sentence; that is, I reject the claim that the process of semantic composition begins by paying attention only to literal semantic values, and turns to derived values only after the literal semantic value *of the whole* (the proposition literally expressed) has been computed. It is this picture which I think is unwarranted.

If I am right, the asymmetric dependence of derived meaning upon literal meaning does not rule out an account according to which literal meaning and derived meaning are on equal footing as far as semantic composition is concerned. Thus we can imagine that the literal meaning and the derived meaning of a given expression are processed in parallel, in constructing an interpretation for the whole utterance. In the model I have in mind, the literal meaning of the expression is accessed first and triggers the activation of associatively related representations. That literal meaning is a natural candidate for the status of semantic value, but there are others: some of the representations activated by association contribute further candidates for the status of semantic value.[9] All candidates, whether literal or derived, are processed in parallel and compete. When an interpretation which fits the broader context of discourse is found, it is selected (that is, it undergoes semantic composition) and the other candidates are suppressed.

On this view, derived meanings still proceed (associatively) *from* literal meanings, which they indeed presuppose; but, although generated serially, they are processed in parallel. The literal meaning has no compositional privilege over derived meanings; they compete and it is possible for some derived meaning to be retained (if it fits the broader context of discourse) while the literal

---

[8] For a detailed critique, see my papers 'Processing Models for Non-Literal Discourse', in Roberto Casati, Barry Smith and Graham White (eds.), *Philosophy and the Cognitive Sciences, Proceedings of the 16th International Wittgenstein Symposium* (Hölder-Pichler-Tempsky, 1994), 277–90, and 'The Alleged Priority of Literal Interpretation', in *Cognitive Science* 19 (1995), 207–232.

[9] By 'semantic value' here I mean what the process of semantic composition operates on. My point is that the semantic value contributed by an expression need not be the literal meaning of that expression – it may be affected by pragmatic processes, including optional pragmatic processes. (Later in this book I will talk of 'pragmatic value' instead of 'semantic value' to stress the fact that such values result from the operation of such processes.)

interpretation is suppressed. In other words, the derived interpretation is *associatively derived* from the literal interpretation, but it is not *inferentially* derived. Inferential derivation entails computation of the literal value of the global sentence, while associative derivation is a 'local' process which does not require prior computation of the proposition literally expressed.[10]

Consider, as an example, Geoff Nunberg's famous ham sandwich. The waiter says 'The ham sandwich has left without paying.' On the Gricean picture the interpreter computes the proposition literally expressed by the sentence – namely the absurd proposition that the sandwich itself has left without paying – and from its absurdity infers that the speaker means something different from what she says. On the parallel model I have outlined the description 'the ham sandwich' first receives its literal interpretation, in such a way that a representation of a ham sandwich is activated; activation then spreads to related representations, including a representation of the man who ordered a ham sandwich.[11] *All these representations activated by the description 'the ham sandwich' contribute potential candidates for the status of semantic value of the expression;* all of which are equally susceptible of going into the interpretation of the global utterance. Now the ham sandwich orderer is a better candidate than the ham sandwich itself for the status of argument for '. . . has left without paying'. It is therefore the derived, non-literal candidate which is retained, while the literal interpretation is discarded.

An important difference between the Gricean model (according to which the literal interpretation is processed first) and the parallel model just outlined is this: on the parallel model it is possible for an utterance to receive a non-literal interpretation *without the literal interpretation of that utterance being ever computed.*[12] The non-literal interpretation of the global sentence does not presuppose its literal interpretation, contrary to what happens at the constituent level. If the non-literal interpretation of some constituent fits the context especially well it may be retained (and the other interpretations suppressed) *before* the literal interpretation of the sentence has been computed. Whether or not this sort of thing actually happens, this is at least *conceivable*, on the parallel model.

---

[10] See my *Direct Reference*, pp. 263–6.

[11] As Ivan Sag ('Formal Semantics and Extralinguistic Context', in Peter Cole (ed.), *Radical Pragmatics* (Academic Press, 1981), 273–94) and Geoff Nunberg ('Transfers of Meaning') pointed out, it is not the description as a whole, but the predicate 'ham sandwich' *in* the description which has a derived, non-literal value; the ham sandwich example is a case of property transfer, not a case of deferred reference (see footnote 19, p. 35). Since nothing hinges on this point, I will simplify matters in this and the next two sections by treating the description itself as a unit susceptible to both a literal and a derived interpretation.

[12] According to R. Bartsch ('Structure of Word Meanings', pp. 29–30), 'there is not always a [literal interpretation] available to start with'. In some instances of metaphor 'a sentence meaning as a whole cannot be constructed because of semantic incompatibility of parts of the sentence'. In any case, 'it is not necessary to arrive at any literal meaning of the metaphorical sentence as a whole, but we arrive at the metaphorical meaning right away'.

2.3   Accessibility

When someone talks of 'wearing rabbit', the literal meaning of the mass term 'rabbit' (namely R A B B I T   S T U F F) is accessed, but it has to compete with other candidates for semantic value. The more specific representation R A B B I T   F U R is also activated since it is associatively connected to the representations encoded by both 'rabbit' and 'wear'. As a result of this multiple activation, it is possible for the representation R A B B I T   F U R to be more active, in this context, than the less specific representation R A B B I T   S T U F F which is linguistically encoded. Whatever we think of this particular example, it seems to me that the following situation can obtain: an expression linguistically encodes a certain representation; that representation becomes active when the expression is uttered, but another, associatively related representation is also activated (in part – but in part only – through the encoded representation) and turns out to be more active in that context than the original representation from which (in part) it derives.[13] If we assume that the candidate for semantic value which is retained and undergoes semantic composition is that which is *most accessible*, that is, that which corresponds to the most active representation when the interpretation process stabilizes, we explain how a derived meaning resulting from enrichment (or loosening, or transfer) can be selected as semantic value, in lieu of the literal meaning from which it is derived.[14]

The same phenomenon can happen dynamically. Some representation may be activated through its associative links to the representation linguistically encoded and *become* more active than the latter as a result of the coming into play of further linguistic material which raises its activation level. Before considering such a case, let us look at a simpler example of accessibility shift along the temporal dimension.

Consider sentence (2) from *Direct Reference* (p. 265):

(2) John was arrested by a policeman yesterday; he had just stolen a wallet.

In order to interpret the utterance one must assign a reference to the pronoun 'he' in the second sentence. The two persons who were mentioned in the first sentence, namely John and the policeman, are obvious candidates, and we may

---

[13] I assume that representations can be activated because they are being processed (or have been recently), or because they receive activation from associatively related representations which are themselves activated. Frequency of processing is another important factor (among several others); it can be conceived of as lowering the activation threshold of a representation. See for example Lawrence Barsalou and Dorrit Billman, 'Systematicity and Semantic Ambiguity', in D. Gorfein (ed.), *Resolving Semantic Ambiguity* (Springer, 1989), 146–203.

[14] The role of accessibility (or activation, or salience) has been stressed in a number of works. See Mira Ariel, 'Accessibility Theory: An Overview', in Ted Sanders, Joost Schilperoord and Wilbert Spooren (eds.), *Text Representation: Linguistic and Psycholinguistic Aspects* (John Benjamins, 2001), 29–87, and Rachel Giora, *On Our Mind: Salience, Context, and Figurative Language* (Oxford University Press, forthcoming).

suppose that there is no other (sufficiently accessible) candidate. (There would be one if, for example, the speaker pointed to someone while uttering the pronoun.) We may suppose that when the pronoun 'he' is uttered one of the two candidates, John or the policeman, is more accessible than the other; John because he is foregrounded (*qua* subject of the sentence), or the policeman because he was mentioned last. For the sake of the argument, let us suppose that the second factor is more important than the first one, so that *the policeman* is slightly more accessible than John when the pronoun is uttered. This may well change when the other constituents of the sentence are processed. When the predicate 'had just stolen a wallet' is uttered, *John* becomes more accessible than the policeman as a candidate for the status of referent of 'he', even if the policeman was more accessible at an earlier stage in the processing of the utterance. For John is the subject of 'was arrested' and therefore occupies the role of the person being arrested; now that role is linked to the role of the person doing the stealing, in some relevant frame.[15] Because of this link, the representation of the referent of 'he' as the person doing the stealing contributes some activation to the representation of the person being arrested and therefore raises the accessibility of John *qua* occupier of this role. John thus becomes the most accessible candidate.

If we turn to a case in which some candidate for semantic value is distinguished from the others by being literally encoded, we see that the same sort of temporal shift in accessibility can occur. When the words 'the ham sandwich' are uttered, we may consider that the representation of the ham sandwich is more active than other, related representations which are activated through their links to that representation. Thus we may suppose that the representation of the ham sandwich is more active than the 'derived' representation of the ham sandwich orderer. This is similar to the fact that the policeman is more accessible than John when the pronoun 'he' in (2) is uttered, except that the policeman is (perhaps) more accessible because he was mentioned last, while the representation of the ham sandwich is more active because it is linguistically encoded and has some form of priority over the ham sandwich orderer (derived value). In both cases, the initial ranking is reversed when further linguistic material comes into play. After the predicate in the sentence 'The ham sandwich has left without paying' has been processed, the ham sandwich is no longer a more accessible candidate than the ham sandwich orderer – the order of accessibility is reversed. The explanation, again, is very simple and does not appeal to inference on the hearer's part. The predicate 'has left without paying' demands a person as argument; this raises the accessibility of all candidates who are

---

[15] On frames, see for example, Charles Fillmore and Beryl Atkins, 'Toward a Frame-Based Lexicon: The Semantics of RISK and its Neighbors', in Adrienne Lehrer and Eva Kittay (eds.), *Frames, Fields and Contrasts: New Essays in Semantic and Lexical Organization* (Lawrence Erlbaum Associates, 1992), 75–102. Other references are provided in footnote 29, p. 94.

(represented as) persons. In this way the representation of the ham sandwich orderer gains some extra activation which makes him more accessible than the ham sandwich, after the predicate has been processed.

2.4   Objections and responses

In the framework I have sketched the interpretation which eventually emerges and incorporates the output of various pragmatic processes results from a blind, mechanical process, involving no reflection on the interpreter's part. The dynamics of accessibility does everything, and no 'inference' is required. In particular, there is no need to consider the speaker's beliefs and intentions.

Dan Sperber objected to me in conversation that accessibility can lead us astray: sometimes the first interpretation that comes to mind (the most accessible one) turns out not to be satisfactory and forces the hearer to backtrack. According to Sperber, the possibility of such garden-path effects shows that success, for a candidate semantic value, cannot be equated with sheer accessibility. This objection is misguided, I think. The most accessible interpretation at some stage s in the interpretation process may well turn out to be unsatisfactory at some later stage s', thereby resulting in a garden path effect and the need to backtrack. This does not show that interpretational success cannot be cashed out in terms of accessibility. At any given stage, the most accessible interpretation will be the winning one (at that stage). In garden path utterances we have *two* successive stages to consider. One interpretation is the most accessible one, hence wins, at s, but that interpretation fails to fit some schema, hence loses, at a later stage s'. In an accessibility based framework, this means that this interpretation's accessibility at s' is no longer sufficient for it to be the winning candidate (at s'). Another candidate (which was less accessible at s, but turns out to be more accessible at s') takes over, hence the garden path effect. The distinction between successive stages of interpretation, together with the notion of an accessibility shift, is sufficient to account for garden path effects within the accessibility based framework.

The notion of an accessibility shift also provides immediate answers to the questions which, according to Kent Bach,[16] my account of the ham sandwich metonymy and similar phenomena in terms of local pragmatic processes raises. Bach writes:

Recanati supposes that the process of metonymical transfer takes place without the intrusion of a thought of the absurd proposition associated with the literal meaning of (i) ['The ham sandwich is getting restless']. That is, the hearer does not have to compute that the speaker does not mean that a certain culinary item is getting restless in order to determine what the speaker does mean. But, I ask, how can the hearer go from the

---

[16] Bach, 'Conversational Impliciture', pp. 157–61.

concept of ham sandwich to that of ham-sandwich-orderer without first entertaining the absurd minimal proposition? What triggers the 'local process' and, for that matter, keeps it from being triggered in a case like (ii) ['The ham sandwich is getting eaten'], uttered in similar circumstances? Recanati's account predicts that the hearer would entertain the proposition that the ham-sandwich-orderer is getting eaten, since the local process it posits would get triggered before a full proposition were reached. And yet (ii) could be understood perfectly well.[17]

But my account does *not* predict that the hearer would understand (ii) ('The ham sandwich is being eaten') as being about the ham sandwich orderer. There *is* something, in my account, which keeps the local process of transfer from being triggered in a case like (ii). What keeps the local process of transfer from being triggered in a case like (ii) is precisely what answers Bach's legitimate question: 'How can the hearer go from the concept of ham sandwich to that of ham-sandwich-orderer without first entertaining the absurd minimal [that is literal] proposition?' In my framework, the process of metonymical transfer is 'local', not global, *yet it is sensitive to the linguistic (and extralinguistic) context in which the expression which receives the metonymical interpretation occurs.* In particular, it is sensitive to the meaning of the predicate expression; this is why it is triggered in (i) but not in (ii).

For the literal proposition to be entertained, the literal semantic value of '(the) ham sandwich' must undergo semantic composition with the semantic value of the predicate; but as soon as the semantic value of the predicate is accessed, the metonymical interpretation of the subject-term becomes more accessible than its literal interpretation, which is therefore prevented from going into the proposition expressed. The activation of the concept which corresponds to the literal interpretation of the predicate is both what triggers the process of metonymical transfer in (i) and what prevents it from taking place in (ii). Yet the transfer's sensitivity to the interpretation of the other constituents in the sentence does not mean that the transfer is a global process involving the computation of the absurd, literal proposition. The interpreter does not go from the concept of ham sandwich to that of ham-sandwich-orderer after having entertained the absurd literal proposition; rather, it is *because* the interpreter goes from the concept of ham sandwich to that of ham-sandwich-orderer (as a result of an accessibility shift resulting from the interpretation of the predicate) that he or she does *not* entertain the absurd literal proposition.

In this account, the metonymical transfer from ham sandwich to ham-sandwich-orderer results from a shift in accessibility triggered by the interpretation of another constituent in the sentence. The literal interpretation of the subject-term was more accessible than the metonymical interpretation before the predicate came into the picture, but the metonymical interpretation becomes

---

[17] *Ibid.*, p. 158.

more accessible as a result of interpreting the predicate. This accessibility shift has two consequences. First, the literal value of the subject term in (i) does not undergo semantic composition with that of the predicate, precisely because the semantic value of the predicate makes the literal value of the subject term less accessible than some other, non-literal interpretation. Second, if the sentence contained *another* predicate which did *not* require a person, but rather a culinary item, as argument, then the accessibility shift would *not* occur and the description 'the ham sandwich' would be given the literal interpretation; this accounts for the difference between (i) and (ii).

2.5   Interactive processing

So far I have considered the interpretation of a given constituent as if the interpretations of the other constituents were fixed; but nothing is fixed. All constituents can be given derived as well as literal interpretations, and how we interpret a constituent cannot but affect how we interpret the others. Consider (3), for instance.

(3) The city is asleep.

A city is not the sort of thing that sleeps (in the normal sense of the term), hence the overall interpretation of (3) is likely to involve some process of non-literal interpretation. There are various possibilities, though. 'The city' can be interpreted metonymically as standing for 'the inhabitants of the city' (transfer); or 'asleep' can be interpreted metaphorically in the sense of 'quiet and showing little activity' (loosening). Given the likelihood of a non-literal interpretation for some constituent, if 'the city' literally applies to a city, 'asleep' will have to be taken non-literally; conversely, if 'asleep' is literal, 'the city' will not be.

The same sort of trade-off applies to seemingly unproblematic examples such as the following:

(4) I finished the book.
(5) John heard the piano.

If 'finish' has its standard sense in (4), its object (what is said to be finished) must be a process, for only processes can start or finish in the standard sense. It follows that 'the book' must be interpreted non-literally – it must be interpreted as standing, not for a certain book, but for the process of, say, *reading* a certain book. Conversely, if 'the book' is interpreted literally and stands for a certain book, 'finish' must have a derived sense and mean something like *finished reading*. Pustejovsky defends the former analysis, Langacker the latter.[18]

[18] James Pustejovsky, 'The Generative Lexicon', in *Computational Linguistics* 17 (1991), 409–41, and *The Generative Lexicon* (MIT Press, 1995); Ronald Langacker, 'Active Zones', in *Proceedings of the Annual Meeting of the Berkeley Linguistics Society* 10 (1984), 172–88. Note that the sentence may also be seen as either 'completed' or 'expanded' into 'I finished reading the book'

(5) is another example (discussed by Langacker) which can be interpreted in two ways. We may construe 'the piano' as standing for *the sounds emitted by the piano* (metonymy), in accordance with the 'postulate' that only sounds can be heard; or we may consider 'hear' as polysemous. When it is said that 'only sounds can be heard', 'hear' is taken in its basic sense ($HEAR_1$), but there is another sense ($HEAR_2$), which can be defined as follows: an object is heard$_2$ whenever the sound it emits is heard$_1$. Langacker analyses (5) as saying that John heard$_2$ the piano, rather than as saying that he heard$_1$ the sounds emitted by the piano.

Though (3), (4) and (5) exhibit the same sort of trade-off, there is an important difference between (3), on the one hand, and (4) and (5) on the other hand. Depending on which constituent receives a non-literal interpretation, the global interpretation of (3) itself will vary. In one case the speaker means that the inhabitants of the city are sleeping, in the other she means that the city itself is quiet and shows little activity; the truth-conditions are distinct. It follows that it is easy to say which constituent is responsible for the non-literal interpretation of the sentence: we have only to consult our intuitions concerning the truth-conditions of the utterance. Examples (4) and (5) are very different, however. Whether one constituent or the other bears the onus of non-literal interpretation, the overall interpretation of the utterance does not seem to change. Hence it is not easy to establish which analysis is right, and one must appeal to indirect evidence, such as, for example, the fact that we can say things like: 'I can both hear and touch the piano.' (This fact tends to support Langacker's view: when we say that we hear the piano, we are referring to the piano. It is the verb, not the noun-phrase, which has a derived sense in this context.)[19]

(on expansion and completion, see Kent Bach, *Thought and Reference* (Oxford University Press, 1987) and 'Conversational Impliciture').

[19] A number of similar tests are offered by Geoff Nunberg in 'Indexicality and Deixis' (in *Linguistics and Philosophy* 16 (1993), 1–43) and 'Transfers of Meaning'. For example, Nunberg argues that (a) and (b) must be analysed in fairly different ways, despite their superficial similarity:
(a) I am parked out back.
(b) This one <pointing to a car key> is parked out back.
Example (b) is a case of 'deferred ostension': an object (the key) is 'demonstrated', but the ultimate 'referent', as opposed to the 'demonstratum', is another object suitably related to the demonstratum, namely the car itself. In contrast, 'I' does *not* refer to the car in (a); it normally refers to the speaker. It's the *predicate* 'parked out back' that bears the onus of non-literality. That the referent is the car rather than the (demonstrated) key in (b) is established by the fact that semantic features of the referring expression such as number or gender do NOT correspond to the key, but to the car; thus we would say 'this one' (in the singular) even if we were exhibiting a whole set of keys for the car in question. Also, we can say things like:
(c) This <pointing to a car key>, which is an old Chevrolet, is parked out back.
The relative clause clearly qualifies the car, not the key. These tests provide evidence that the referent is the car, even if it is the key which is 'demonstrated'. When we turn to (a), the situation is totally different. Gender and number correspond to the speaker, not to the car. We would not say 'We are parked out back' if there was a single car owner and several cars (whereas we can say 'Those <pointing to a key> are parked out back' if there is a single key and several cars). And we can't say 'I, who am an old Chevrolet, am parked out back.'

The trade-off talked about in this section is a particular case of a more general and fairly complex phenomenon: the search for coherence in interpretation. The examples involve two constituents, A and B, each with (at least) two possible interpretations (Ai and Aj, and Bi and Bj). Now there is a better 'fit' between Ai and Bj or between Aj and Bi than there is between either Ai and Bi or Aj and Bj, hence the 'trade-off' effect: the two global interpretations $<$Ai, B$j>$ and $<$Aj, B$i>$ are favoured, in such a way that the choice of either Aj or Ai as the correct interpretation for A 'coerces' a particular interpretation (Bi or Bj) for B. The tendency to prefer coherent interpretations (with a high degree of fit between the various semantic values) is what we must now try to account for. But first, we must introduce the notion of a schema.[20]

2.6   The role of schemata

To say that two semantic values α and β 'fit together' is to say that there is an abstract schema which $<\alpha$, $\beta>$ instantiates. The particular case discussed above, 'coercion', can be analysed as follows. An expression E activates an abstract schema in which there is a slot for a value of a certain type; as a result, the semantic value of E will preferably enter into composition with a semantic value of the relevant type. Thus in a sentence like 'The city is asleep', if we give to 'asleep' its literal value (thereby activating the SLEEP schema), the value of 'the city' will have to be of the relevant type (for example, human or animal), hence non-literal.

The role of schemata in interpretation is best seen in connection with more complex examples. Consider example (2) once again:

(2) John was arrested by a policeman yesterday; he had just stolen a wallet.

As I said earlier, John is selected as the referent for 'he' in the second clause because (i) the referent of 'he' is said to have stolen and John is known to have been arrested, and (ii) there is a frame or schema in which the two roles (stealing, and being arrested) are linked. This schema is jointly activated by the predicates 'was arrested' and 'had stolen'. An interpretation in which the same person steals and is arrested (and in which he is arrested because he has stolen – see below) satisfies the schema, and is more likely to be selected than one which violates it.

---

[20] On schemata, see David Rumelhart, 'Some Problems with the Notion of Literal Meanings', in Andrew Ortony (ed.), *Metaphor and Thought* (Cambridge University Press, 2nd edn, 1993), 71–82, and 'Schemata: the Building Blocks of Cognition', in R. Spiro, B. Bruce and W. Brewer (eds.), *Theoretical Issues in Reading Comprehension* (Lawrence Erlbaum, 1980), 33–58; see also Ronald Langacker, *Foundations of Cognitive Grammar*, vol. 1 (Stanford University Press, 1987). For further references and a historical overview (with, unfortunately, no mention of Fillmore's work on 'frames'), see David Rumelhart, Paul Smolensky, James McClelland and Geoffrey Hinton, 'Schemata and Sequential Thought Processes in PDP Models', in James McClelland and David Rumelhart (eds.), *Parallel Distributed Processing: Explorations in the Microstructure of Cognition*, vol. 2 (MIT Press, 1986), pp. 17–21.

Given the link we have established between coherence (or fit) and schemata, the question we must answer becomes: why are schema-instantiating interpretations more successful than others? In line with what has been said so far, the following answer suggests itself. Interpretational success – what brings a 'candidate' or potential semantic value into the actual interpretation of the utterance – to a large extent depends on the candidate's accessibility or degree of activation. Now a schema is activated by, or accessed through, an expression whose semantic value corresponds to an aspect of the schema. The schema thus activated in turn raises the accessibility of whatever possible semantic values for other constituents of the sentence happen to fit the schema. The schema itself gains extra activation from the fact that some other constituent of the sentence has a possible interpretation which fits the schema. In such a case all 'candidates' or potential semantic values which fit the schema evoked by some of them mutually reinforce their accessibility and therefore increase the likelihood that they will be globally selected as part of the interpretation of the utterance. Coherent, schema-instantiating interpretations therefore tend to be selected and preferred over non-integrated or 'loose' interpretations. As a result, schemata drive the interpretation process.

The role played by schemata explains why the process of utterance interpretation is to such a large extent top down and driven by world knowledge. The interpreter unconsciously enriches the situation described by the utterance with many details which do not correspond to any aspect of the uttered sentence but are contributed in order to fit an evoked schema.[21] Thus, in the policeman example above, not only is the reference of 'he' determined by the $STEAL$ (X) – IS $ARRESTED$ (X) schema, but (among other things) the causal interpretation of the relation between the two events mentioned – the fact that the referent was arrested because he had stolen – is also determined by the schema.

---

[21] Think of an example like (6):

(6) John hates the piano.

Contrary to (4)–(5), this example cannot be described in terms of 'coercion'. I mentioned earlier various contentions to the effect that only sounds can be heard and only processes finished. By virtue of these principles, some process of non-literal interpretation must take place in order to make sense of phrases such as 'finish the book' or 'hear the piano'. But a piano is certainly an object that *can* be hated, however strictly one construes the predicate 'hate'. Still, some contextual enrichment is in order, because to hate the piano is to hate it *under some aspect or dimension*. One may hate the sounds emitted by the piano, or one can hate playing the piano, or one can hate the piano as a piece of furniture, etc. The relevant dimension is contextually provided through the process of enrichment.

3   Relevance-theoretic objections

3.1   One or two systems?

There is much that is common between the view so far presented and 'relevance theory'.[1] The emphasis upon the psychological dimension of utterance interpretation, and the rejection of Minimalism, are among the important features that the two frameworks share. But there are also some differences.

One difference that has been recently the focus of attention on the part of relevance theorists is this. According to me, the primary pragmatic processes involved in comprehension are not 'inferential'.[2] Only when the unreflective, normal process of interpretation yields weird results does a genuine inference process take place whereby we use evidence concerning the speaker's beliefs and intentions to work out what he means. There is no doubt that our ability to do so is an important part of our conversational competence, but the question at issue is: *how essential* is that inferential ability? Can linguistic communication proceed without it, at some basic level, or is it from the very start constituted by it? Following Millikan and Burge, I reply that communication is not constitutively inferential.[3] As Burge writes,

We seem normally to understand content in a way whose unconscious details (. . .) are not accessible via ordinary reflection. To be entitled to believe what one is told, one need not understand or be able to justify any transition from perceptual beliefs about words to understanding of and belief in the words' content. One can, of course, come to understand certain inferences from words to contents. Such empirical meta-skills do enrich communication. But they are not indispensable to it.[4]

In my framework, however, conversational implicatures *are* inferentially derived from premises concerning the speaker's intentions in saying what he

---

[1] On relevance theory, see Sperber and Wilson, *Relevance*, Diane Blakemore, *Understanding Utterances: An Introduction to Pragmatics* (Blackwell, 1992), and Carston, *Thoughts and Utterances*.

[2] See my paper 'The Alleged Priority of Literal Interpretation', and more recently 'Does Linguistic Communication Rest on Inference?', in *Mind and Language* 17 (2002), 105–26.

[3] Ruth Millikan, *Language, Thought, and Other Biological Categories* (MIT Press, 1984), pp. 60–70; Tyler Burge, 'Content Preservation', in *Philosophical Review* 102 (1993), 457–88.

[4] Burge, 'Content Preservation', p. 477.

says. They are arrived at by answering questions such as, 'Why is the speaker saying what he says?' Instead of merely retrieving what is said through the operation of unconscious, primary pragmatic processes, we reflect on the fact that the speaker says what he says and use that fact, together with background knowledge, to infer what the speaker means without saying it. The retrieving of conversational implicatures therefore involves reflective capacities that are not exercised in what Millikan calls 'normal language flow'.[5]

As I emphasized in chapter 2, the contrast between primary and secondary pragmatic processes corresponds to different levels of processing. The determination of what is said takes place at a sub-personal level, like the determination of what we see. But the determination of what the speaker implies takes place at the personal level, like the determination of the consequences of what we see.

Relevance theorists do not accept my distinction between the two sorts of process. They advocate a unified view, according to which 'the various different pragmatic tasks are performed by processes that comprise a single system, which takes decoded linguistic meaning as its input and delivers the propositions communicated'.[6] And they insist that the processes in question are uniformly inferential, though in a sense that does not entail reflectiveness.

According to relevance theorists, there is nothing 'special' about implicatures. They accept that in some cases a conscious, explicit process of inference takes place, which disrupts normal language flow;[7] but it would be a mistake, they argue, to think of implicature derivation on this model. Implicature derivation is as automatic and unconscious as the other processes I treat as 'primary', viz. enrichment or loosening. In other words, there are two forms of inference: a spontaneous, automatic, unconscious form of inference which is involved *both* in explicature[8] and implicature derivation, and an effortful, conscious form which is involved only in cases in which something goes wrong and there is disruption of normal language flow. As Carston puts it,

The appropriate distinction within modes of processing and levels of explanation would seem to be between, on the one hand, a modular (sub-personal) pragmatic processor which, when all goes well, quickly and automatically delivers speaker meaning

---

[5] Millikan, *Language, Thought, and Other Biological Categories*, p. 69.
[6] Robyn Carston, 'Linguistic Meaning, Communicated Meaning, and Cognitive Pragmatics', in *Mind and Language* 17 (2002), p. 141.
[7] 'There clearly are times at which the normal communicative flow is disrupted: certain instances of garden-path utterances, especially when exploited by speakers for particular, often humorous, effects; some cases of complex figurative use which require an effortful conscious search for interpretation; other cases where there is some apprehended difficulty in satisfying oneself that the intended interpretation has been reached (it doesn't seem sufficiently relevant, for instance)' (*Ibid.*, p. 145).
[8] 'Explicature' is the relevance-theoretic word for 'what is said' in the rich, non-minimal sense. See Carston, *Thoughts and Utterances*, pp. 116–19.

(explicatures and implicatures), and, on the other hand, processes of a conscious reflective (personal-level) sort which occur only when the results of the former system are found wanting.[9]

In what follows I will discuss the arguments offered by relevance theorists in support of their position. This will enable me to clarify my view and to clear up some misunderstandings.

3.2 Personal and sub-personal inferences

Communication, in its most basic form, is non-inferential in the sense that it does not rest on reasoning. Reid defines 'reasoning' as

the process by which we pass from one judgment to another which is the consequence of it. Accordingly, our judgments are distinguished into intuitive, which are not grounded upon any preceding judgment, and discursive, which are deduced from some preceding judgment by reasoning.[10]

Evidently, comprehension is intuitive rather than discursive, except in the special situations in which one adopts a reflective stance towards the ongoing discourse. Normally we do not have to reason to understand what others are saying: the judgment that the speaker has said that p is made directly upon hearing the utterance, without being inferentially grounded in some prior judgment to the effect that the speaker has uttered sentence S.

Relevance theorists do not deny that comprehension is intuitive rather than discursive. When they say that communication is fundamentally inferential, they mean it in a sense which is compatible with its being intuitive. According to them, there are two sorts of inference (figure 3.1). One is conscious, explicit inference – what Reid calls 'reasoning'. But there is also a type of inference that occurs unconsciously, in such a way that the judging subject is aware only of the conclusion of the inference (which is, therefore, available not as the conclusion of an inference but as an immediate, intuitive judgment).

Relevance theorists admit, indeed emphasize, that the inferential procedure underlying ordinary understanding is unconscious. As Sperber says, 'when most of us talk of reasoning, we think of an occasional, conscious, difficult, and rather slow mental activity. What modern psychology has shown is that something like reasoning goes on all the time – unconsciously, painlessly, and fast.'[11] It is in that modern psychological sense that communication is said to be 'inferential'.

---

[9] 'Linguistic Meaning, Communicated Meaning, and Cognitive Pragmatics', p. 146.
[10] Thomas Reid, *Essays on the Intellectual Powers of Man* (MIT Press, 1969), p. 710.
[11] Dan Sperber, 'How Do We Communicate?', in J. Brockman and K. Matson (eds.), *How Things Are: A Science Toolkit to the Mind* (Morrow, 1995), p. 195. See also Kent Bach and Mike Harnish, *Linguistic Communication and Speech Acts* (MIT Press, 1979), pp. 92–3.

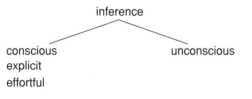

Figure 3.1 A taxonomy of inferences according to Relevance Theory

That there is such a liberal notion of inference in contemporary cognitive science is beyond question. For example, Marr writes that 'the true heart of visual perception is the inference from the structure of an image about the structure of the real world outside'.[12] That is a *very* liberal sense of 'inference' indeed. Nothing prevents the input to an inference in that sense from being non-conceptual.[13] Sperber and Wilson use 'inference' more restrictively. For there to be inference, they claim, the transition must be from a conceptual representation to a conceptual representation. Moreover, the transition must be truth-preserving. Only if these conditions are satisfied will a cognitive transition count as a genuine 'inference'.[14] According to Sperber and Wilson, pragmatic inferences are genuine inferences by this criterion.[15] Still, they are not explicit, conscious inferences conducted at the personal level. They are inferences only in the liberal, psychological sense. That is true whether we talk of the inferences which underlie my 'primary pragmatic processes' (enrichment, saturation and so on) or of those through which conversational implicatures are generated.

As far as I am concerned, I wish to maintain that implicature generation rests on a process of *conscious* inference, corresponding to Reid's description of 'reasoning'. But the notion of conscious inference that is relevant here does not quite correspond to the description given by relevance theorists. Sperber contrasts explicit, conscious reasoning, which is a voluntary, effortful and slow activity, with spontaneous inference, which is effortless, fast, and takes place

---

[12] David Marr, *Vision: A Computational Investigation into the Human Representation and Processing of Visual Information* (Freeman, 1968), p. 68.

[13] Representations of intensity changes in terms of zero-crossings are clearly non-conceptual (as pointed out by Tim Crane in *The Contents of Experience* (Cambridge University Press, 1990)), yet Marr describes the transition from such proximal representations to distal representations of edges as an inference. Fodor uses 'inference' in the same broad way in *The Modularity of Mind* (MIT Press, 1983).

[14] '[Whenever] the input and the output of a [computation] are not related as premiss and conclusion in an argument, the computation is not interpretable as inferential' (Dan Sperber and Deirdre Wilson, 'Précis of *Relevance: Communication and Cognition*', in *Behavioral and Brain Sciences* 10 (1987), p. 737).

[15] This is debatable. In 'Does Linguistic Communication Rest On Inference?', pp. 122–3, I have questioned the claim that primary pragmatic processes can be described as truth-preserving operations on conceptual representations.

unconsciously. This distinction I find misleading in the present context, for it mixes distinct issues. According to me, a *conscious inference* takes place if and only if (i) one judgment (the conclusion) is grounded in another judgment (the premiss), and (ii) both judgments, as well as the fact that one is grounded in and justified by the other, are available (consciously accessible) to the judging subject. Secondary pragmatic processes are inferential in the narrow sense of 'conscious inference' because they satisfy that essential condition – the *availability condition*. But it would be wrong to claim that conscious inferences are necessarily effortful, slow and under voluntary control. Among conscious inferences as I have just defined them, some – including those that underlie the retrieval of conversational implicatures – are typically spontaneous: the inference is drawn more or less automatically.

Consider Sperber's own example of spontanous inference: you hear the doorbell ringing, and you form the belief 'There is someone at the door.'[16] That belief is inferentially derived from a prior belief (to the effect that the doorbell is ringing) directly based on perception, but it does not issue from a process of explicit reasoning:

> If challenged, you might be able to produce, *ex post facto*, a missing premiss that, together with the perceptual belief, warrants the inferential belief. However, the fact is that you arrived at the inferential belief without engaging in deliberate or conscious inference.[17]

I grant that there is a difference between spontaneous inference and explicit reasoning, but I deny that this corresponds to the distinction between conscious (personal) and unconscious (sub-personal) inferences. On my view, spontaneous inferences of the sort mentioned by Sperber *are* conscious inferences.

In all the examples given by Sperber in the passage from which I've just quoted, including the doorbell example, the availability condition *is* satisfied: the subject makes two judgments, one based on perception, the other based on inference from the first belief. The two judgments are conscious and available to the subject. Moreover, the subject is aware that the second judgment is grounded in, and justified by, the first. If she says, 'There is someone at the door', and is asked 'How do you know?', she will reply something like: 'The doorbell is ringing.' The perceptual judgment to the effect that the doorbell is ringing justifies, and is known to justify, the non-perceptual judgment that there is someone at the door. Since there are two judgments standing in the appropriate relation to each other, Reid's definition of 'reasoning' applies, even though this piece of reasoning is spontaneous, effortless and fast. The only thing that is not conscious here are the inferential steps needed to bridge the gap between

---

[16] Sperber, Dan, 'Intuitive and Reflective Beliefs', in *Mind and Language* 12 (1997), pp. 77–8.
[17] *Ibid.*, p. 78.

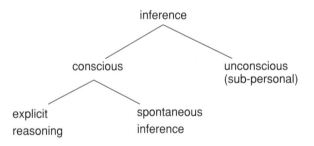

Figure 3.2 A revised taxonomy

the first, perceptual belief and the second, inferential belief. Still, the inference, though not *explicit*, is *conscious* in the sense that the availability condition is satisfied.[18] This is in contrast to cases in which the availability condition is *not* satisfied: cases, for example, where the subject is aware only of one judgment, the alleged inferential source of that judgment being unavailable to consciousness; or cases in which both judgments are available, but the subject is unaware of one being inferentially derived from the other.

I conclude that there are two sorts of conscious inference: explicit reasoning, and spontaneous inference (figure 3.2). *In both cases the availability condition is satisfied.* Unconscious, sub-personal inferences are characterized by the fact that the availability condition is *not* satisfied. Now it is my contention that, if primary pragmatic processes are indeed 'inferential' (in the liberal sense), the inferences at issue are unconscious and sub-personal. The interpreter is not aware that his judgment, to the effect that the speaker has said that *p*, is inferentially derived from a prior judgment (for example, a judgment to the effect that the speaker has uttered sentence S). Similarly, some theorists claim that perceptual judgments themselves are inferential, but the inferences at issue do not satisfy the availability condition: the perceiver is not aware that his perceptual judgment that *p* is based on a prior judgment (to the effect that

---

[18] The distinction between the two notions is crucial. Overlooking it leads to fallacies, as in this passage from Michael Thau's *Consciousness and Cognition* (p. 149): 'Once we abandon the idea that conversational participants consciously calculate what's implicated from what is said, there's no reason to think that they should always have the ability to consciously distinguish the former from the latter.' This is fallacious because the main reason for denying that conversational participants consciously calculate what's implicated from what is said is that they don't do so explicitly. (As Thau rightly points out, p. 145, 'when I understand that your utterance [Fergie was sober today] is intended to convey that Fergie is often drunk, I don't have any explicit thoughts about conversational maxims, nor do I perform any explicit inferential reasoning.') But this has no bearing at all on the issue, whether or not the availability condition is satisfied. In this particular case I take it as obvious that the availability condition *is* satisfied: the interpreter is aware that the speaker has said that Fergie is sober today (thereby implying that he is often drunk).

things seem thus and so, or whatever).[19] In contrast, when I judge that John is still here because I can see his car, that judgment is transparently or consciously inferential: the availability condition is satisfied. Similarly, secondary pragmatic processes are transparently or consciously inferential, because the availability condition is satisfied: the subject is aware of the relation between the implicature and what is said. That is true even though (normally) conversational implicatures are not generated through a process of *explicit* reasoning. As relevance theorists rightly emphasize, implicature generation is often as automatic, as effortless as primary pragmatic processes. But this is irrelevant to the distinction *I* want to make. Despite their spontaneous and automatic character, secondary pragmatic processes are conscious in the minimal sense that the availability condition is satisfied. In primary pragmatic processes, the availability condition is not satisfied.

3.3   Implicature or enrichment?

Relevance theorists have provided a couple of arguments supporting their view that implicatures and explicatures are not processed by separate systems, a 'primary' pragmatic system that works blindly and in parallel, and a 'secondary' system that takes as input the output of the primary system. Those arguments attempt to show that the computation of what is said does not have to precede the derivation of implicatures, contrary to what my account suggests.

Following Herb Clark, Carston points out that 'there is a class of widely recognized implicatures, known as "bridging" implicatures, which *have to* precede the full derivation of an explicature'.[20] One of Clark's original examples was (1), which is said to implicate (2).

(1) The picnic was awful. The beer was warm.
(2) The beer was part of the picnic.

Carston writes: 'in the absence of any argument that denies the status of implicature to assumptions like those in (2), they seem to present strong evidence in

---

[19] Searle gives the following example: 'Suppose I am standing in front of a house looking at it; in so doing I will have a certain visual experience with a certain Intentional content, that is certain conditions of satisfaction; but suppose now as part of the background assumptions I assume I am on a Hollywood movie set and all of the buildings are just papier maché façades. This assumption would not only give us different conditions of satisfaction; it would even alter the way the façade of the house looks to us' ('The Background of Meaning', in John Searle, Ferenc Kiefer and Manfred Bierwisch (eds.), *Speech Act Theory and Pragmatics* (Reidel, 1980), p. 231). This sort of example shows that what we see (in the cognitive sense, involving identification of the seen object) depends upon background assumptions and can be modified by manipulating them even though the optical stimuli remain unchanged. This can be described in terms of an 'inference' using the relevant assumption as 'premiss', but, clearly, the inference at issue is not available to the perceiving subject.

[20] Carston, 'Linguistic Meaning, Communicated Meaning, and Cognitive Pragmatics', p. 143.

favour of a system of pragmatic interpretation which derives explicatures and implicatures in parallel'.[21]

Now I am puzzled by this particular example because it is so strikingly similar to other examples of 'bridging' which Carston herself (rightly) treats as instances of enrichment. If 'She took out her key and opened the door <with the key>' is an instance of bridging enrichment (a *primary* pragmatic process, in my account), the same thing should be said of the Clark example, since the only significant difference between the two cases is the fact that there is conjunction in one case, parataxis in the other. Conversely, if (2) is treated as a conversational implicature of (1), then 'the door was opened with the key' ought to be treated as a conversational implicature of 'She took out her key and opened the door', contrary to Carston's own analysis in terms of enrichment. As far as I am concerned, I opt for the enrichment account, and I therefore deny that (2) is a conversational implicature of (1). (The enrichment of incomplete descriptions is a standard phenomenon, which I have already mentioned. The enrichment of 'the beer' into something like 'the beer that was part of the picnic' is like the enrichment of 'the table' into 'the table of the living room'.)[22]

Another example of implicature invoked by Carston in arguing against my view turns out to be best treated as a case of enrichment. She writes:

Let's consider some examples of utterances which clearly communicate an implicature, starting with the first example Grice gave when illustrating the role of his conversational maxims:

    (3) A I am out of petrol.
          B There is a garage around the corner.
          (*Gloss*: B would be infringing the maxim 'Be relevant' unless he thinks, or thinks it possible, that the garage is open, and has petrol to sell; so he implicates that the garage is, or at least may be, open, etc.)

Now, B could have given a more explicit response to A, one in which the information that petrol is currently being sold at a garage round the corner is part of what is said by the utterance. For instance he could have uttered the sentence in (4):

    (4) B There is a garage round the corner which sells petrol and is open now.

According to [Recanati's view], this utterance would have maintained the normal language flow while the one B actually gave, in (3), disrupts that normal language flow. It is perhaps difficult to have a sure sense of what is meant by the notion of 'normal' language flow, but the exchange in (3) seems to be about as natural, normal and flowing a conversation as there is, while, arguably, the implicature-less one in (4) is somewhat awkward, being quite unnecessarily explicit (in the absence of any doubt about the functioning of the garage).[23]

---

[21] *Ibid.*

[22] Carston would probably argue that examples like (1) involve *both* enrichment and implicature generation. In (1), for example, the speaker implicates that there was beer at the picnic, and the explicature of (1) is enriched on the basis of that 'implicated premiss': 'the beer' is understood as 'the beer that was part of the picnic'. As far as I am concerned, however, I am unwilling to treat what relevance theorists call 'implicated premisses' as genuine implicatures (see §3.5).

[23] *Ibid.*, p. 144.

I have already said in what sense I mean that implicatures are special: their distinctness from what is said is grasped, while the aspects of meaning that are contextually provided through primary pragmatic processes are phenomenologically undiscriminated. Be that as it may, I deny that a conversational implicature is involved in the Gricean example mentioned by Carston. The content of B's utterance in (3) is enriched into the proposition which (4) explicitly articulates. This is very standard. In the relevance-theoretic framework favoured by Carston herself the word 'garage' can be taken to contextually express the ad hoc concept GARAGE*, paraphrasable as 'a garage that is presumably open and has petrol to sell'.[24]

The inappropriateness of the alleged counterexamples should not blind us to the important issue raised by relevance theorists: if there are cases in which the derivation of an implicature must come before the computation of what is said, does this not argue against my account? To this issue I now turn.

3.4   Mutual adjustment of explicature and implicature

According to relevance theorists, I am committed to a sequential view of the derivation of implicatures and am therefore unable to account for the phenomenon of 'mutual adjustment' between implicature and explicature. My view, it is said,

assumes that explicature derivation precedes implicature derivation, and, thereby, commits [me] to a sequential processing model. By contrast, a relevance-based comprehension model is not a sequential model: the implicature derivation may coincide with, precede, or follow the implicature derivation, and the content of derived implicatures may affect the way explicatures are developed.[25]

---

[24] Grice's 'garage' example is often treated as the paradigm case of conversational implicature. In 'Gricean Rational Reconstructions and the Semantics/Pragmatics Distinction' (*Synthèse* 128 (2001), 93–131), Manuel Garcia-Carpintero invokes that example to discredit the 'Scope Principle': that genuine conversational implicatures (in contrast to pragmatic constituents of what is said) are not 'inherited' when the sentence conveying the implicature is placed under the scope of logical operators (*Direct Reference*, pp. 269–74). As against the principle, Carpintero argues as follows: 'Uncontroversial cases of implicated contents are also inherited. In another famous example by Grice, an utterance of 'there is a gas station around the corner' implicates that there is gas available around the corner. This implicated content is inherited in some longer utterances: just consider 'if there is a gas station around the corner, I do not need to worry any more'; and 'there is no gas station nearby' can be regarded as not falsified by the existence of a closed gas station around the corner.' ('Gricean Rational Reconstructions', p. 113).

But who said that that example was an uncontroversial case of implicated content? The very fact that the alleged implicature is inherited in complex sentences makes it controversial that it is a genuine implicature. (I am indebted to Robyn Carston for mentioning Carpintero's use of that example, and this possible line of reply, in her talk 'Semantics and Conversational Implicature', forthcoming in the Proceedings of the Genoa conference *WOC 2002: The Semantics/Pragmatics Distinction*, to be published by CSLI Publications.)

[25] Tomoko Matsui, 'Experimental Pragmatics: Towards Testing Relevance-Based Predictions about Anaphoric Bridging Inferences', in Varol Akman, Paolo Bouquet, Richmond Thomason and Roger Young (eds.), *Modeling and Using Context* (Springer, 2001), p. 250.

Relevance theorists have documented the phenomenon of 'mutual adjustment' between implicature and explicature. As Sperber and Wilson say, 'expectations of relevance warrant the derivation of specific implicatures, for which the explicit content must be adequately enriched'.[26] One of their examples is the following exchange:

A Do you want to go to the cinema?
B I am tired.

A primary pragmatic process of enrichment maps the lexical concept TIRED to the ad hoc concept TIRED*, which can be paraphrased as something like TIRED TO AN EXTENT THAT MAKES GOING TO THE CINEMA UN-DESIRABLE TO B. Enrichment here is driven by the need to derive from B's utterance an implicated response to A's question. Similarly, at the end of chapter 1 (pp. 21–2), I mentioned the connection between enrichment and implicature derivation:

> By saying that she's had breakfast, the speaker implies that she is not hungry and does not want to be fed. By saying that the child is not going to die, the mother implies that the cut is not serious; and so forth. Now those implicatures can be worked out only if the speaker is recognized as expressing the (non-minimal) proposition that she's had breakfast *that morning*, or that the child won't die *from that cut*. Clearly, if the speaker had had breakfast twenty years ago (rather than that very morning), nothing would follow concerning the speaker's present state of hunger and her willingness or unwillingness to eat something. The implicature could not be derived, if what the speaker says was not given the richer, temporally restricted interpretation.

So I agree with Sperber and Wilson about the phenomenon they call 'mutual adjustment'. Carston concludes that 'there is no generalization to be made about which of the two kinds of communicated assumption (explicature and implicature) is recovered first and functions as input to the recovery of the other; the parallel adjustment process entails that neither is wholly temporally prior to the other'.[27] Rather, the proper generalization to make is this:

> Any interpretation . . . results from mutual adjustment of the explicit and implicit content of the utterance. This adjustment process stabilises when the hypothesised explicit content is warranted by the hypothesised explicit content together with the context.[28]

But there is nothing with which I find that I have to disagree here. So I deny that my view commits me to a 'sequential model' in the sense under discussion. What matters from my point of view is only this: there is an *asymmetry* between implicature and explicature, in that the implicature must be grounded in, or warranted by, the explicature. Both Carston and Sperber and Wilson grant this point, at least as far as 'implicated conclusions' are concerned. So there is no

---

[26] Sperber and Wilson, 'The Mental and the Public Lexicon', p. 194.
[27] Carston, 'Linguistic Meaning, Communicated Meaning, and Cognitive Pragmatics', p. 143.
[28] Sperber and Wilson, 'The Public and the Mental Lexicon', p. 197.

disagreement on this score. (I shall return to the mutual adjustment issue in §3.6.)

3.5   Implicated premisses

Deirdre Wilson once objected to me that implicatures may be premisses as well as conclusions, hence they need not be 'grounded in' or 'warranted by' the explicature. Implicated premisses are background assumptions that either serve as auxiliary premisses in deriving the implicatures from the explicature, or, possibly, are appealed to in enriching the content of the utterance so as to yield an appropriate explicature. Wilson gave as example the following exchange:

A Why didn't you invite me to your party?
B I only invited nice people.

The implicature here is the premiss that A is not nice. (B's utterance provides a relevant answer to A's question only if this is assumed.) The alleged 'bridging implicature' invoked by Carston as counterexample to my view is also an implicated premiss. That there was beer among the beverages served at the picnic is an implicated premiss by appeal to which one can enrich 'the beer' into 'the beer served at the picnic'.

In general I don't think so-called 'implicated premisses' are genuine implicatures in the sense in which I am using that term. They are not part of what the speaker means, that is, intentionally communicates, but part of what he takes for granted (presupposes) and expects the hearer to take for granted. Thus I draw a distinction between the common ground to which such premisses belong, and the explicit or implicit content of the utterance – what the speaker specifically intends to communicate. Implicatures are, by definition, an aspect of content. Since that is not true of implicated premisses, they do not count as genuine implicatures (in my framework).

To be sure, there are cases in which an implicated premiss is part of what is meant. Thus in the above exchange we may imagine that B's point precisely is to convey to A that he (A) is not nice. Even in that case I would not treat that as an instance of implicature, but, rather, as an instance of 'staging' (§5.5). The speaker ostensively speaks as if it were common ground that A is not a nice person. The mechanism at work here is more similar to that which underlies irony than to the inferential mechanism characteristic of implicature. However, let us assume that there is a genuine implicature here. What, exactly, is implicated? Wilson says it is the premiss that A is not nice. But there is an alternative construal. We may consider that what the speaker implicates is that he considers A as not a nice person. Is this a premiss or a conclusion? Arguably, like other implicatures it is the conclusion of an inference taking as premiss the speaker's saying what he says. *The speaker's saying that only nice persons were invited, in response to the question 'Why didn't you invite me?', implies that he considers the hearer as not a nice person.* If this is an implicature, one may argue that it is, indeed, grounded in or warranted by the speaker's locutionary act (that is, his saying of what is said), just as ordinary implicatures are.

3.6   Personal-level inferences: occurrent vs dispositional

Commenting on a first version of this chapter, Robyn Carston has expressed incredulity. It is not enough, she said, merely to *assert* that I accept the relevance theorist's (RT) account of the derivation of explicatures and implicatures in terms of processes of 'mutual adjustment'. This must be substantiated, for there is a prima facie incompatibility between my account and the RT account. On my account, there are quite distinct types of processes involved in deriving these different types of communicated assumption: local associative processes, governed solely by accessibility considerations, in the case of what is said; properly inferential processes operating over propositions, and governed by Gricean-type maxims, in the case of implicatures. Furthermore, statements occur throughout my book (especially in chapter 5) which strongly encourage an understanding of these processes as taking place in a sequential order.[29] 'At the very least', Carston concludes,

> Recanati should acknowledge that these details of his account seem to lead naturally to the conclusion that the two types of process are sequential in nature. It would be even better if he would give some explanation of how these details can, after all, be reconciled with the parallel mutual adjustment account.[30]

Let me (try to) satisfy Carston's request. To do so I need to introduce a distinction, sketched by Carpintero, between two ways for an inference to be 'tacit' rather than explicit. Tacit inferences, in general, are contrasted with what Carpintero calls 'conscious, explicit, occurrent' (CEO) inferences, that is, 'reasonings which we make by carefully going through their steps'.[31] An inference is tacit in the first, *sub-personal* sense, if it is ascribed to a cognitive system merely on the grounds that 'the causal processes constituting the system, mirror the processes of someone who [performed] the relevant [inferences] in an explicit form' (p. 122).[32] An inference is tacit in a second, *personal* sense if

---

[29] 'In order to derive the implicature, we need the premiss that the speaker has said what he has said; therefore we need to have identified the primary content of his utterance' (p. 70); '. . . derived from some antecedently determined meaning by an inferential process akin to that which is involved in conversational implicature' (p. 72); 'it is a two-step procedure instead of being a one-step procedure. The interpreter first determines the utterance's primary meaning, then infers some additional meaning' (p. 74).

[30] 'Report on typescript by François Recanati called *Literal Meaning*' (November 2002), p. 3.

[31] Garcia-Carpintero, 'Gricean Rational Reconstructions', p. 120.

[32] *Ibid.*, p. 122. That is the notion of tacit inference appealed to by Scott Soames in *Beyond Rigidity: The Unfinished Semantic Agenda of 'Naming and Necessity'* (Oxford University Press, 2002). Soames writes: 'In talking of inference here, I don't mean to suggest any conscious or unconscious process of inferring conclusions from premises one consciously or unconsciously

the cognitive agent to which it is ascribed on those grounds is *itself* capable of making the inference explicitly and of rationally justifying whatever methods it spontaneously uses in arriving at the 'conclusion'.

In terms of this distinction, here is my proposal. It is constitutive of conversational implicatures that the inference which gives rise to them is available to the interpreters; but this availability need not be cashed out as requiring on the part of the subject a CEO-inference. A tacit inference is ok, provided it is of the 'personal' sort, that is, provided the subject herself has the reflective capacities for making the inference explicit. To say that this capacity is constitutive, in the case of conversational implicatures, is to say that there would be no conversational implicature if the interpreters did not have that reflective capacity. On the other hand, I maintain that the reflective capacity to rationally justify one's interpretation is not constitutive when the interpretation involves only primary pragmatic processes.[33] We can ascribe to unsophisticated subjects the form of communicative competence which enables them to understand utterances in the normal way (by unreflectingly exploiting pragmatic processes such as saturation, enrichment, loosening or transfer), even if, because of their lack of sophistication, they cannot be ascribed the reflective capacities for explicitly justifying those interpretations. But in the case of conversational implicatures, the reflective capacity is constitutive of the competence. This does not mean that whenever the competence is exercised, the reflective capacity is also exercised. Far from it: often we understand an implicature intuitively, without going through a CEO-inference.[34] The cases of mutual adjustment focused on by relevance theorists fall into that category: in the actual mental process of the interpreter, there is no step by step, linear reasoning leading from the premiss to the conclusion. Still, the availability condition is satisfied: that means that the inferential link between premiss and conclusion is grasped by the interpreter, who can, on reflection, make it explicit.

---

represents to oneself and takes to be true. What happens is that a sentence is uttered in a context in which many things are assumed. As a causal result of this, the hearer typically comes to accept . . . a sequence of sentences . . . The psychological process by which this happens is not something that can be determined by armchair philosophizing. However, we can construct an idealized model whose inputs and outputs correspond to those of the real psychological process. In the idealized model, rational speaker-hearers extract information from utterances by explicitly representing premises and rationally inferring conclusions from them. When we show that the inputs and outputs of the real psychological process match those of the idealized model, we show that our actual methods for gathering information from utterances make sense, and are rationally justified' (*Beyond Rigidity*, p. 335).

[33] Here I depart from Carpintero, who thinks the reflective capacity is constitutive of our communicative competence in general. I will return to that issue in the concluding chapter (§10.3).

[34] That does not show that implicatures are not 'available', contrary to what Jonathan Berg asserts ('In Defense of Direct Belief: Substitutivity, Availability, and Iterability', in *Lingua e Stile* 33 (1998), pp. 462–3). Berg uses a simple distinction between conscious and tacit (sub-personal) inferences and misses the intermediate category unearthed by Carpintero.

4   The Syncretic View

4.1   Four levels?

In chapter 1 I described two approaches to what is said: the standard approach, based on the minimalist principle, and the availability based approach, which entails rejecting Minimalism. The two pictures are summarized in figure 1.3 (p. 21). Now an intermediate position is available, according to which *there are two equally legitimate notions of what is said*: a purely semantic, minimalist notion, and a pragmatic notion ('what is stated' as opposed to what is implied). If we accept this suggestion, we end up with four levels instead of three:

$$
\begin{array}{ll}
\text{literal} & \left\{ \begin{array}{l} \text{sentence meaning} \\ \text{what is said}_{\text{min}} \end{array} \right. \\
\text{meaning} & \\
\text{vs} & \\
\text{speaker's} & \left\{ \begin{array}{l} \text{what is said}_{\text{prag}} \\ \text{what is implied} \end{array} \right. \\
\text{meaning} &
\end{array}
$$

Such a compromise would seem to be acceptable to both parties. The minimalist wants to isolate a purely semantic notion of content, that is, a notion of the content of a sentence (with respect to a context) which is compositionally determined and takes pragmatic elements on board only when this is necessary. His opponent wants to capture the intuitive notion of 'what is said' (as opposed to what is implied) and stresses that what is said in that sense is, to a large extent, determined in a top down manner by the context. The two notions can be integrated within a unified framework if one agrees to replace the traditional triad by a four-level picture (fig. 4.1).

Several authors have made proposals to that effect. In 'The Pragmatic Fallacy',[1] Nathan Salmon distinguishes two senses of the phrase 'what is said': what is said in the strict and philosophical sense (the semantic content of the sentence, with respect to the context at hand) and what is said in the loose and popular sense (the content of the speaker's speech act). What is said in the loose and popular sense is typically richer than the sentence's semantic content, yet it does not encompass what the speaker merely conveys or implicates in Grice's

---

[1] Nathan Salmon, 'The Pragmatic Fallacy', in *Philosophical Studies* 63 (1991), 83–97.

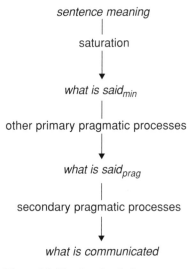

sentence meaning

|

saturation

|

what is said$_{min}$

|

other primary pragmatic processes

|

what is said$_{prag}$

|

secondary pragmatic processes

|

what is communicated

Figure 4.1 The four-level picture

sense. Salmon, in effect, draws a threefold distinction between (i) what is said in the minimalist sense (the semantic content of the sentence, in the speaker's context), (ii) what the speaker asserts, and (iii) what he or she implies. When the conventional meaning of the sentence-type is added, this yields something very much like the four-level picture above.

Kent Bach defends a similar view, with one more level.[2] 'What is said' is so minimal, in Bach's conception, that it need not even be propositional. It may be a 'propositional radical'. Thus if, pointing to Tipper, I say 'He is ready' what I say is *that Tipper is ready*. This becomes a full-fledged proposition only if an answer is provided to the question: ready for what? A pragmatic process of 'completion' must therefore take place to make the Bachian 'what is said' into a complete proposition. To go from that proposition (resulting from completion) to what is actually asserted, a further pragmatic process of *expansion* often comes into play. That process is clearly non-minimalist: it is neither triggered by a linguistic constituent, nor necessary in order to achieve propositionality. ('Expansion' is Bach's word for free enrichment.) So in Bach's framework there are five distinct notions: the sentence's linguistic meaning; what is said in the less-than-minimal sense; the minimal proposition resulting from completion (= what is said in the minimalist sense); the non-minimal proposition resulting from expansion (= what is said in the pragmatic sense, that is, the 'explicature', in relevance-theoretic terminology); and, finally, the

---

[2] See his 'Conversational Impliciture' and 'Semantic Slack'.

conversational implicatures of the utterance (not to mention what the speaker non-literally communicates). The contextual components of meaning generated through completion and expansion are called by Bach 'conversational implicitures' because they are 'implicit in' what is said, in contrast to the implicatures which are 'implied by' what is said (or the saying of it).

A third author worth mentioning in this connection is Scott Soames. In *Beyond Rigidity* he writes:

> When speaking of the information carried by an assertive utterance of a sentence in a context, one must distinguish (i) the semantic content of the sentence uttered in the context; (ii) what the speaker says (asserts) by uttering the sentence; (iii) what the speaker implies, implicates, or suggests . . . (i) is standardly included in (ii), but . . . in the case of many utterances, (ii) is not exhausted by (i).[3]

Like Salmon and Bach, Soames contrasts what is said in the semantic sense with what is said in the pragmatic sense (that is, what is stated or asserted). It is what is said in the pragmatic sense which arguably serves as input to secondary pragmatic processes and satisfies the availability condition. As we have seen, that entails that what is said (in the pragmatic sense) cannot satisfy Minimalism. But nothing follows regarding what is said in the semantic sense; hence there is no reason to give up Minimalism when dealing with semantic content.

Whatever we think of the details of the views held by Bach, Salmon or Soames, it is clear that, by freeing us of the limitations of the traditional three-level picture, they make a reconciliation of Minimalism and Availability possible. One can be a minimalist with respect to what is said in the strict and literal sense, and at the same time give up Minimalism when it comes to what the speaker asserts, which is subject to the availability constraint.

The Syncretic View promises to give us the best of both worlds. It sounds appealing and reasonable. As Jonathan Berg pointed out, I myself have proposed something along similar lines.[4] Yet I think there is a problem with that view – a problem which makes it rather unattractive, despite its initial appeal.

The weak point in the Syncretic View is the very notion of 'what is said in the strict and literal sense', that is, the minimalist notion of what is said. How are we to understand that notion? A natural and widespread interpretation runs as follows: 'What is said' in the minimalist sense is what *the sentence* says (with respect to the context at hand), as opposed to what *the speaker* says by uttering the sentence. Thus interpreted, however, the Syncretic View is closely related to a highly dubious, literalist construal of the semantics/pragmatics distinction. In the next two sections of this chapter, I will spell out that conception and show what is wrong with it.

---

[3] Soames, *Beyond Rigidity*, p. 86. [4] Berg, 'In Defense of Direct Belief', pp. 466–7.

4.2   Semantics and pragmatics: the literalist picture

On the literalist picture, knowing a language is like knowing a theory by means of which one can deductively establish the truth-conditions of (or the proposition expressed by) sentences which one has never encountered before. *Semantic interpretation* is the process whereby an interpreter exploits his or her knowledge of a language, say L, to assign to an arbitrary sentence of L its truth-conditions. *Pragmatic interpretation* is a totally different process. It is not concerned with language per se, but with human action. When someone acts, there is a reason why he does what he does. To provide an interpretation for the action is to find that reason, that is, to ascribe the agent a particular intention in terms of which we can make sense of the action.

A distinguishing characteristic of pragmatic interpretation is its defeasibility. The best explanation we can offer for an action given the available evidence may be revised in the light of new evidence. Even if an *excellent* explanation is available, it can always be overridden if enough new evidence is adduced to account for the subject's behaviour. It follows that any piece of evidence may turn out to be relevant for the interpretation of an action. In other words, there is no limit to the amount of contextual information that can affect pragmatic interpretation.

A particular class of human actions is that of communicative actions. That class is defined by the fact that the intention underlying the action is a *communicative* intention – an intention such that (arguably) its recognition by the addressee is a necessary and sufficient condition for its fulfilment.[5] To communicate that *p* is therefore to act in such a way that the addressee will explain one's action by ascribing to the agent the intention to communicate that *p*. For communication to succeed, the addressee must not only understand *that* the agent does what he does in order to communicate something to her; she must also understand *what* the agent tries to communicate. To secure that effect the communicator will do something which will evoke in the addressee's mind that which he wants to communicate. To that purpose the communicator may use icons, or indices, or symbols, that is, conventional signs. It is, of course, symbols that are used when the communicator and the addressee share a common language.

At this point semantic interpretation and pragmatic interpretation make contact with each other. A speech act is an action performed by uttering a sentence in some language, say L. Let us assume that the sentence has a certain

---

[5] See John Searle, *Speech Acts* (Cambridge University Press, 1969), p. 47; Bach and Harnish, *Linguistic Communication and Speech Acts*, p. 15. For a discussion, see my 'On Defining Communicative Intentions', in *Mind and Language* 1 (1986), 213–42, and Bach's response, 'On Communicative Intentions: A Reply to Recanati', in *Mind and Language* 2 (1987), 141–54.

semantic interpretation in L: it means that *p*. Since the speaker utters a sentence which means that *p* and manifests the intention to communicate something to the hearer, one reasonable hypothesis is that he intends to communicate that *p*. If that is the best explanation for the action given the available evidence, the hearer will settle for it and (if that was indeed the speaker's intention) the communicative intention will be fulfilled: the speaker will have succeeded in communicating that *p* to the hearer. In this case the speech act will be assigned a particular content as a result of pragmatic interpretation; and that content will coincide with the content which comes to be assigned to the sentence as a result of semantic interpretation. That is not really a coincidence, of course; for the semantic interpretation of the sentence was part of the evidence used in pragmatically determining the content of the speech act. But there are cases in which the two contents do not coincide: the sentence means that *p*, but that is not what the speaker means – what he manifestly intends to communicate.

So far I have expounded the literalist picture of the relation between semantic and pragmatic interpretation. I will criticize it shortly (§4.3). Before doing so, let me spell out the connection between that picture and the Syncretic View talked about in the first section.

On the literalist picture, as we have just seen, there is a basic distinction between what the sentence says and what the speaker means, even when they coincide. *What the sentence says* is determined by semantic interpretation, that is, deductively and without paying any regard to the speaker's beliefs and desires. Of course, one needs to make sure that the speaker utters what he does as a sentence of L; and that may require a good deal of pragmatic interpretation. But once it is determined that the utterance at issue counts as an utterance of a particular sentence of L, semantic interpretation takes over, and the content of that sentence is mechanically determined. On the other hand *what the speaker means* is determined by pragmatic interpretation. Pragmatic interpretation involves an assessment of the speaker's communicative intentions, given an overall assumption of rationality. As I pointed out, any piece of contextual information may turn out to be relevant to establishing the correct interpretation for the speech act.

In this framework there is room for the notion of *what the speaker says* – what is said in the pragmatic sense, or, as Bach puts it, 'what is stated'. Sometimes we can distinguish two components within what the speaker means: what he states, and what he implies by virtue of stating it. What is stated may, but need not, be identical to what the sentence says. Often what is stated is richer than what the sentence says, as we have seen. Be that as it may, there are two notions of what is said: one is the output of semantic interpretation. It is what the sentence says. The other is a particular aspect of speaker's meaning. It is what the speaker states. That distinction is the core of the Syncretic View.

4.3   Semantic underdeterminacy

I think there is something deeply wrong with the literalist picture (and the Syncretic View insofar as it is based on it). What is wrong – or one of the things that are wrong – is the assumption that semantic interpretation can deliver something as determinate as a complete proposition. On my view semantic interpretation, characterized by its deductive character, does not deliver complete propositions: it delivers only semantic schemata – propositional functions, to use Russell's phrase.[6]

By saying that semantic interpretation properly conceived delivers only schemata, not complete propositions, I do not mean that it delivers only characters in Kaplan's sense.[7] When a sentence contains an indexical like 'I' or 'tomorrow', the meaning of the indexical (its character) contextually determines its content in a very straightforward manner. There is no reason not to consider that aspect of content-determination as part of semantic interpretation. For the type of context-dependence exhibited by (pure) indexicals has nothing to do with the radical form of context-dependence which affects speaker's meaning. The hallmark of the more radical form of context-dependence is the fact that any piece of contextual information may be relevant. But the context that comes into play in the semantic interpretation of indexicals is not the total pragmatic context; it is a very limited context which contains only a few aspects of the pragmatic context: who speaks, when, where, and so forth. As Bach puts it,

There are two quite different sorts of context, and each plays quite a different role. Wide context concerns any contextual information relevant to determining the speaker's intention and to the successful and felicitous performance of the speech act . . . Narrow context concerns information specifically relevant to determining the semantic values of [indexicals] . . . Narrow context is semantic, wide context pragmatic.[8]

But most context-sensitive expressions are *semantically underdeterminate* rather than indexical in the strict sense. A possessive phrase such as 'John's car' means something like *the car that bears relation R to John*, where 'R' is a free variable. The free variable must be contextually assigned a particular value; but that value is not determined by a rule and it is not a function of a particular aspect of the narrow context. What a given occurrence of the phrase 'John's car' means ultimately depends upon what the speaker who utters it means. It therefore depends upon the wide context. That is true of all semantically underdeterminate expressions: their semantic value varies from occurrence to

---

[6] This should be qualified; for the schemata themselves can be represented as 'reflexive propositions' (see §4.7). Still, the propositions in question don't quite correspond to what one standardly means by a 'complete' proposition.

[7] See David Kaplan, 'Demonstratives', in Joseph Almog, Howard Wettstein and John Perry (eds.), *Themes from Kaplan* (Oxford University Press, 1989), 481–563.

[8] From the handout of a talk on 'Semantics vs Pragmatics', delivered in 1996.

occurrence, just as the semantic value of indexicals does, yet it varies not as a function of some objective feature of the narrow context but as a function of what the speaker means. It follows that semantic interpretation by itself cannot determine what is said by a sentence containing such an expression: for the semantic value of the expression – its own contribution to what is said – is a matter of speaker's meaning, and can only be determined by pragmatic interpretation.

Even if we restrict our attention to expressions traditionally classified as indexicals, we see that they involve a good deal of semantic underdeterminacy. This is true, in particular, of demonstratives. The reference of a demonstrative cannot be determined by a rule, like the rule that 'I' refers to the speaker. It is generally assumed that there is such a rule, namely the rule that the demonstrative refers to the object which happens to be demonstrated or which happens to be the most salient, in the context at hand. But the notions of 'demonstration' and 'salience' are pragmatic notions in disguise. They cannot be cashed out in terms merely of the narrow context. Ultimately, a demonstrative refers to *what the speaker who uses it refers to by using it.*

To be sure, one can make that into a semantic rule. One can say that the character of a demonstrative is the rule that it refers to what the speaker intends to refer to. As a result, one will add to the narrow context a sequence of 'speaker's intended referents', in such a way that the nth demonstrative in the sentence will refer to the nth member of the sequence. Formally that is fine, but philosophically it is clear that one is cheating. We pretend that we can manage with a limited, narrow notion of context of the sort we need for handling indexicals, while in fact we can only determine the speaker's intended referent (hence the semantic referent, which depends upon the speaker's intended referent) by resorting to pragmatic interpretation and relying on the *wide* context.[9]

We encounter the same sort of problem even with expressions like 'here' and 'now' which are traditionally considered as *pure* indexicals (rather than demonstratives). Their semantic value is the time or place of the context respectively. But what counts as the time and place of the context? How inclusive must the time or place in question be? It depends on what the speaker means, hence,

---

[9] One may acknowledge the need to appeal to the wide context in interpreting demonstratives while arguing that the appeal thus made is 'pre-semantic'. The speaker's directing intention is necessary to endow a demonstrative with a character in the first place, one might say. We need the wide context to fix the expression's character, but once the character is thus determined, through a pragmatic procedure akin to disambiguation, it maps the narrow context onto the proposition expressed by the utterance in that context. (See David Braun, 'Demonstratives and their Linguistic Meaning', in *Noûs* 30 (1996), 145–73.) Similarly, we might say that whenever there is semantic underdeterminacy, some form of pragmatic disambiguation must take place before the process of semantic interpretation can start. To argue in this way, it seems to me, *is* to acknowledge that semantic interpretation by itself cannot determine the content of a sentence containing a semantically underdeterminate expression.

again, on the wide context. As is well known, 'here' can refer to this room, this building, this city, this country, and so on, and the same underdetermination affects 'now'. We can maintain that the character of 'here' and 'now' is the rule that the expression refers to 'the' time or 'the' place of the context – a rule which automatically determines a content, given a (narrow) context in which the time and place parameters are given specific values; but then we have to let a pragmatic process take place to fix the values in question, that is, to determine *which* narrow context, among indefinitely many candidates compatible with the facts of the utterance, serves as argument to the character function. On the resulting view the (narrow) context with respect to which an utterance is interpreted is not *given*, it is not determined automatically by objective facts like where and when the utterance takes place, but it is determined by the speaker's intention and the wide context. Again, we reach the conclusion that pragmatic interpretation has a role to play in determining the content of the utterance, in such a case.

To sum up, either semantic interpretation delivers something gappy, and pragmatic interpretation must fill the gaps until we reach a complete proposition. Or we run semantic interpretation only after we have used pragmatic interpretation to pre-determine the values of semantically underdeterminate expressions, which values we artificially feed into the narrow context. Either way, semantic interpretation by itself is powerless to determine what is said, when the sentence contains a semantically underdeterminate expression.

Now I take it that such expressions can be found all over the place. Moreover, semantic underdeterminacy is not limited to particular lexical items. One can follow Waismann and argue that the satisfaction conditions of any empirical predicate are semantically underdeterminate and subject to pragmatic interpretation (§9.4). There is also constructional underdeterminacy. For example consider something as simple as the Adjective + Noun construction, as in 'red pen'. What counts as a red pen? A pen that is red. But when does a pen count as red? That depends upon the wide context. The satisfaction conditions of 'red pen' can only be determined by pragmatic interpretation (§9.3).

Suppose I am right and most sentences, perhaps all, are semantically underdeterminate. What follows? That there is no such thing as 'what the sentence says' (in the standard sense in which that phrase is generally used). There is a single notion of what is said, and that is a pragmatic notion: saying, as Grice claimed, is a variety of non-natural meaning, characterized by the role which conventional meaning of the sentence plays in the hearer's intended recognition of the speaker's communicative intention.

4.4   The minimal proposition as 'common denominator'

My conclusion at this point should not be overstated. I am not saying that the Syncretic View cannot be made sense of, only that a particular interpretation (the literalist interpretation) must be rejected. There is, I claimed, no such thing as 'what the sentence says' in the literalist sense, that is, no such thing as a complete proposition autonomously determined by the rules of the language with respect to the context but independent of the speaker's meaning. As Bach points out, what the sentence says, in the purely semantic sense, 'excludes anything that is determined by [the speaker's] communicative intention (if it included that, then what is said would be partly a pragmatic matter)'.[10] It is for that reason that I say there is no such thing: in order to reach a complete proposition through saturation, we *must* appeal to the speaker's meaning. That is the lesson of semantic underdeterminacy.

There is another possible interpretation for the semantic notion of 'what is said', however. Instead of construing what is said as a non-pragmatic property of the sentence, independent of the speaker's meaning, we can start with the pragmatic notion of what is said, and define the semantic notion in terms of it. What is said in the minimal sense can thus be defined as what is said in the full-fledged, pragmatic sense *minus* the contextual ingredients that are optional and whose provision is context-driven. To filter out the optional ingredients, while retaining the contextual ingredients that are necessary for propositionality (reference of indexicals, and so on), one may follow Soames and define the semantic content of a sentence *s* relative to a context C as

that which would be asserted and conveyed by an assertive utterance of *s* in any normal context in which the reference of all indexicals in *s* is the same as their reference in C.[11]

The strategy now consists in *abstracting* what is said in the semantic sense *from* what is said in the pragmatic sense. That seems possible if, like Soames, we take the semantic content of the sentence to be *included in* the content of the assertion. To get to the semantic content, one only has to filter out those aspects of assertion content that go beyond semantic content and are tied to specific contexts of utterance. What remains, that is, the 'common denominator', is the minimal proposition expressed by the sentence itself:

The semantic content of a sentence relative to a context is information that a competent speaker/hearer can confidently take to be asserted and conveyed by an utterance of the sentence in the context, no matter what else may be asserted, conveyed, or imparted. It is a sort of minimal common denominator determined by the linguistic knowledge shared by all competent speakers, together with contextually relevant facts such as the time, place, and agent of the context; the identity of individuals demonstrated by the speaker; and the referents of the names, as used in the context. As such, the semantic content of a sentence functions as a sort of minimal core around which speaker/hearers can structure the totality of information the sentence is used to communicate in a given context.[12]

---

[10] Bach, 'You Don't Say?', p. 21.
[11] Soames, *Beyond Rigidity*, p. 106. A similar idea is expressed in section 4 of Jason Stanley, 'Modality and What is Said', forthcoming in *Philosophical Perspectives* 16.
[12] Soames, *Beyond Rigidity*, p. 109.

This alternative strategy also raises a problem, however. What is said in the minimal, semantic sense cannot be abstracted from what is said in the pragmatic sense simply because *it need not be part of it*.[13] Soames's claim that semantic content is included in assertion content passes muster only because he focuses on cases in which the asserted content is richer than the alleged semantic content. He gives the following sort of example:

A man goes into a coffee shop and sits at the counter. The waitress asks him what he wants. He says, 'I would like coffee, please.' The sentence uttered is unspecific in several respects – its semantic content does not indicate whether the coffee is to be in the form of beans, grounds, or liquid, nor does it indicate whether the amount in question is a drop, a cup, a gallon, a sack, or a barrel. Nevertheless, it is obvious from the situation what the man has in mind, and the waitress is in no doubt about what to do. She brings him a cup of freshly brewed coffee. If asked to describe the transaction, she might well say, 'He ordered a cup of coffee' or 'He said he wanted a cup of coffee', meaning, of course, the brewed, drinkable kind. In so doing, she would, quite correctly, be reporting the content of the man's order, or assertion, as going beyond the semantic content of the sentence he uttered.[14]

Soames thinks that in such cases several propositions are asserted, including (i) the unspecific proposition literally expressed (to the effect that the man wants coffee in some form or other) and (ii) more specific propositions recoverable from the literal proposition and the context. Those more specific propositions resulting from enrichment are tied to the particular context in which they are generated, hence they can be filtered out by considering other contexts in which that sentence would be uttered and the indexicals would be given the same semantic values. Soames equates the minimal proposition expressed by the sentence with the proposition which would be asserted in *all* such contexts.

The problem is that enrichment is only one optional process among others. Only in the case of enrichment, however, is it plausible to suggest that the minimal proposition itself is part of what is asserted. Soames glosses assertion in terms of commitment: 'assertively uttering a sentence with the intention to assert or convey p involves doing so with the intention of committing oneself to p'.[15] Since one cannot commit oneself to the truth of a specific proposition p without committing oneself to the truth of a less specific proposition q which it entails, it makes sense to say that the minimal proposition q is asserted when one (intuitively) asserts an enriched proposition p. But the principle that the minimal proposition is part of what is asserted (hence can be abstracted from it) does not hold when the primary processes at issue are instances of loosening or transfer. The speaker who assertively utters 'The ham sandwich left without paying', thereby referring to the ham sandwich orderer, does not assert the

---

[13] See Oswald Ducrot, *Le Dire et le Dit* (Minuit, 1984), pp. 56–7.
[14] *Beyond Rigidity*, p. 78.   [15] *Ibid.*, p. 73.

minimal proposition that the sandwich itself left without paying! Hence the minimal proposition cannot be defined as the common denominator – what is asserted in all contexts in which the sentence is uttered and the indexicals are given the same semantic values as in the current context.

To be sure, the counterexamples involving loosening or transfer are taken care of, in Soames's framework, by the notion of a 'normal' context, that is, of a context in which the sentence 'is used with its literal meaning', 'is not used metaphorically, ironically, or sarcastically', and so on. However this qualification can hardly be invoked in support of the 'abstractive' strategy I am presently discussing. We are supposed to start with the intuitive (non-minimalist) notion of what is said, which sometimes *is* affected by loosening or transfer. If, conforming to the abstractive strategy, we want to build the notion of the minimal proposition out of what is said in that sense, we cannot arbitrarily set aside the cases that potentially threaten the enterprise.

4.5   Interaction between saturation and optional pragmatic processes

The problem with the 'minimal proposition' is that it results from, and presupposes, the process of saturation (that is, the contextual assignment of semantic values to indexicals and other context-sensitive expressions) – a process that, in most cases, is impossible without appealing to the speaker's meaning. It follows that the minimal proposition is not independent of the speaker's meaning. On the other hand, the alleged minimal proposition does not necessarily correspond to *an aspect of* what the speaker means or asserts, hence it cannot be abstracted from what is asserted.

Another, related difficulty is this. To get the minimal proposition, we must separate those aspects of the speaker's meaning which are provided in the course of saturation, that is, which fill gaps in the representation associated with the sentence as a result of purely semantic interpretation, and those aspects of the speaker's meaning which are optional and enrich or otherwise modify the representation in question. The former, but not the latter, contribute to the minimal proposition. Those aspects of the speaker's meaning cannot easily be separated, however. They are indissociable, often mutually dependent aspects of a single process of pragmatic interpretation. This can be seen by considering yet another example in which the interpretation of various constituents in a sentence proceeds in an interactive manner.

As we saw in §2.4, how we interpret a particular constituent often depends upon how we interpret the other constituents in the sentence. The cases described in §2.4 were cases in which one constituent had to be interpreted non-literally if the others were interpreted literally. There are also cases in which a non-literal interpretation for a constituent prompts a non-literal interpretation for another constituent, and cases of interaction involving for example saturation.

Thus in interpreting an utterance of: 'Mike finished John's book', we have to assign a contextual value to 'finish' (FINISH READING, FINISH WRITING, FINISH BINDING, and so on) and a contextual value to 'John's book' (BOOK OWNED BY JOHN, WRITTEN BY JOHN, READ BY JOHN, and so on). There is an obvious interaction between the two values respectively assigned to the two constituents; the overall assignment must be coherent. If 'John's book' is interpreted as meaning THE BOOK WRITTEN BY JOHN, it's unlikely that 'finished' will be interpreted as meaning FINISHED WRITING.

The cases of interaction that are relevant to the present discussion are cases in which the primary pragmatic processes which interact respectively belong to the two broad classes I have distinguished: the primary pragmatic processes which are semantically *mandatory* because no proposition would be expressed without them (saturation), and the processes which are *optional*, that is, non-mandatory (enrichment, loosening, and transfer). We naturally interpret 'He took out his key and opened the door' as meaning that he opened the door *with the key*, but even if we did not 'enrich' the interpretation of the utterance in this way it would still express a complete proposition (namely the proposition that he did two things: take out his key, and open the door in some way or other). In this regard enrichment is optional and differs from saturation; for 'I read John's book' does not express a complete proposition if a certain relation between John and the book is not contextually provided.

Now it is possible for two pragmatic processes respectively belonging to the two classes distinguished above to interact in such a way that *the mandatory process depends upon the optional one*, and cannot operate until the latter has. For example, take the construction 'the x of y', or even better the possessive construction 'y's x'. For the sentence where such a construction occurs to express a definite proposition, a certain relation between x and y must be contextually provided. Which relation is actually provided as part of the interpretation of the utterance obviously depends upon the identity of the relata and what we know about them. The relata, x and y, will themselves be referred to by means of linguistic expressions, say NP_1 and NP_2. Now it's easy to imagine a case in which, say, NP_2 can undergo a process of non-literal interpretation. For example a definite description such as 'the lion' can be either interpreted literally (as referring to a lion) or non-literally (as referring metonymically to, say, the warrior whose shield carries a picture of a lion). How we interpret the description determines the identity of one of the relata, and we have seen that (in some cases at least) how we interpret the relation expressed by the possessive construction depends upon the identity of the relata. I want to argue that, in such a case, if the description is used non-literally (if it refers to the warrior), then a pragmatic process which must take place for the utterance to express a complete proposition (namely the assignment to the possessive construction of a particular relation as contextual value) cannot take place unless a non-literal interpretation has been antecedently provided for some other constituent in the sentence. It follows that the utterance is *semantically indeterminate at the purely literal level*, for the mandatory process of saturation – without which no complete proposition would be expressed – itself depends on some feature of the *non-literal* interpretation of the utterance and therefore cannot be achieved at the literal level. This is a case in which it is not possible (even in principle) to determine the proposition literally expressed before one has determined what the speaker non-literally means.

Let us actually construct the example by filling in the context. Suppose that there has been a ritual fight between respectively five warriors and five beasts. The beasts are a wolf, a lion, a hyena, a bear, and an alligator; the warriors are armed with swords, and carry shields with distinctive decorations (the first warrior has the moon on his shield, the second one has the Eiffel Tower, the third one has the Metro-Goldwyn-Mayer roaring lion, and so on). Each warrior is assigned a particular beast which he or she must stab to death. After the ritual fight, the five beasts lie on the ground with swords through their bodies. This is the context. Now suppose that in this context I utter

Bring me the lion's sword – I want to have a look at it.

In this context I think there are two accessible interpretations for 'the lion'; 'the lion' can be interpreted literally as referring to the lion (one of the beasts), or non-literally as referring to the warrior who has (a picture of) a lion on his shield. If we choose the first interpretation, the relation which will be contextually assigned to the possessive construction will be one of the salient relations which hold between the lion (the animal) and the sword which can be seen emerging from its pierced body. If we choose the second interpretation, the relation will be totally different; it will be one of the salient relations between the warrior and the sword which he used in his fight against, say, the bear.

Now suppose the correct interpretation is the second one: the speaker actually refers to the warrior with a lion on his shield and wants to see his sword (that is, the sword which emerges from the bear's body). What *is* the minimal proposition expressed by the utterance, in this context? I doubt that there is one, but if the minimalist insists, here is the only available procedure for determining it: to get the minimal proposition, we must give the word 'lion' its *literal* interpretation, because the non-literal interpretation results from an optional, non-minimalist process; and we must assign a particular value to the variable 'R' carried by the possessive construction. Which value? Well, the value which corresponds to what the speaker actually means. (Remember: there is no other way to determine contextually a value for the genitive, than by appeal to a speaker's meaning.) But that value is that which goes together with the intended *non*-literal interpretation of 'lion'! The result is a monster: what the phrase 'the lion's sword' contributes to what is said in the minimalist sense is something like THE SWORD WHICH

THE LION (THE ANIMAL) USED DURING THE FIGHT. The minimal proposition thus determined is absurd and evidently corresponds to no stage in the actual process of understanding the utterance.

4.6   Do we need the minimal proposition?

We have seen that the minimal proposition which the Syncretic View posits as the semantic content of the utterance, and which results from saturation alone, is not 'what the sentence says' in the objectionable sense glossed in §4.2 and criticized in §4.3. It is not autonomously determined by the rules of the language independent of speaker's meaning. At the same time, the minimal proposition does not necessarily correspond to an aspect of what the speaker asserts and cannot be abstracted from it (§4.4). The minimal proposition is a hybrid which goes beyond what is determined by the rules of the language yet has no psychological reality and need not be entertained or represented at any point in the process of understanding the utterance (§4.5).

Do we need such a notion in theorizing about language and communication? Many semanticists claim that we do, but I can hardly understand why. In a recent paper, King and Stanley argue against semantic theories which ascribe (functional) characters to sentences on the basis of the characters of their parts, on the grounds that 'the job of character is to give us content, and we can assign contents to complex expressions in contexts using only the characters of the parts, and combining the contents they determine in those contexts.'[16] They conclude that

> Both a semantics that assigns characters to simple expressions and recursively assigns characters to complex expressions *and* a semantics that assigns characters to only simple expressions allow for an assignment of the same contents in contexts to simple and complex expressions. So unless the functional characters of complex expressions have some *additional* job to do, they are unnecessary. But there seems to be no such additional job.[17]

The same sort of argument seems to me to rule out the minimal proposition as unnecessary. What must ultimately be accounted for is what speakers say in the pragmatic sense. The job of characters, contents and so on is to contribute to the overall explanation. But it is sufficient to assign semantic contents (in context) to simple expressions. Pragmatic processes will operate on those contents, and the composition rules will compose the resulting pragmatic values, thereby yielding the content of the speaker's assertion. Of course it is possible to let the composition rules compose the semantic contents of the constituent expressions,

[16] Jeffrey King and Jason Stanley, 'Semantics, Pragmatics, and the Role of Semantic Content', forthcoming.
[17] *Ibid.*

thereby yielding the minimal proposition expressed by the sentence. (An absurd proposition, in the lion's sword case and many others.) However, the content of the speaker's assertion will still be determined by composing the pragmatic values resulting from the operation of pragmatic processes on the contents of the constituent expressions; so it is unclear what additional job the minimal proposition is supposed to be doing.

4.7 The reflexive proposition

If one insists on using a purely semantic notion of 'what is said', that is, a notion of what is said which is propositional (truth-evaluable) yet 'excludes anything that is determined by the speaker's communicative intention', there is a better candidate than the alleged minimal proposition. For every utterance, there arguably is a proposition which it expresses in virtue solely of the rules of the language, independent of the speaker's meaning: that is the 'reflexive' proposition in the sense of John Perry (a variant of Stalnaker's diagonal proposition).[18] The main difference between the minimal proposition and the reflexive proposition is that the reflexive proposition is determined *before* the process of saturation takes place. The reflexive proposition can't be determined unless the sentence is tokened, but no substantial knowledge of the context of utterance is required to determine it. Thus an utterance *u* of the sentence 'I am French' expresses the reflexive proposition that *the utterer of u is French*. That it does not presuppose saturation is precisely what makes the reflexive proposition useful, since in most cases saturation proceeds by appeal to speaker's meaning. If one wants a proposition that's determined on purely semantic grounds, one had better not have it depend upon the process of saturation.

Soames considers the possibility of equating 'what the sentence says' with the reflexive proposition or something close to it, but he rejects that option with the following argument:

Consider . . . the first-person singular pronoun as it occurs in a sentence *I am F*. There is no such thing as 'what this sentence says' independent of the context of utterance in which it is used. The competence conditions associated with the first-person singular pronoun guarantee that when I assertively utter the sentence, I use it to say something about me, whereas when you assertively utter it, you use it to say something about you. One might be tempted to suppose that there is some more general thing that the sentence 'says' in every context – namely, the proposition expressed by *the speaker is F* (or some

---

[18] See Robert Stalnaker, *Context and Content* (Oxford University Press, 1999); John Perry, *Reference and Reflexivity* (CSLI Publications 2001), and *The Problem of the Essential Indexical*, chapters 11 and 13, and postscript to chapter 2. As Perry points out in *The Problem of the Essential Indexical*, p. 246, the notion goes back to Reichenbach's *Elements of Symbolic Logic*. (See also François Recanati, *La Transparence et l'Enonciation* (Editions du Seuil, 1979), pp. 161–3.)

such thing). But this will not do. Our notion of 'what a sentence says' is tied to what speakers who assertively utter the sentence say. Typically, when I assertively utter *I am F*, I don't assert that I am speaking or using language at all. Further, the proposition that I assert when I assertively utter such a sentence may be true in a possible circumstance in which no one is using language, and someone may believe this proposition without believing anything about me being a speaker.[19]

Soames's main objection is that the alleged reflexive proposition is not (part of) what the speaker asserts. As we have seen, however, the same thing often holds for the minimal proposition posited by the syncretists. The advantage of the reflexive proposition over the minimal proposition is that it (the reflexive proposition) is determined solely by the rules of the language, independent of the speaker's meaning, in such a way that there *is* a path to the reflexive proposition that does not go through the speaker's meaning; hence it does not matter much if that proposition can't be reached by abstraction from what the speaker asserts.

The reflexive proposition is admittedly distinct from that which the speaker asserts – they have different possible worlds truth-conditions, as Soames points out – but why is this an objection? Are we not supposed to draw a sharp distinction between *the proposition expressed by the sentence* and *the proposition asserted by the speaker who utters that sentence*? Note that we can, if we wish, incorporate into the reflexive proposition something to the effect that the linguistic mode of presentation associated with the first person pronoun will not be part of the proposition asserted, while the reference it contextually determines will be. Thus we might take the reflexive proposition expressed by an utterance *u* of 'I am French' to be the proposition that *there is an x such that x utters u and u is true iff x is French*. This comes as close as one can get to capturing, in propositional format, the information provided by the utterance in virtue solely of the linguistic meaning of the sentence 'I am French.'[20] Such a reflexive proposition determines that the proposition contextually asserted by 'I am French' will consist of the reference of 'I' and the property of being French. The reflexive proposition is therefore 'tied to what speakers who assertively utter the sentence say', even if it is not (part of) what they say.

I conclude that there may be a way of preserving the notion of 'what the sentence says', in the purely semantic sense, if one wants to; but it does not support the Syncretic View with its four levels. What characterizes the reflexive proposition is that, although fully propositional, it does not incorporate those contextual ingredients whose provision is linguistically mandated; it is much

---

[19] Soames, *Beyond Rigidity*, p. 104.
[20] See my 'Rigidity and Direct Reference' in *Philosophical Studies* 53 (1988), 103–17, and *Direct Reference*, chapter 2, for an analysis along those lines.

closer to the linguistic meaning of the sentence – indeed it is directly and immediately determined by the linguistic meaning of the sentence. Appealing to the reflexive proposition instead of the minimal proposition takes us back to the non-minimalist picture with its three basic levels (figure 1.2): the linguistic meaning of the sentence (and the reflexive proposition it directly and immediately determines); what is said in the pragmatic sense; and what is implied or otherwise conveyed by the utterance.

5   Non-literal uses

It may be thought that the pragmatic approach to what is said advocated in the first four chapters of this book blurs the commonsensical distinction between what is (literally) said and what is non-literally conveyed. What is said, in the pragmatic sense, already incorporates the derived, non-literal values resulting from primary pragmatic processes of the optional variety. Is there still room for a contrast between literal and non-literal speech? Wilson and Sperber think this distinction belongs to folk-linguistics and must be repudiated.[1] In this chapter, however, I will attempt to show that the ordinary, folk-theoretical notion of *non-literal use* can be rescued. It corresponds to a range of phenomena which constitute a natural class, from a phenomenological point of view.

5.1   Non-literal uses as non-minimal departures from literal meaning

Let us start with a sense of the phrase 'literal meaning' which is reasonably clear and raises no particular problem. In that sense, the literal meaning of a linguistic expression is its *conventional* meaning: the meaning it has in virtue of the conventions which are constitutive of the language. Thus understood literal meaning is a property of the expression-type; for it is the expression-type which the conventions of the language endow with a particular meaning. Literal meaning, in that sense, I will dub '*t*-literal meaning' (with '*t*' standing for 'type'), in order to distinguish the sense just introduced from other possible senses of the phrase 'literal meaning'.

Particular *occurrences* of an expression also possess meaning. First, every occurrence inherits the meaning of the expression-type of which it is an occurrence. Every occurrence of a meaningful expression-type therefore possesses a *t*-literal meaning. Second, an occurrence also possesses a meaning which depends not merely upon the conventional significance of the expression-type, but also on features of the context of use. That meaning is, by definition, not *t*-literal. Insofar as it departs from the meaning of the expression-type, it may even be said to be '*t*-non-literal'. Yet it need not be 'non-literal' in the *ordinary*

---

[1] 'Truthfulness and Relevance', pp. 622–4.

68

sense. When we speak of 'non-literalness', in the ordinary sense, we mean that what is meant departs from t-literal meaning in a fairly specific way. Not any old departure from t-literal meaning adds up to non-literalness in the ordinary sense.

Consider the following example. Suppose that Paul is thirsty, and I tell you, while pointing to him: 'He is thirsty.' I thereby say of Paul that he is thirsty. What is thus said is not t-literal because the reference to Paul is something that is achieved by partly contextual means. The demonstrative pronoun 'he', *qua* expression-type, does not refer to Paul. The semantic conventions of the language do not assign that expression a reference, but merely a rule of use in virtue of which it may, in context, acquire a reference. Since the reference of the expression is not fixed by the semantic conventions of the language, independent of context, it is not part of the t-literal meaning of the sentence. The proposition that Paul is thirsty (at the time of utterance) therefore counts as t-non-literal, but of course no one wants to say that there is anything 'non-literal' in the ordinary sense going on in that example (as described so far). The speaker is speaking literally, in the ordinary sense of the word. It may be that he is communicating something non-literally by his utterance, but that can only be something different from the proposition that Paul is thirsty. If the speaker means that Paul should be offered a drink, *that* aspect of the meaning of his utterance will indeed count as non-literal in the ordinary sense. The proposition that Paul should be offered a drink is conveyed without being literally expressed.

What is the difference between the proposition that Paul is thirsty and the proposition that he should be offered a drink, in the above example? The former departs from the t-literal meaning of the sentence since it includes something (the reference of 'he') which depends upon the context and not merely upon the conventional significance of the uttered words. Yet it is the words themselves which, in virtue of their conventional significance, make it necessary to appeal to context in order to assign a reference to the demonstrative. It is part of the t-literal meaning of indexical expressions that they should be assigned a reference in context. In interpreting indexical sentences, we go beyond what the conventions of the language give us, but *that step beyond is still governed by the conventions of the language*. The rule of use which constitutes the t-literal meaning of indexical expressions is what triggers the search for a contextual value. (This is the process I call 'saturation'.) The departure from t-literal meaning is therefore pre-determined by t-literal meaning. Whenever that is so, I say that the departure is 'minimal'. When the meaning of an utterance only minimally departs from t-literal meaning, that meaning does not count as non-literal in the ordinary sense. *Only non-minimal departures make for non-literalness in the ordinary sense.* That is precisely what we have in the other case – when the speaker says that Paul is thirsty and implies that he should be offered a drink. For there is nothing in the sentence-type 'He is thirsty' that triggers the contextual generation of the implicature that Paul should be offered a drink.

Let me define: the meaning conveyed by an utterance is '*m*-literal' iff it involves only minimal departures from *t*-literal meaning. (The case in which no departure is involved may count as a limiting case of *m*-literalness. I doubt that there are such cases, however.) Standard cases of non-literalness, in the ordinary sense, are cases of *m*-non-literalness: they involve *non-minimal* departures from *t*-literal meaning. Yet, as we shall see, not all cases of *m*-non-literalness (that is, not all cases involving such departures) count as 'non-literal' in the ordinary sense.

5.2   Non-literal uses and secondary meaning

More often than not, non-literal meaning is *secondary* meaning – meaning derived from some more basic, primary meaning which it presupposes. In the above example, the proposition that Paul is thirsty is primary. By asserting that proposition, the speaker indirectly conveys something more: that Paul should be offered a drink.

Conversational implicatures and indirect speech acts obviously have a secondary character. Let us start with conversational implicatures. They are a special case of pragmatic implication. Pragmatic implications are the implications of actions. When I do something, my so doing may imply various things. For example, my taking an umbrella implies that I think it will rain. Conversational implicatures are pragmatic implications of *an act of speech*. They fall under the schema: the speaker's saying that *p* implies that *q*. Not all implications of an act of speech are implicatures, however. My saying that Frege died in 1940 implies that I am ignorant, but that is not something I *mean* by my utterance. Arguably, a necessary condition for something to count as an implicature is that it be part of what the speaker means by his utterance. For that condition to be satisfied, the speaker must overtly intend the hearer to recognize the pragmatic implication of his utterance, and to recognize it as intended to be recognized. (Other conditions may have to be satisfied for a pragmatic implication of a speech act to count as a genuine conversational implicature, but I will be content with what I have just said.)

Since what is conversationally implicated is implied by the speaker's saying what he says, it immediately follows that conversational implicatures have a secondary character. The speaker implies that *q by saying that p*. In order to derive the implicature, we need the premiss that the speaker has said what he has said; therefore we need to have identified the primary content of his utterance.

The same thing holds, even more obviously, for indirect speech acts. As their name indicates, indirect speech acts are performed 'indirectly', via the performance of another speech act which falls within the illocutionary-act potential of the uttered sentence and is said to be performed directly. For example, I may make a request either directly ('Pass me the salt, please') or indirectly, by asking a question ('Can you reach the salt?') or by making a statement ('I can't reach the salt'). Twenty years ago I suggested that indirect speech acts are nothing but a special case of conversational implicature, where the speaker's intention to perform the indirect speech act is conversationally implicated by his performance of the direct speech act.[2] Be that as it may, everyone agrees that there is much in common between conversational implicatures and indirect speech acts. What they have in common is, in effect, their secondary character: the interpretation of both conversational implicatures and indirect speech acts involves an inference from the utterance's primary meaning to its derived meaning.

In both conversational implicatures and indirect speech acts, the meaning of the utterance involves something over and above its primary meaning – something whose derivation presupposes the primary meaning. In other cases, like irony, the situation is more complex. Suppose the speaker says 'Paul really is a fine friend', in a situation in which just the opposite is known to be the case. The speaker does not really say, or at least she does not assert, what she 'makes as if to say' (Grice's phrase). Something is lacking here, namely the force of a serious assertion. While in conversational implicature, the speaker asserts something and conveys something more as well, in irony the speaker does *less* than assert what she would normally be asserting by uttering the sentence which she actually utters. What the speaker does in the ironical case is merely to *pretend* to assert the content of her utterance. Still, there is an element of indirectness here, and we can maintain that irony also possesses a secondary character. By pretending to assert something, the speaker conveys something else, just as, in the other types of case, by asserting something the speaker conveys something else. By pretending to say of Paul that he is a fine friend in a situation in which just the opposite is obviously true, the speaker manages to communicate that Paul is everything but a fine friend. She shows, by her utterance, how inappropriate it would be to ascribe to Paul the property of being a fine friend. The utterance has a primary meaning – it expresses the proposition that Paul is a fine friend; and it is by expressing that primary meaning (under the 'pretence' mode, and without the force of a serious assertion) that the speaker is able to convey what she conveys.

Whenever the meaning conveyed by an utterance is secondary and derived from some antecedent meaning expressed by the utterance, it is 'non-literal' in the ordinary sense. Let us therefore introduce a third notion alongside *t*-literalness and *m*-literalness: that of *p*-literal meaning, where '*p*' stands

[2] François Recanati, 'Insinuation et Sous-Entendu', *Communications* 30 (1979), 95–106; *Meaning and Force: The Pragmatics of Performative Utterances* (Cambridge University Press, 1987), pp. 121–6.

for 'primary'. An interpretation for an utterance is *p*-literal just in case it directly results from interpreting the sentence (in context), without being derived from some antecedently determined meaning by an inferential process akin to that which is involved in conversational implicatures, indirect speech acts, and so on.

The question I want to raise concerns the relation between *p*-literalness and *m*-literalness. We have seen that a meaning is *m*-literal if it departs from the *t*-literal meaning of the sentence only minimally. Now we have another notion, that of *p*-literal meaning. To what extent do they coincide? In the example I used ('He is thirsty'), the proposition that Paul is thirsty was both *m*-literal and *p*-literal, in contrast to the other proposition (the implicature), which was neither. How general is this coincidence? More specifically: is a primary meaning necessarily a meaning that only minimally departs from the *t*-literal meaning of the sentence? A positive answer to that question tends to be assumed in the literature on this topic, but it should be clear, from what I said in previous chapters, that I think that is a mistake.

5.3   Non-minimal departures without secondariness

There are, I hold, meanings that are *primary* yet involve *non-minimal* departures from the conventional meaning of the sentence. Examples abound in the pragmatic literature. Let us start with two conjunctive utterances which have been analysed and discussed many times:

(1) They got married and had many children.
(2) The policeman raised his hand and stopped the car.

We naturally interpret (1) as depicting a situation in which marriage took place before the coming of the children. Yet, according to Grice, this is not encoded in the meaning of the sentence. Not only is the temporal ordering of the events not part of *t*-literal meaning; it is not even part of *m*-literal meaning.[3] Remember how *m*-literal meaning was characterized: *m*-literal meaning is not fully conventional since it involves, or may involve, contextual ingredients (for example, assignment of values to indexicals), yet it departs from *t*-literal meaning only minimally, where a 'minimal' departure from *t*-literal meaning is a departure that is itself governed by the conventions of the language. But the temporal order between the events described by the conjuncts in (1) is not something that the *t*-literal meaning of the sentence forces an interpreter to specify. There are conjunctive utterances similar in all formal respects to (1) which can be given a quite satisfactory interpretation without specifying that order. Grice concludes that the temporal ordering of the events, though strongly suggested by the order of the conjuncts, is not part of 'what is said' by the utterance. ('What is said' is Grice's term for the *m*-literal meaning.)

---

[3] This is controversial. See §6.2 for an alternative analysis.

The contextual provision of that component of the meaning of the utterance constitutes a 'non-minimal' departure from *t*-literal meaning.

Example (2) is similar. As Rumelhart pointed out,[4] we naturally interpret the sentence as depicting a scene in which the stopping of the car was caused by the raising of the policeman's hand. Moreover, we interpret the relevant form of causation as involving no direct physical contact between hand and car but rather the mediation of intentional states: the raising of the policeman's hand is understood to have caused the driver (i) to recognize the policeman's intention that she should stop the car and (ii) to stop the car so as to comply with the policeman's request. In other words, we understand (2) as saying that the policeman stopped the car by signalling to the driver that she was to stop. Yet neither the form of causation, nor even the existence of a causal link between hand-raising and car-stopping, is encoded in sentence (2). Nor is the contextual provision of those elements of utterance meaning required in virtue of some aspect of the *t*-literal meaning of the sentence. Once again we find that the interpretation of the utterance involves non-minimal departures from *t*-literal meaning.

Still, I maintain that the meanings thus conveyed by (1) and (2) are *p*-literal. In conversational implicatures, indirect speech acts, irony etc., there is something which is said (or which the speaker 'makes as if to say'), and something else that is implied by saying what is said. This distinction between two separate components, one inferentially dependent upon the other, is actually part of the meaning of the utterance: whoever understands the utterance realizes that something is said and something else is implied by saying it. For example, if I am asked whether I talked to Freddy, and I reply

I don't talk to crooks

a normal hearer will understand me as saying that I don't talk to crooks and thereby implying that I did not talk to Freddy. (Someone who does not understand that does not understand the utterance.) Moreover, as Grice insisted, the understander will grasp the inferential connection between what is said (or the saying of it) and what is implied. (In this particular case, the connection involves the premiss: 'Freddy is a crook.') Faced with (1) and (2), however, an interpreter does not construct an *m*-literal interpretation – an interpretation that differs only minimally from *t*-literal meaning – and use it to infer the *m*-non-literal elements. The *m*-non-literal interpretations are arrived at directly, as a result of the interaction of the *t*-literal meaning of the words (and constructions), salient features of the speech situation, expectations created by the discourse, schemata stored in memory and evoked by the words, and so on. As I pointed out in chapters 1 to 3, there is no inference here, or at least no inference of which the interpreters themselves are aware.

---

[4] Rumelhart, 'Problems with Literal Meanings', p. 78.

Consider a third (and last) example, which I already mentioned several times:

(3) You are not going to die.

In the context imagined by Kent Bach, a boy is crying because of a minor cut and his mother utters (3). What she means is: 'You're not going to die from that cut.' But m-literally, Bach points out, the utterance expresses the proposition that the kid will not die *tout court*. The extra element contextually provided (the implicit reference to the cut) is not a component of m-literal meaning: it is not triggered by anything in the sentence, nor is it necessary for the utterance to express a complete proposition. On the other hand, that element is not 'inferred' on the basis of m-literal meaning: the hearer does not construct the m-literal interpretation, realize that the utterance, thus interpreted, would violate Grice's maxim of quality by entailing something blatantly false (that the child is immortal), and infer what the speaker actually means; rather, she directly understands the mother's utterance as characterizing the situation created by the cut.[5] Once again, the conveyed meaning turns out to be m-non-literal, but p-literal nonetheless.

5.4   The transparency condition

In the sort of case I have just discussed (the policeman example, and so on), the interpretation of the utterance goes well beyond what the conventions of the language dictate. The conventional meaning of the sentence is not only 'completed' from the bottom up by assigning contextual values to indexicals and other free variables, it is also *enriched* in a top-down manner by appealing to background assumptions and world-knowledge. That process of enrichment yields an output that is not m-literal, yet there is nothing non-literal in the ordinary sense in that output. Non-literal interpretations (in the ordinary sense) are 'special', by definition, but there is nothing special about the interpretations of utterances like (2). Utterance interpretation, *in general,* proceeds by matching the linguistic meaning of the sentence to the particular situation or sort of situation the speaker intends to talk about. The output of this matching process typically is a richer meaning, as (2) clearly illustrates: a number of features which are not linguistically encoded are nonetheless incorporated into the described scene as a result of top down pressures. This is the phenomenon of sense modulation, to be described in chapter 9.

In contrast, there *is* something special about the interpretation of p-non-literal utterances; it is a two-step procedure instead of being a one-step procedure. The interpreter first determines the utterance's primary meaning, then infers some additional meaning. This two-step process (which, even when short-circuited,

---

[5] See my 'Situations and the Structure of Content', in Kumiko Murasugi and Robert Stainton (eds.), *Philosophy and Linguistics* (Westview, 1999), p. 122.

can always be made explicit)[6] does not take place all the time: it takes place only when the speaker conveys something indirectly. But processes like enrichment or loosening are universal: there is no utterance, however explicit, whose interpretation does not involve adjusting the conventional meanings of words to the particulars of the situation talked about. Communication would be impossible if things were not so.

The 'special' character of non-literal communication is not the whole story, however. Even if there were something special about m-non-literalness – if, say, most uses of words were m-literal – a use of words would still not count as non-literal in the ordinary sense merely in virtue of the fact that it is m-non-literal. A use of words counts as non-literal in the ordinary sense only if there is something special about that use *that is, or can be, perceived by the language users themselves.* That is so because non-literalness is a feature of the interpretation of utterances, and the interpretation of utterances is something that is bound to be available to the language users who do the interpreting. Now m-non-literalness per se is not transparent to the language users. The speaker and hearer need not be aware that in their understanding of the uttered words they are going beyond what the conventions of the language dictate. It is not part of their competence to reflect upon the complex cognitive processes through which the meaning of an utterance gets built up from a number of distinct sources. On the other hand, we have seen that whenever a meaning is accessed via an inference from a primary meaning, as in (genuine) conversational implicatures, the language users themselves are aware of the distinction between the two layers of meaning as well as of the connection between them. In other words, p-non-literalness is transparent to the language users; hence it counts as non-literalness in the ordinary sense. (This transparency is not a contingent property of p-non-literalness. It is definitive of p-non-literalness that the sort of inference at issue is conducted at the 'personal', rather than 'sub-personal', level and is therefore available to the language users.)

To sum up, for something to count as non-literal in the ordinary sense it must not only go beyond the conventional significance of the uttered words (m-non-literalness), but it must be felt as such: the language users must be aware that the conveyed meaning exceeds the conventional significance of the words. That condition I dub the 'transparency condition'. It is satisfied whenever the conveyed meaning has a secondary character, as in conversational implicatures and indirect speech acts.

5.5   Varieties of non-literal meaning

Is secondariness a necessary, or merely a sufficient condition of transparency? If it is necessary, then only p-non-literal instances of m-non-literal meaning

---

[6] See section 3.6.

(conversational implicatures, indirect speech acts, and so on) will count as non-literal in the ordinary sense. If it is merely sufficient, then presumably there will be *p*-literal instances of *m*-non-literal meaning which will count as non-literal in the ordinary sense, because the transparency condition has been satisfied through something other than indirectness. I see no reason to deny that there are such instances.

The paradigm case of non-literal meaning is metaphor. Now metaphor, in its most central varieties, I count as *p*-literal. To re-use an example from chapter 2, if I say that the ATM swallowed my credit card, I speak metaphorically; there can be no real 'swallowing' on the part of an ATM, but merely something that resembles swallowing. Still, an ordinary hearer readily understands what is said by such an utterance, without going through a two-step procedure involving the prior computation of the 'literal' meaning of the utterance (whatever that may be) and a secondary inference to the actual meaning. Knowing the linguistic meaning of 'swallow', and knowing what sometimes happens with ATMs, the hearer unreflectively constructs the sense in which the ATM can be said to 'swallow' the card by adjusting the meaning of the word to the situation talked about. This is not very different from what goes on when the meaning of words is enriched so as to fit the specific situation of discourse, as in the policeman example from §5.3. In both cases, as Langacker persuasively argued, the situation talked about is 'categorized' by means of the words which are used to describe it. In enrichment the situation talked about is a straightforward instantiation of the schema encoded in the words, which schema therefore gets 'elaborated' through its application to the situation. That defines what Langacker calls full schematicity: 'the target is compatible with the sanctioning unit (= the word, with its conventional meaning), and is therefore judged by a speaker to be an unproblematic instantiation of the category it defines'.[7] In contrast, partial schematicity occurs when 'there is some conflict between the specifications of the sanctioning and target structures, so that the former can be construed as schematic for the latter only with a certain degree of strain':[8]

Because partial schematicity involves conflicting specifications, the sanctioning and target structures cannot merge into a single, consistent conceptualization; in a categorizing judgement of the form [[SS —> TS]], the discrepancy between SS and TS keeps them at least partially distinct. The result is a bipartite conceptualization including what we recognize as a literal sense (SS) and a figurative sense (TS). On the other hand, nothing prevents the sanctioning and target structures from merging into a unified conceptualization when there is full consistency between their specifications. In the schematic relationship [[SS —> TS]], SS is in effect 'swallowed up' by TS, since all of the specifications of the former are implicit in the latter, which simply carries them down to a greater level of precision.[9]

---

[7] Langaker, *Foundations of Cognitive Grammar*, p. 68.   [8] *Ibid.*, p. 69.
[9] *Ibid.*, pp. 92–3. 'SS' stands for 'sanctioning structure' and 'TS' for 'target structure'.

The picture that emerges is this. As words are applied, in context, to specific situations, their meaning is adjusted. Depending on whether the conventional meaning is fully or only partially schematic for the situation talked about, adjustment will take one of two forms: sense elaboration (enrichment), or sense extension (loosening). In sense elaboration the meaning carried by the words is made more specific through the interaction with contextual factors. In sense extension, those dimensions of meaning which stand in conflict to the specifications of the target are filtered out, but they remain somewhat active and may generate a feeling of discrepancy between the evoked schema and the sense constructed by (partially) applying the schema to the situation at hand. That feeling, like the conflict which underlies it, comes in degrees. Hence there is a continuum between ordinary cases of sense extension that we don't even perceive (the ATM swallowing the credit card) and more dramatic cases of metaphor whose non-literal character cannot be ignored.[10] The more noticeable the conflict, the more transparent the departure from *t*-literal meaning will be to the language users. Beyond a certain threshold, cases of sense extension will therefore count as special and non-literal in the ordinary sense, despite their *p*-literal character. They will count as *figurative* uses of language (fig. 5.1).[11]

Irony and non-serious uses of language are another type of case in which, I think, the transparency condition is satisfied through something other than indirectness. To be sure, irony possesses a secondary character (§5.2): by pretending to say of Paul that he is a fine friend in a situation in which just the opposite is obviously true, the speaker manages to communicate that Paul is everything but a fine friend. She shows, by her utterance, how inappropriate it would be to ascribe to Paul the property of being a fine friend. But let us put aside what is thus implied by saying something ironically – let us concentrate on the *primary* meaning of the ironical utterance. In order to understand the utterance at the primary level one must recognize that the act of asserting that Paul is a fine friend is staged or simulated rather than actually performed. And that means that one must discern two 'layers' within the primary meaning of the utterance: the surface speech act which the speaker pretends to perform, and the ironical act of staging the performance of that speech act.[12] This layering, internal to the primary meaning of the utterance, characterizes 'staged communicative acts',

---

[10] On this continuum, see Dan Sperber and Deirdre Wilson, 'Loose talk'. Note that metonymic transfers also admit of a continuum of cases: some cases count as 'above threshold' in the same sense in which metaphors do. (I am indebted to Robyn Carston for pointing this out to me.)

[11] To make the ATM example figurative, we have only to belabour the metaphor so as to make it conspicuous, as in 'The ATM swallowed my credit card, chewed it up and spat it out.' (Kent Bach suggested this figurative development of the example.) On the distinction between 'unconscious metaphorical use of language, as exhibited mainly by young children but also by adults' and 'conscious metaphorical use' in which 'the awareness of people . . . is caused by the feeling of discrepancy', see Bartsch, 'Word Meanings', pp. 31–3.

[12] Herb Clark, *Using Language* (Cambridge University Press, 1996), pp. 353–4.

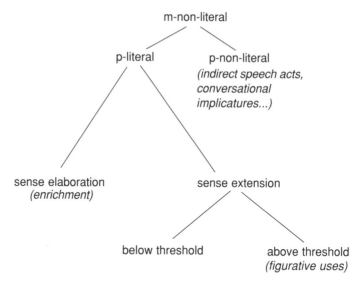

Figure 5.1 Non-literal uses

a large family which includes not only irony but also 'sarcasm, teasing, over-statement, understatement, rhetorical questions, and their relatives'.[13] Insofar as the duality of layers is internal to the (primary) meaning of the utterance and is recognized by whoever understands it, the transparency condition is eo ipso satisfied: the utterance is intuitively recognized as special, as exhibiting a duality which is absent from standard ('serious') uses of language. That duality, characteristic of staged communicative acts, is a third type of duality, distinct both from the 'two-step procedure' at work in the recovery of secondary meanings, and from the 'bipartite conceptualization' induced by metaphorical discrepancy. (Of course, nothing prevents a single utterance from exhibiting the three types of duality, in various patterns of interaction.)

5.6   Internal vs external duality

Commenting on an earlier version of this chapter, Robyn Carston has objected that

there is (at least on the face of it) a tension or conflict between the earlier discussion of availability and the current discussion of transparency: a number of cases of transparent non-literalness fall within the class of what are labeled 'p-literal uses'. So we seem to

---

[13] *Ibid.*, p. 369. See also Helga Kotthoff, 'Irony, Quotation, and Other Forms of Staged Intertextuality', in Carl Graumann and Werner Kallmeyer (eds.), *Perspective and Perspectivation in Discourse* (Benjamins, 2002), 201–29.

have some instances of utterance meaning that are, on the one hand, elements of what is said$_{prag}$ (primary meaning), hence the result of subpersonal (unconscious, unavailable) processes, and are, on the other hand, transparently non-literal, i.e. phenomenologically salient to speakers/hearers as figurative, i.e. as derived from a more basic meaning, so that the derivability of the one from the other is consciously available (hence, arguably, a matter of personal level processing).[14]

Though I understand Carston's reaction, I deny that there is a conflict between the earlier discussion of availability and the discussion of transparency and figurativeness in this chapter. As I have insisted throughout in this book, and again in section 5.4, 'the interpretation of utterances is something that is bound to be available to the language users who do the interpreting' (see above, p. 75). This applies both to the primary meaning of the utterance – what is said – and to the secondary meaning that, in some cases, can be derived from it. Both I take to be available to the speakers/users (in a normal situation of communication). What is *not* available, according to me, is the sub-personal machinery – the processes through which the primary meaning is computed. All that I maintain.

The cases that Carston sees as problematic I myself describe as cases in which there is a felt duality *internal to the primary meaning of the utterance*. That is not the same thing as the primary/secondary duality, or *external* duality, which characterizes implicatures and indirect speech acts. Normal interpreters are aware of the (secondary) processes through which the secondary meaning is derived, but they are not aware of the (primary) processes through which the primary meaning is derived. That is true *even if the primary meaning in question exhibits an internal duality which is transparent to normal interpreters* (figure 5.2).

In my framework, summarized in figure 5.2, the duality which characterizes figurative uses is internal to the output of the primary pragmatic processes, and we are aware of it because we are aware of that output. Thus the primary interpretation of the 'figurative' version of the ATM example, 'The ATM swallowed my credit card, chewed it up and spat it out'[15] is a scene in which the ATM machine exhibits genuine human-like properties. In the scene the ATM is both a machine and a human being – hence the feeling of discrepancy.[16] The discrepancy should not be construed (merely) as a tension between two of the ingredients which enter into the determination of primary meaning (as in ordinary cases of sense extension, like the initial, non-figurative ATM example, where the very process of sense extension is meant to resolve the tension): rather, it is a tension between two aspects or components of the primary interpretation. This is the crucial point: the duality which is said to be transparent

---

[14] Carston, 'Report', pp. 4–5.   [15] See footnote 11, p. 77.
[16] See Gilles Fauconnier and Mark Turner, *The Way We Think: Conceptual Blending and the Mind's Hidden Complexities* (Basic Books, 2002) for more examples of metaphorical 'blending'.

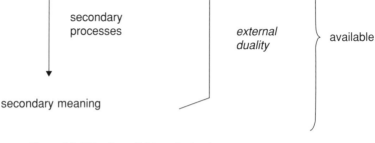

Figure 5.2 What is available and what is not

to normal interpreters is internal to the *output* of the (primary) interpretation process, hence its availability does not entail the availability of the processes which give rise to that interpretation. Thus there is no inconsistency between my earlier account of the primary/secondary distinction, and my discussion in section 5.5. Both the external duality characteristic of implicatures and indirect speech acts, and the internal duality characteristic of ironies, above-threshold metaphors and other figurative uses, are transparent to the language users. They are transparent because, in both cases, the duality is an aspect of the interpretation of the utterance, hence it is bound to be available to normal interpreters. What is not available, in both types of case, are the sub-personal processes underlying and generating the primary interpretation.

At this point one may wonder whether the distinction I have drawn between an 'external' and an 'internal' duality is not ad hoc. Is this not a verbal manoeuvre, designed to protect the theory? What is the substance of the distinction if, in both types of case (figurative uses in which the duality is said to be internal to the primary meaning, and implicature-like cases exhibiting secondariness), the subject is aware of a distinction between the literal meaning of the utterance and a non-literal, derived meaning? In ordinary (non-figurative) cases of enrichment and loosening, there is no felt duality at all; hence the contrast between such cases and cases exhibiting phenomenological secondariness is striking. But as soon as we bring figurative uses into the picture, the contrast becomes elusive. So the objection goes.

Here again, I plead not guilty. There is something special to cases in which the duality is of the primary/secondary variety. What is special is the *perceived inferential link* between the primary and secondary meanings. In internal-duality cases, there is a duality but no inferential relation between the two components. The extra element – the perceived inferential link – is what gives substance to the distinction between the two types of case.

5.7   Conclusion

The literal/non-literal distinction turns out to cover two quite different things:

- For the semanticist, the literal meaning of an expression is the semantic value which the conventions of the language assign to that expression ('with respect to context', if the expression is indexical). Whenever the meaning which the expression actually conveys departs from that literal meaning, it is said to be 'non-literal'.
- In the ordinary sense of the term, non-literal meaning contrasts with normal meaning. Non-literal meaning is special, it involves a form of deviance or departure from the norm; a form of deviance or departure which must be transparent to the language users.

Both distinctions are legitimate. We need both the distinction between conventional meaning and conveyed meaning, and that between normal meaning and the special meanings assigned to words when the speaker speaks figuratively or non-seriously or conveys something indirectly. But it is all too easy to confuse the two distinctions, which should be kept separate. Indeed I think it is because the two distinctions have been confused that the same terms have been used for both distinctions.

The culprit here is the tacit, but very widespread, assumption that the m-literal meaning of words is what, in context, they normally express. In semantics (as opposed to psychology), departures from m-literal meaning tend to be treated as special, on the pattern of figurative language, non-serious speech or indirect communication. I think that assumption is mistaken. In context, words *systematically* express meanings that are richer than (or otherwise different from) what the conventions of the language dictate. Contrary to what formal semanticists tend to assume, the (intuitive) truth-conditions of our utterances are not compositionally determined by the meanings of words and their syntactic arrangement, in a strict bottom-up manner. They are shaped by contextual expectations and world-knowledge to a very large extent. That is true of all utterances, however 'literal' they are (in the ordinary sense). If we abstract from those top-down factors, what we get – the utterance's m-literal meaning – no longer corresponds to the intuitive truth-conditions which the language users themselves associate with their own utterances. In other words, there is a gap between the deliverances of semantic theory and the intuitive content of utterances. That gap is bridged by pragmatic processes which take place normally and do not generate 'non-literal meanings', except in special cases.

6   From Literalism to Contextualism

6.1   Five positions

I take it that there currently are five basic positions concerning the role of context in the determination of truth-conditions. I have already attempted to refute two of these positions. Before proceeding, it will be helpful to identify all five, and to take a bird's eye view of the theoretical landscape.

The five positions I am about to list can be ordered on a scale, one end of which is occupied by the extreme position I call Literalism, and the other end by another extreme position, which I call Contextualism. Of the intermediate positions I will describe, some fall on the literalist side and others on the contextualist side, depending on where they are situated on the scale (see table 6.1, p. 86).

The debate between Literalism and Contextualism was at the forefront of attention in the philosophy of language of the middle of the twentieth century. It is widely believed to have been settled (in favour of Literalism in some version or other) but I think that is a mistake. The alleged refutations of Contextualism that have been offered actually refute nothing;[1] while Literalism strikes me as by and large indefensible. So I think the history of twentieth-century philosophy of language ought to be rewritten. I will not do so in this book, however.

What is the Literalism/Contextualism debate exactly about? The basic question, I think, is whether we may legitimately ascribe truth-conditional content (the property of 'saying' something, of expressing a thought or a proposition) to natural-language sentences, or whether it is only speech acts, utterances in context, that have content in a basic, underived sense. Consider the type of formal language philosophers of the first half of the century were concerned with. In these languages, sentences are given an interpretation that is fixed and does not depend on the context of use. Natural language sentences, by contrast, express a complete thought (say something definite) only with respect to a context of utterance – in many cases at least. This difference between natural language and a certain type of formal language is well known, and no one has ever attempted to deny it. But there was disagreement as to the *importance* of the distinction.

---

[1] See §10.1 below (pp. 154–8), for a discussion of two famous anti-contextualist arguments.

Contextualists[2] held that the difference between the two types of language was all-important; natural-language sentences, according to them, were *essentially* context-sensitive, and did not have determinate truth-conditions. Literalists, on the other hand, believed that the difference between the two types of language could be abstracted from through a legitimate idealization.

The literalist idealization was based on the following claim:

(L) For every statement that can be made using a context-sensitive sentence in a given context, there is an eternal sentence that can be used to make the same statement in any context.

To obtain an eternal sentence from a context-sensitive one, one has only to replace its indexical constituents by non-indexical constituents with the same semantic value. Owing to (L), the difference between natural languages and the formal languages in which the context of utterance plays no role turns out not to be essential. Using natural language, we could behave so as to abolish the difference – simply by choosing to utter only eternal sentences. The reason why we also (and mainly) use context-sensitive sentences is that this enables us 'to speak far more concisely than otherwise' (Katz 1977: 20).[3]

The contextualists denied (L), if only because they did not really believe that there *were* eternal sentences. Against eternal sentences, it can be argued, on contextualist grounds, that fundamental semantic mechanisms such as reference, quantification, or predication are essentially context-sensitive: there is no way to refer, or to predicate, or to quantify without relying on features of the context of utterance. It follows that sentences, by themselves, don't express propositions.

---

[2] The contextualists I am talking about here are the so-called ordinary language philosophers: Wittgenstein, Austin, Strawson among others.

[3] Note that (L) is much weaker than another principle of effability, namely (T):

(T) Every entertainable *thought* may be expressed by means of an eternal sentence the sense of which corresponds exactly to that thought.

Many philosophers have (rightly) argued against (T). For example, Sperber and Wilson write: 'It seems plausible that in our internal language we often fix time and space references not in terms of universal coordinates, but in terms of a private logbook and an ego-centred map; furthermore, most kinds of reference – to people and events for instance – can be fixed in terms of these private time and space coordinates. Thoughts which contain such private references could not be *encoded* in natural languages but could only be incompletely represented' (*Relevance*, p. 192).

(L) is not subject to that Perry-type criticism. (L) says only that every *statement* can be made using an eternal sentence, not that every *thought* can be literally expressed by an eternal sentence. Now, a statement may be *of* an object, in the sense that it may be about a certain object without involving a particular mode of presentation of that object. Such a *de re* statement corresponds to a *class* of thoughts, each involving a particular (and, perhaps, private) mode of presentation of the object referred to. The fact that, in the thought, there are private modes of presentation attached to the objects referred to implies that there are thoughts that cannot be totally and adequately represented by means of eternal sentences, but does not imply that there are *statements* that cannot be made by means of eternal sentences.

Whatever we think of Contextualism, there are not many supporters of eternal sentences nowadays. It is more or less accepted that natural language sentences are irreducibly context-sensitive. But there are fallback positions for Literalism. The strongest fallback position consists in acknowledging the extent of context-dependence, while insisting that it still is the *sentence* which, in virtue of the rules of the language, expresses a proposition with respect to the context. This semantic notion of the content of a sentence (with respect to context) is distinct from the pragmatic notion of the content of a speech act. For it is the linguistic rules, not the speaker's beliefs and intentions, which fix the content of the sentence with respect to context. So Literalism in its modern form holds that *the truth-conditions of a sentence are fixed by the rules of the language (with respect to context) quite independently of the speaker's meaning.*

So construed, Literalism must be rejected because, as we have seen, semantic underdeterminacy makes appealing to speaker's meaning in determining truth-conditions unavoidable (§4.3). Even though there still are theorists who argue in its favour, I think Literalism is clearly a non-starter and I will not be concerned with it in what follows.

The next two fallback positions correspond to weaker forms of literalism. According to them, we need to appeal to the speaker's meaning in determining truth-conditions, but *we do so only when the sentence itself demands it*. In other words, optional pragmatic processes are not allowed to affect what is said; what is said obeys the Minimalist constraint (§1.2).

The weaker of the two positions in question is what I dubbed the Syncretic View (chapter 4). It acknowledges the fact that what is said, in the intuitive sense, may be affected by primary pragmatic processes of the optional variety; but it draws a distinction between what is said in the intuitive sense (the input to secondary pragmatic processes), and what is strictly and literally said. What is strictly and literally said, at least, obeys the minimalist constraint.

The other position is not as weak as that. For reasons that will become apparent, I call it Indexicalism. It denies that what is said, in the intuitive sense, can be affected by pragmatic processes of the optional variety. No contextual influences are allowed to affect the intuitive truth-conditional content of an utterance unless the sentence itself demands it. This position can be thought of as a research programme: whenever it is argued that the truth-conditions of an utterance are affected by context in a top-down manner, the indexicalist feels compelled to re-analyse the example so as to show that the pragmatic process at issue is an instance of saturation after all.

So far I have listed three positions. Full-fledged *Literalism* denies that the speaker's meaning plays any role in fixing the truth-conditions of sentences. *Indexicalism* is a weaker form of literalism that allows the speaker's meaning to play a role, but only when there is a slot to be filled in logical form; no top down influences can affect truth-conditions. The *Syncretic View*

Table 6.1

• Literalism	
• Indexicalism	*literalist side*
• The Syncretic View	
• Quasi-Contextualism	*contextualist*
• Contextualism	*side*

acknowledges such influences, but limits their effects to what is said in the intuitive sense, as opposed to what is strictly and literally said (the minimal proposition).

The next two positions I want to consider fully acknowledge the role of pragmatic processes, including pragmatic processes of the optional variety, in the determination of what is said. What is said is taken to be pragmatically determined, in a way that is sensitive to top-down influences. In contrast to the Syncretic View, those positions do not postulate a level of content that is unaffected by top-down factors. So they fall on the contextualist side. They differ from each other in their respective attitudes towards the minimal proposition posited by the Syncretic View. One position, which I call *Quasi-Contextualism*, simply considers the minimal proposition as a theoretically useless entity which plays no role in communication (§4.5). Full-fledged *Contextualism* goes further and denies that the notion even makes sense.

To sum up, the five positions in the ballpark are shown in table 6.1. Literalism and the Syncretic View have been explicitly criticized, and I have implicitly endorsed Quasi-Contextualism in arguing against the Syncretic View in chapter 4. So two positions remain to be introduced and discussed: Indexicalism, and Contextualism.

6.2   Indexicalism

The pragmatics literature is replete with examples in which what is said in the intuitive sense seems to be affected by pragmatic processes of the optional (top-down) variety – what King and Stanley call 'strong pragmatic effects'.[4] Yet, as Stephen Levinson (one of the providers of examples) puts it, 'there will always be doubt about whether a better semantic analysis of the relevant construction might not accommodate the apparent pragmatic intrusion in some other way'.[5] Indeed, in most cases, there are different ways of analysing a given example. Some of those analyses may well suggest that the pragmatic process at issue is not a primary pragmatic process of the optional variety, but a regular instance of saturation.

---

[4] See King and Stanley, 'Semantics, Pragmatics, and the Role of Semantic Content'.
[5] Stephen Levinson, *Presumptive Meaning*, p. 214.

Consider the phenomenon of quantifier domain restriction. I may utter the sentence 'Most students are male' in order to assert that most students *in my class* are male. This is arguably a case in which what is asserted goes beyond what is linguistically encoded, for I *tacitly* refer to my class. Moreover, the additional ingredient in the meaning of the utterance which is thereby provided seems to be optional, for there is a possible reading of 'Most students are male' in which no such contextual restriction of the domain occurs. (I call that an 'absolute' reading for the quantifier phrase.) So quantifier domain restriction is a prima facie candidate for the status of 'strong pragmatic effect': a truth-conditionally relevant aspect of what is asserted seems to result from an optional pragmatic process. There are many ways of analysing the phenomenon, however. We may consider that the predicate 'student' is contextually enriched and expresses the ad hoc concept S T U D E N T_I N_M Y_C L A S S. We may also consider the class as an unarticulated constituent of what is said, like the location of rain in 'It's raining.' But it is also possible to consider that, in the logical form of the sentence, there is a slot to be contextually filled: a variable corresponding to the domain of quantification, which variable can be associated either with the determiner or (more plausibly perhaps) with the common noun 'student'. On such a view the semantic analysis of the sentence-type will reveal a hidden quasi-indexical component, namely the domain variable d:

Most$_d$ (students) (are male)
Most (students$_d$) (are male)

The suggestion is that, when the sentence is uttered, a value has to be contextually assigned to the variable, thereby restricting the domain of quantification. If we take this line, we treat quantifier domain restriction as, in effect, a case of saturation.[6] In this framework, the cases in which the quantifier phrase is given an 'absolute' reading are treated as cases in which a value *is* contextually assigned to the variable, but intuitively no restriction takes place because the contextually selected domain is the whole universe (or the entire domain relevant to the variable, in case we use sorted variables).

Or consider the examples of enrichment with which our discussion of Minimalism began:

I've had breakfast <this morning>
You're not going to die <from that cut>

The contextually provided ingredients (within angle brackets) seem to correspond to no element in the sentence; they are putative 'unarticulated constituents'. But this is not the only possible analysis. According to event semantics, such sentences quantify over events, hence it is possible to extend the

---

[6] See for example, Jason Stanley and Zoltán Szabó, 'On Quantifier Domain Restriction', in *Mind and Language* 15 (2000), 219–61.

analysis in terms of quantifier domain restriction to them. In 'The Pragmatics of What is Said' I suggested that the intuitive difference between 'I've had breakfast' ('restricted' reading) and 'I've been to Tibet' ('absolute' reading) can be handled in those terms:

In both cases what is conveyed by virtue of linguistic meaning alone is that, in some temporal domain x prior to the time of utterance,[7] there is a certain event, viz. the speaker's having breakfast or his going to Tibet; but in the first case, the time interval is contextually restricted to the day of utterance, while in the second case the relevant interval is more extended and covers the speaker's life (up to the time of utterance).[8]

If that is so then the intuitive understanding of 'I've had breakfast' in the relevant context results from saturation rather than free enrichment.[9] The same sort of thing can be said about the other example. If the sentence is interpreted as quantifying over events ('you're not going to die' = 'there is no future event e such that e is your death'), we can say that the contextually selected domain of quantification is *the set of events which causally follow from the cut*. In 'The Pragmatics of What is Said' I offered a similar analysis for Sperber and Wilson's favourite example of enrichment, 'It will take us some time to get there.'

Another type of example for which two sorts of analysis are possible involves the temporal understanding of conjunction, as in

They got married and had many children.

In chapter 5 I said that the temporal order of the events which is intuitively part of the truth-conditions corresponds to nothing in the sentence and is provided through free enrichment. Indeed there is a possible reading of that sentence (or formally similar sentences) in which no temporal order is implied. But an alternative analysis in terms of saturation is available.[10] Barbara Partee famously suggested that the role of the past tense is, or may be, to refer to a particular time in the past.[11] Let's take that for granted. Then, to determine what is said by means of the sentence 'They got married and had many children', the hearer must assign a reference to each of the referring expressions, *including the past tense 'got married' and 'had'*. Just as pragmatic principles are employed in ascertaining the referent of 'they', so, Carston says, they are used in assigning temporal reference. The hearer goes beyond the strict semantic content of the sentence

---

[7] The domain in question is 'a set of events defined by a time interval'.

[8] Recanati, 'The Pragmatics of What is Said', pp. 305–6.

[9] The same sort of analysis can be provided even if we don't take the sentence to quantify over events, but, in virtue of the tense it contains, over times. 'I've had breakfast' then says that there is a past time t such that the speaker has breakfast at t. The contextually specified domain of quantification now is a set of times (rather than a set of events). Like the event-theoretic analysis, this analysis can be extended to 'You're not going to die.'

[10] See Carston, 'Implicature, Explicature, and Truth-Theoretic Semantics'.

[11] Barbara Partee, 'Some Structural Analogies Between Tenses and Pronouns in English', *Journal of Philosophy* 70 (1973), pp. 602–3.

uttered, and on the basis of contextual assumptions and pragmatic principles recovers from 'they got married and had many children' a representation such as 'John and Mary got married at t and had many children at $t + n$.'

t is some more or less specific time prior to the time of utterance and $t + n$ is some more or less specific time, later than t. The temporal ordering of the events described in the conjuncts is thus treated as a by-product of the reference assignment process involved in determining [what is said].[12]

As I pointed out in 'The Pragmatics of What is Said', this analysis faces difficulties when the past tense is replaced by the present perfect, as in Jonathan Cohen's example 'The old king has died of a heart attack and a republic has been declared.'[13] That is so because the present perfect can hardly be considered as referring to a specific time. But if, plausibly enough, we construe the present perfect as *quantifying* over times, we can extend the analysis in terms of quantifier domain restriction to that type of example also. The sentence will be understood as saying that there is a time t in the past such that the old king dies of a heart attack at t, and there is a time t' in the past such that a republic is declared at t'. If the domain to which the second quantifier is indexed is contextually restricted to *the set of times that are posterior to t*, we account for the relevant temporal reading. So it seems that there always is a way of analysing Gricean examples of temporally understood conjunctions in terms of saturation rather than enrichment.

Examples can be multiplied at will. The indexicalist position consists in systematically offering an analysis in terms of saturation, whenever the intuitive truth-conditions of an utterance are affected by contextual factors. As Jason Stanley, the chief representative of this research program, puts it, 'all effects of extra-linguistic context on the truth-conditions of an assertion are traceable to elements in the actual syntactic structure of the sentence uttered'.[14] To maintain such a sweeping claim, one must deal with every putative counterexample, in order to establish, in each case, the conclusion that 'we have been given no reason to abandon the thesis that the only truth-conditional role of context is the resolution of indexicality, broadly construed'.[15]

At this point the debate becomes technical (and, fortunately, empirical). It's a matter of detailed analyses of particular examples (or classes of examples). Without going into those details, it is fair to say that the indexicalist starts with a significant disadvantage; for he makes a universal claim while his opponent only makes an existential claim. For his opponent to win, it is sufficient to produce

---

[12] Carston, 'Implicature, Explicature, and Truth-Theoretic Semantics', p. 161.
[13] Cohen, 'Grice's Views about the Logical Particles', p. 54.
[14] Jason Stanley, 'Context and Logical Form', in *Linguistics and Philosophy* 23 (2000), p. 391.
[15] *Ibid.*, p. 401; see also Stanley and Szabó, 'On Quantifier Domain Restriction', and King and Stanley, 'Semantics, Pragmatics, and the Role of Semantic Content'.

one convincing example of a strong pragmatic effect. But the indexicalist is condemned to deal with *all* putative cases, and to show that they are not what they seem to be. A hopeless task, unless the indexicalist can develop methods, or strategies, for dealing with large classes of cases at once. Unsurprisingly, such general methods are what the indexicalist is after. Stanley has come up with one strategy, in particular, that seems very powerful and which he has applied both to the case of quantifier domain restriction and to 'unarticulated constituents' more generally. In chapter 7, I will discuss that strategy and show that it is not as successful as Stanley thinks.

6.3   Contextualism

According to Contextualism – a provocative view which certainly deserves to be explored – there is no level of meaning which is both (i) propositional (truth-evaluable) and (ii) minimalist, that is, unaffected by top-down factors. As I put it in *Direct Reference*, 'no proposition could be expressed without some unarticulated constituent being contextually provided'.[16] Such a radical view has been defended by Charles Travis, John Searle, Julius Moravcsik and a few others. Searle, for example, argues that a determinate proposition can be expressed only against a background of unarticulated assumptions. He gives the following example of unarticulated assumptions at work in understanding a simple utterance:

Suppose I go into the restaurant and order a meal. Suppose I say, speaking literally, 'Bring me a steak with fried potatoes.' (. . .) I take it for granted that they will not deliver the meal to my house, or to my place of work. I take it for granted that the steak will not be encased in concrete, or petrified. It will not be stuffed into my pockets or spread over my head. But none of these assumptions was made explicit in the literal utterance.[17]

Though unarticulated, those assumptions contribute to determining the intuitive conditions of satisfaction (obedience-conditions, truth-conditions, and so on) of the utterance. The order 'Bring me a steak with fried potatoes' does not count as satisfied if the steak is delivered, encased in concrete, to the customer's house. It is mutually manifest to both the hearer and the speaker that the speaker intends the ordered meal to be placed in front of him on the restaurant table he is sitting at, and so on.

In that sort of case a syncretist will insist that what is strictly and literally said is free from the relevant assumptions: the order 'Bring me a steak with fried potatoes' would be literally satisfied if the steak was delivered, encased in concrete, to the customer's house. (See Soames's treatment of the 'coffee' example in §4.4.) That is precisely what the contextualist denies. Another example given by Searle will help to make sense of the contextualist position. The

---

[16] Recanati, *Direct Reference*, p. 260.
[17] John Searle, *The Rediscovery of the Mind* (MIT Press, 1992), p. 180.

word 'cut' is not ambiguous, Searle says, yet it makes quite different contributions to the truth-conditions of the utterance in 'Bill cut the grass' and 'Sally cut the cake'. That is because background assumptions play a role in fixing satisfaction-conditions, and different background assumptions underlie the use of 'cut' in connection with grass and cakes respectively. We (defeasibly) assume that grass is cut in a certain way, and cakes in another way. The assumed way of cutting finds its way into the utterance's truth-conditions:

Though the occurrence of the word 'cut' is literal in (both) utterances . . . and though the word is not ambiguous, it determines different sets of truth-conditions for the different sentences. The sort of thing that constitutes cutting the grass is quite different from, e.g., the sort of thing that constitutes cutting a cake. One way to see this is to imagine what constitutes obeying the order to cut something. If someone tells me to cut the grass and I rush out and stab it with a knife, or if I am ordered to cut the cake and I run over it with a lawnmower, in each case I will have failed to obey the order. That is not what the speaker meant by his literal and serious utterance of the sentence.[18]

Now the syncretist will insist that a sentence such as 'Cut the grass' expresses something that has literal conditions of satisfaction quite independent of any background assumption; something very abstract, involving the constant, underspecified meaning of 'cut' and not the definite sense it takes on particular uses (or types of use). Stabbing the grass with a knife and running over it with a lawnmower are two ways of literally obeying the order 'Cut the grass', on this view. But the contextualist remains sceptical. To get something genuinely evaluable, he claims, that is, something which enables us to partition possible worlds into those in which the relevant condition is satisfied and those in which it is not, we need background assumptions. We cannot specify a determinate proposition which the sentence can be said literally to express, without building unarticulated assumptions into that proposition. The best we can do is to construct a disjunction of the propositions which could be determinately expressed by that sentence against alternative background assumptions.

In support of this claim, Searle sets up an example for which no background assumption is readily available: 'Cut the sun.' What counts as obeying that order? We don't quite know. The abstract condition we can associate with that sentence (involving some form of linear separation affecting the integrity of the sun) is, precisely, too abstract to enable us to tell the worlds in which the condition is satisfied from the worlds in which it is not. It is not determinate enough to give us specific truth-conditions or obedience-conditions.[19]

[18] Searle, 'The Background of Meaning', pp. 222–3.
[19] In 'La Polysémie Contre le Fixisme' (*Langue Française* 113, 1997), p. 120, I gave a real-life example of the phenomenon Searle is drawing our attention to. Consider the following dialogue from *Desire*, a film by Frank Borzage (1936):
– 'Pedro!' – 'Yes sir.' – 'Take the plate to the kitchen and disarm the fricassee.'
    What does the complex phrase 'disarm the fricassee' literally mean? It is hard to tell. To make sense of that phrase, we must know the context. In the film, the context is as follows:

6.4   Literalist responses to the contextualist challenge

According to Emma Borg (who follows the lead of other radical syncretists, such as Herman Cappelen and Ernie Lepore),[20] the fact that we are unable to specify intuitive conditions of application for the predicate 'cut the sun' does not support the contextualist conclusion that sentences per se do not have truth-conditions. There is, she claims, a crucial difference between 'knowledge of truth-conditions and the knowledge that truth-conditions are satisfied'.[21] We may know the obedience-conditions of 'Cut the sun' in a purely 'disquotational' manner (that is we may know that 'Cut the sun' is obeyed iff the addressee cuts the sun), without knowing *what counts as* cutting the sun, in the context at hand. So there is no reason to deny sentences genuine truth-conditions. The sentence 'Oscar cuts the sun' does possess truth-conditions; such truth-conditions are determined by a recursive truth-theory for the language, which issues theorems such as '*Oscar cuts the sun* is true iff Oscar cuts the sun.' We know those truth-conditions provided we know the language. What we don't know, simply in virtue of knowing the language, is 'a method of verification for those truth-conditions'. This, then, is the syncretist's ultimate reply to the contextualist. According to the syncretist, the contextualist is guilty of endorsing a form of (so-called) 'verificationism'.[22]

This move strikes me as an unacceptable weakening of the notion of truth-condition. The central idea of truth-conditional semantics (as opposed to mere 'translational semantics') is the idea that, via truth, we connect words and the

(i) Gary Cooper (the speaker) is handing a fricassee plate to the waiter (Pedro); (ii) the fricassee plate contains a gun; (iii) that gun has just fallen from the hands of someone during a brief fight around the dinner table. With respect to that situation, the phrase 'disarm the fricassee' makes sense: it means that the waiter is to remove the gun from the plate. Without a proper background, however, we no more know the obedience conditions of Cooper's utterance 'Disarm the fricassee' than we know the obedience conditions of 'Cut the sun.'

[20] As King and Stanley point out in their forthcoming paper 'Semantics, Pragmatics, and the Role of Semantic Content', Syncretism – what they call 'semantic modesty' – 'is a position that comes in degrees. On the one extreme, there are those who hold that most of our intuitions about what is said by a sentence in a context are affected by strong pragmatic effects. On the other end of the spectrum, are theorists who hold that while generally intuitions about what is said by a sentence are reliable guides to semantic content, there are a restricted range of cases in which strong pragmatic effects may affect speaker intuitions about what they take to be the semantic content of a sentence.' Cappelen and Lepore are radical syncretists. They argue for *systematically* disconnecting the semantic content which the theorist assigns to a sentence from what is intuitively said by uttering that sentence (see Cappelen and Lepore, 'On an Alleged Connection Between Indirect Speech and the Theory of Meaning').

[21] Borg, 'Saying What You Mean'.

[22] *Ibid.* The first occurrence of this line of reply to contextualism can be found in Marcelo Dascal's discussion of Searle's 'Literal Meaning': see Marcelo Dascal, 'Contextualism', in Parret, Sbisà and Verschueren (eds.), *Possibilities and Limitations of Pragmatics*, pp. 173–4. The most recent occurrence I have seen is in Herman Cappelen and Ernie Lepore, 'Radical and Moderate Pragmatics: Does Meaning Determine Truth-Conditions?' (forthcoming).

world.[23] If we know the truth-conditions of a sentence, we know *which state of affairs must hold for the sentence to be true*.[24] T-sentences display knowledge of truth-conditions in that sense only if the right-hand side of the biconditional is *used*, that is, only if the necessary and sufficient condition which it states is transparent to the utterer of the T-sentence. If I say *'Oscar cuts the sun* is true iff Oscar cuts the sun', without knowing what it is to 'cut the sun', then the T-sentence I utter no more counts as displaying knowledge of truth-conditions than if I utter it without knowing who Oscar is (for example, if I use the name 'Oscar' deferentially, in such a way that the right-hand side is not really *used*, but involves some kind of mention).[25]

One may doubt the feasibility of referential or truth-conditional semantics and defend translational semantics as a viable alternative. I have heard (or read) arguments to that effect.[26] My point however is that *if* we stick to the standard truth-conditional project (as Davidsonians like Cappelen and Lepore surely ought to do) then we should not accept the syncretist's claim that we somehow know the truth-conditions of 'Harry cut the sun.' (For we don't.)

The contextualist challenge is likely to elicit another unsatisfactory response, this time from the indexicalist. To each dimension of underdeterminacy, the indexicalist may argue, there corresponds a slot in logical form, which must be filled for the utterance to say something definite. To illustrate that point, let us consider another contextualist example from Searle.[27]

When we ask someone to open the door, the content of the request goes beyond what is linguistically encoded. Not only is it necessary for the addressee to identify the relevant door (that is, to complete or otherwise enrich the incomplete definite description 'the door'). She must also determine in what sense the door must be 'opened'. Besides doors and windows, eyes and wounds can

---

[23] See Donald Davidson, 'Truth and Meaning', in his *Inquiries into Truth and Interpretation* (Clarendon Press, 1984), p. 24; Jaakko Hintikka, 'Semantics for Propositional Attitudes', in his *Models for Modalities* (Reidel, 1969), pp. 87–8; David Lewis, 'General Semantics', in *Synthèse* 22 (1970), pp. 18–19; and especially Gareth Evans and John McDowell, 'Introduction' to *Truth and Meaning: Essays in Semantics* (Clarendon Press, 1976), pp. vii–xi.

[24] In §1.5 I gave an example of the way knowledge of truth-conditions can be tested, by asking subjects to pair sentences with situations. Pure 'disquotational' knowledge of the sort invoked by Emma Borg does not suffice to pass that sort of test.

[25] As Harman pointed out, if pure disquotational knowledge counts as knowledge of truth-conditions (in a suitably weak sense), then knowledge of truth-conditions (in that sense) does not count as knowledge of meaning. 'There is a sense in which we can know the truth-conditions of an English sentence without knowing the first thing about the meaning of the English sentence. To borrow David Wiggins's (1972) example, we might know that the sentence "All mimsy were the borogroves" is true if and only if all mimsy were the borogroves. However, in knowing this we would not know the first thing about the meaning of the sentence, "All mimsy were the borogroves." ' (Gilbert Harman, 'Meaning and Semantics', in his *Reasoning, Meaning, and Mind* (Clarendon Press, 1999), p. 196).

[26] See for example Edwin Martin Jr, 'Truth and Translation', in *Philosophical Studies* 23 (1972), 125–30, and Marco Santambrogio, 'Translational Semantics', forthcoming.

[27] John Searle, *Intentionality* (Cambridge University Press, 1983), pp. 145–7.

be opened. Now if the addressee 'opened' the door by making an incision in it with a scalpel, as when opening a wound, she would not have satisfied the request. Still, in a special context, it could be that the request to open the door must be satisfied precisely by incising it by means of a scalpel. The manner of opening is thus defeasibly indicated by context, it is not determinable on the basis of just the linguistic meaning of the sentence (including the direct object of the verb). To be sure, we can make it explicit in the sentence itself by introducing supplementary details, but each addition of this sort cannot fail to introduce other underdeterminacies. If, for example, we add that the door must be opened 'with a key', we don't specify whether the key must be inserted into the lock or rather used like an axe to break the door open.[28] However explicit the sentence, there will always be some aspect of truth-conditional content that is contextually determined without being explicitly articulated.

At this point, the imagined indexicalist response consists in saying that, like all verbs, 'open' is associated with a complex frame[29] – the opening frame – involving a certain number of argument roles: a location playing the role of INSIDE; another location operating as OUTSIDE; a BOUNDARY separating the two; a MOVING OBJECT liable to pass from inside to outside (or the other way round); an OBSTACLE, that is, an entity preventing the passage of the moving object; an AGENT liable to free the passage by means of ACTION on the obstacle; an INSTRUMENT serving to accomplish the action; and so on and so forth. In context, each of the variables I have enumerated must be assigned a particular value: the INSIDE, the OUTSIDE, the OBSTACLE, the PATH and so on, all must be contextually identified. In the case of 'opening a wound', the INSIDE is the interior of the wound, the OUTSIDE is the exterior of the body, the MOVING OBJECT is the internal secretions of the wound and so on. This contextual instantiation of the variables is what determines the specific interpretation assigned to 'open' in a given context, and it is no different from what is required for interpreting 'John's boat' or 'He came' or any other context-sensitive expression in need of saturation. It is therefore unnecessary to modify semantic theory in order to give an account of Searle's examples; it is enough to extend the list of context-sensitive expressions, so as to include all verbs (insofar as they are all associated with frames which comprise a number of argument roles, the fillers of which must be contextually assigned).

This indexicalist response is no more convincing than the syncretist response was. Let's admit that the verb 'to open' is associated with the complex frame

---

[28] Searle, *The Rediscovery of the Mind*, p. 182.
[29] The notion of frame which I am using is that elaborated by Fillmore in a series of papers. See Charles Fillmore, 'Frame Semantics and the Nature of Language', in *Annals of the New York Academy of Sciences* 280 (1976), 20–32; 'Frame Semantics', in The Linguistic Society of Korea (ed.), *Linguistics in the Morning Calm* (Hanshin, 1982), 111–38; 'Frames and the Semantics of Understanding', in *Quaderni di Semantica* 6 (1985), 222–54; and Atkins and Fillmore, 'Toward a Frame-Based Lexicon'.

I have mentioned. Does that make it an indexical or context-sensitive expression, whose use triggers, indeed mandates, a primary pragmatic process of saturation? No. There is an important difference between the argument roles of a frame and the indexical variables associated with context-sensitive expressions.[30] Indexical variables *must* be contextually assigned values for the expression to acquire a definite semantic content. If the referent of 'he' in 'He boarded John's boat' is not contextually specified, or if the relation between John and the boat remains indefinite, the utterance does not have definite truth-conditions. In contrast, the argument roles of a frame may but need not be assigned contextual values. The contextual assignment process is optional; it may, or may not, take place, depending on what is contextually relevant. In other words, it is the context (not the sentence) which determines which, among the many argument roles of a given frame, are contextually assigned particular values, and which remain indefinite (existentially quantified). In many contexts, it is of no importance whether the door is opened with a key or in another way; what counts is simply that it is opened. To be sure, for any given verb (or verb plus syntactic context), there is a small number of argument roles in the frame for which the contextual assignment of value is linguistically mandated; but the indexical response presupposes something much stronger: that the verb 'open' is like an indexical expression, which acquires a definite content only when the argument roles of the associated frame (*all* the argument roles, insofar at they can all be contextually foregrounded) are contextually assigned values. That is evidently too strong. In a given context, many of the argument roles which feature in the frame are existentially quantified rather than contextually assigned values. This does not prevent the verb 'open' from expressing a definite content, in such a context.

To sum up, for indexicals it is the conventional meaning of the expression which triggers the process of saturation and makes it mandatory. With ordinary expressions such as 'open', it is the context, not the conventional meaning of the expression, which is responsible for foregrounding certain aspects of the described situation and triggering a process of contextual specification which goes well beyond what is linguistically encoded. The process in question is top-down, not bottom up. It is a pragmatically controlled pragmatic process, rather than a linguistically controlled pragmatic process, like saturation.

6.5   Where Indexicalism and Contextualism meet

In §6.1 I described Indexicalism as the strongest fallback position for a literalist forced to acknowledge that speaker's meaning plays a role in fixing

---

[30] See Robyn Carston, 'Explicature and Semantics', in *UCL Working Papers in Linguistics* 12 (2000), p. 34; Claudia Bianchi, *La Dipendenza Contestuale: Per una Teoria Pragmatica del Significato* (Edizioni Scientifiche Italiane, 2001), pp. 163–7; and François Recanati, 'Déstabiliser le sens', in *Revue Internationale de Philosophie* 55 (2001), p. 206.

truth-conditional content. According to Indexicalism, it is the sentence which, via the conventional meaning of the context-sensitive expressions it contains, triggers and controls the appeal to the speaker's meaning. The speaker's meaning thus plays a role in the determination of truth-conditional content, but it does so only when the sentence itself sets up slots to be pragmatically filled (Minimalism). The Syncretic View is a weaker form of literalism since it concedes that the intuitive truth-conditions of an utterance may not satisfy the minimalist constraint, which holds only for 'what is strictly and literally said' (the minimal proposition). Next comes Quasi-Contextualism, which differs from the Syncretic View in downplaying the minimal proposition. For the quasi-contextualist, the minimal proposition literally expressed by the sentence exists in semantic heaven but plays no role in the actual process of communication. Finally, Contextualism denies the very existence and possibility of the minimal proposition, insofar as it is determined in a purely bottom-up manner: without pragmatic intrusions of the optional (top-down) variety, no determinate proposition could be expressed.

Even though it is useful and illuminating to order the five positions on the scale from Literalism to Contextualism, as I have done, their relations are more complex than a simple ordering can suggest. In particular, there is a dimension along which Indexicalism and Contextualism are close neighbours.

One must not forget that the gist of Literalism is an attempt to minimize context-sensitivity, while Contextualism takes it to be an essential feature of natural language (as opposed to formal languages). From this point of view, the indexicalist position is somewhat ambiguous. On the one hand, by rejecting contextual influences on content that are not linguistically controlled, the indexicalist does his best to preserve the literalist doctrine that linguistic entities are genuine bearers of content, context-sensitivity notwithstanding. On the other hand, by multiplying indexical variables, the indexicalist widens the gap between sentence meaning and propositional content, in the spirit of Contextualism. Indexicalism can thus be seen as a natural ally of Contextualism.[31]

Likewise, Contextualism can be construed as an extreme form of Indexicalism that generalizes context-sensitivity so as to rule out eternal sentences not merely de facto but de jure. It's not just that there are expressions whose meaning is schematic and involves contextual variables; it is *linguistic meaning in general* which suffers from a form of underdeterminacy which makes it unfit to carry content save against a rich contextual background. Owing to that underdeterminacy, some form of enrichment or contextual elaboration becomes mandatory for the sentence to express a definite proposition. The reason why Contextualism and Indexicalism become so close is precisely that, with

---

[31] In 'The Pragmatics of What is Said', pp. 308–9 n., I argued that the Minimalist Principle can serve as a methodological weapon in the hand of the contextualist.

Contextualism, the distinction between mandatory and optional pragmatic processes is somewhat blurred.

According to Contextualism, the meaning of words and/or phrases (whether indexical or not) is not determinate enough to yield even a minimal proposition. In chapter 9 I will consider various arguments in favour of that claim, and various contextualist positions corresponding to these arguments. One extreme position denies that words have meanings in anything like the traditional sense. Another, less extreme view takes polysemous words such as 'open' or 'cut' as paradigmatic and generalizes the form of underdeterminacy they reveal. According to both of these views, the meaning of a predicate is not a determinate concept: it is a 'semantic potential', which only determines a concept against a rich pragmatic context.[32] At this point Contextualism becomes hard to distinguish from (an extreme form of) Indexicalism. Nearly all words are like indexicals, whose contents must be contextually determined. As Sperber and Wilson say, "words are used as pointers to contextually intended senses'.[33]

---

[32] A third contextualist position to be discussed in chapter 9 construes the process of semantic composition as, to a large extent, pragmatically sensitive, in such a way that complex phrases must be *assigned* a sense, in context, even if the constituent words all possess a definite sense.

[33] Sperber and Wilson, 'The Mental and the Public Lexicon', p. 200. The difference between the contextualist positions mentioned in the text and the view of Sperber and Wilson is that Sperber and Wilson take words also to *encode* concepts (in many cases). Sperber and Wilson are *quasi*-contextualists. They accept that ordinary words have contents, in and by themselves, and that sentences containing them express propositions (once indexicals etc. have been assigned semantic values) – even though they take these contents and these propositions to be communicationally irrelevant. In the same article (p. 185) they write: 'Many words seem to encode not a full-fledged concept but what might be called a pro-concept. (. . .) As with pronouns, their semantic contribution *must* be contextually specified for the associated utterance to have a truth-value. (. . .) All words behave *as if* they encoded pro-concepts: that is, whether or not a word encodes a full concept, the concept it is used to convey in a given utterance has to be contextually worked out.' In contrast, a genuine contextualist denies that words have full-fledged contents or encode concepts. All words – or, more cautiously, nearly all words – encode only 'pro-concepts' (semantic potentials) and serve as pointers to intended senses. In *Thoughts and Utterances*, pp. 359–64, Robyn Carston tentatively amends relevance theory along those lines.

7 Indexicalism and the Binding Fallacy

7.1 Mandatory vs optional

What characterizes contextual ingredients of the optional variety is the fact that their contextual provision is not mandatory – it is not required in virtue of a linguistic convention governing the use of a particular construction (or class of constructions). *In context*, it may be that that ingredient is 'required'; but then it is required *in virtue of features of the context*, not in virtue of linguistic properties of the expression-type. A contextual ingredient is mandatory in the relevant sense, and is provided through saturation, only if *in every context* such an ingredient has to be provided (precisely because the need for saturation is not a contextual matter, but a context-independent property of the expression-type). This, then, is the criterion we must use for deciding whether a contextual ingredient results from an optional pragmatic process or from saturation: can we imagine a context in which the same words are used normally, and a truth-evaluable statement is made, yet no such ingredient is provided?

To illustrate the contrast between the two types of pragmatic process, let us consider the phenomenon of 'null instantiation' (to use Fillmore's terminology), where the direct object of a transitive verb is not syntactically realized, or at least not overtly. There are two sorts of case, which must be sharply distinguished.[1] In *indefinite* null instantiation (INI), the argument role corresponding to the direct object is existentially quantified instead of being assigned a particular value. In that type of case the suppression of the direct object arguably changes the semantic value of the verb: it denotes not the original two-place relation, but a property generated by existentially quantifying the object argument-role

---

[1] See Barbara Partee, 'Compositionality', in Fred Landman and Frank Veltman (eds.), *Varieties of Formal Semantics* (Foris, 1984), p. 299; Charles Fillmore 'Pragmatically Controlled Zero Anaphora', in *BLS* 12 (1986), 95–107; Michele Prandi, *Grammaire Philosophique des Tropes* (Minuit, 1992), pp. 48–9, fn. 34; Charles Fillmore and Paul Kay, *Construction Grammar Coursebook* (University of California at Berkeley, 1993), §7.2; and Marjolein Groefsema, 'Understood Arguments: A Semantic/Pragmatic Approach', in *Lingua* 96 (1995), 139–61. As Cresswell pointed out (after Partee), we observe the same contrast between two sorts of relational nouns: 'Unlike nouns like *mother* and *sister* whose default cases are existentially quantified the default cases of *enemy* and of *representative* appear to have the second argument supplied contextually' (Max Cresswell, *Semantic Indexicality* (Kluwer, 1996), p. 39).

of the original relation. As Quine pointed out, from any n-place predicate P, one can generate an $n - 1$ place predicate by applying to P an operator he calls 'Derelativization', which he describes as follows:

$$(\text{Der } P) x_1 \ldots x_{n-1} \text{ iff there is something } x_n \text{ such that } P x_1 \ldots x_n$$

If 'P' is a two-place predicate, 'Der P' will be a genuine one-place predicate, denoting a property rather than a relation.[2] In the case of 'eat' and other verbs subject to INI, suppressing the direct object in surface syntax amounts semantically to the same result as applying 'Der' to the original two-place predicate. Intransitive 'eat' thus denotes the property of eating (EAT_1), namely the property one has in virtue of filling the EATER argument-role in some instance of the dyadic EAT relation (EAT_2). One eats$_1$ iff there is something that one eats$_2$.

In *definite* null instantiation (DNI) the situation is quite different. Like 'eat', 'hear' and 'notice' are transitive verbs which have an intransitive use: they can be used without a direct object, as in 'I heard' or 'I noticed'. When that is the case, however, there must be something definite, in context, which the speaker is said to have heard or noticed. To understand what is said, an interpreter must identify that thing. This shows that *the objectless verb still denotes the original two-place relation*, even though the second argument-role is not realized in surface syntax.[3] Unless a particular filler is contextually assigned to the unrealized argument role, the utterance remains semantically incomplete. Thus 'I heard' or 'I noticed' cannot be interpreted as meaning that the speaker has heard or noticed *something or other*. This is what it means to say that, in contrast to 'eat', 'hear' is not subject to INI, but to DNI. 'John eats' is true iff there is something that John eats$_2$. The fact that the relevant thing does not have to be specified supports the conclusion that intransitive 'eat' denotes the property of eating$_1$. In contrast, 'x noticed' is definitely *not* true iff *there is* something y which x noticed. Rather, it is true, for some contextually specified thing y, iff x noticed *that thing*. The relevant y has to be specified for the utterance to be truth-evaluable. That is an instance of saturation, even though the constituent to be contextually provided is 'unarticulated' in surface syntax.[4]

---

[2] Willard van Orman Quine, 'Variables Explained Away', in his *Selected Logic Papers* (Harvard University Press, 1995), pp. 229–31.

[3] In the situation-theoretic framework I will sketch in chapter 8, an alternative account of DNI is available. The missing argument can be construed as belonging to the 'circumstance of evaluation' rather than to the 'articulated content'. Thus, instead of maintaining that the objectless verb still denotes the original two-place relation, we can say that the objectless DNI-verb is an *indexical* one-place predicate: the property it denotes is relativized to, and varies with, the 'circumstantial' constituent that is contextually provided. Thus in a context c_1 intransitive 'notice' will denote the property of *noticing the accident*, while in another context c_2 it will denote the property of *noticing the man*. See my 'Unarticulated Constituents', p. 312, footnote 11 for an analogous suggestion concerning another type of implicit argument.

[4] Insofar as it is mandatory and provided through saturation, the constituent is unarticulated only in a weak sense. For the distinction between two senses of 'unarticulated', see my 'Unarticulated Constituents', pp. 307–13.

To sum up, it is a conventional property of the English verb 'eat' that (i) it can be used intransitively (in contrast to 'devour'), and (ii) when so used it does not require saturation of the unarticulated argument-role. That argument role is best thought of as suppressed: the two-place relation has been replaced by a property. Likewise, it's a conventional property of the English verb 'finish' that (i) it too can be used intransitively (in contrast to 'complete'), but (ii) when so used it does require saturation of the unarticulated argument-role. The latter is not suppressed, though it remains implicit.

The fact that the suppressed argument role of intransitive 'eat' does not require saturation does not entail that a value *cannot* be contextually provided for that role. What the DNI/INI contrast suggests is only this: *if* a value is provided for the suppressed argument role of 'eat', it is provided through an optional pragmatic process of enrichment. This is different from the mandatory provision of a contextual value for the implicit argument-role in need of saturation, in cases of DNI such as 'finish' or 'notice'. Verbs subject to DNI carry something like a free variable in semantic structure, which must be assigned a definite value in context. Verbs subject to INI do not carry such a free variable, hence the contextual provision of a value for the suppressed argument role cannot be treated as an instance of saturation, but as a case of enrichment.

Let me give an example. We can imagine a context in which 'Look! He's eating!' would be understood as stating not merely that the individual denoted by 'he' is eating something or other, but that he is eating *a certain salient piece of food*, for example, a dangerous mushroom which has been the focus of attention for some time. The eaten object would then be contextually provided without being linguistically required, since the intransitive verb only denotes the property and does not require saturation. In such a case the contextual specification of the eaten object would result from free enrichment. But in the above cases of DNI ('I heard', 'I finished', 'I noticed'), the contextual provision of the relevant ingredient is a bottom-up pragmatic process – a variety of saturation – rather than a top-down pragmatic process of free enrichment. This is established by the fact that the provision of an object filling the second argument role is required in *every* context, not just in the contexts in which it turns out to be relevant.

7.2   Two criteria

I have argued that, whenever a contextual ingredient of content results from a pragmatic process of the optional variety, we can imagine contexts in which the lack of such an ingredient would not prevent the sentence from expressing a complete proposition. This gives us a criterion for telling apart cases in which a contextual ingredient results from saturation and cases in which it does not:

Optionality Criterion
Whenever a contextual ingredient of content is provided through a pragmatic process of the optional variety, we can imagine another possible context of utterance in which no such ingredient is provided yet the utterance expresses a complete proposition.

Systematically used, that criterion may give surprising results. Thus it is common to hold that the sentence 'It's raining' expresses a complete proposition only if a location is contextually provided. If that's right, then the contextual specification of the location of rain is an instance of saturation, much like the contextual provision of the thing heard in 'I heard'.[5] Using the Optionality Criterion, however, I have established that the location of rain is not provided through saturation; for there are contexts in which the sentence 'It is raining' expresses a complete proposition, even though no location is contextually provided as that which the utterance concerns (see §1.3, pp. 9–10).

Applying the Criterion is not always easy, however. For it is not always easy to tell whether or not a contextual ingredient is actually provided. In §6.2 I gave an example of that difficulty. There are two ways to look at contextual restrictions of the domain of quantification. First possibility: we say that a contextual ingredient is provided only when the domain of quantification is implicitly restricted. The cases in which the quantifier ranges over the entire domain of discourse, without contextual restriction, are treated as cases in which no pragmatic process takes place – the sentence is simply taken at face value. The fact that there are such 'absolute' readings of quantified sentences can then be considered as showing that the process of contextual domain restriction is not mandatory but optional. Second possibility: we consider that a primary pragmatic process of saturation must take place to assign a value to the domain variable in logical form. Absolute readings themselves result from a particular assignment of value to the variable, but that is not visible because of the nature of the assignment: the entire domain is assigned to the variable, hence no contextual restriction intuitively occurs. A contextual ingredient is nonetheless provided. The Optionality Criterion, by itself, cannot help us with the choice between the two possibilities. It's only after the choice has been made that we can apply the Optionality Criterion. That is, we must decide, first, whether or not a contextual ingredient is provided when the quantified sentence is given

---

[5] Thus Ken Taylor writes ('Sex, Breakfast, and Descriptus Interruptus', p. 53): 'The view which I favor supposes that the verb 'to rain' has a lexically specified argument place which is θ–marked THEME and that this argument place takes places as values. This is a way of saying that the subatomic structure of the verb "to rain" explicitly marks rainings as a kind of change that places undergo. (. . .) Thus though "It is raining" is missing no syntactically mandatory sentential constituent, nonetheless, it is semantically incomplete. The semantic incompleteness is manifest to us as a felt inability to evaluate the truth value of an utterance of [that sentence] in the absence of a contextually provided location (or range of locations). This felt need for a contextually provided location has its source, I claim, in our tacit cognition of the syntactically unexpressed argument place of the verb "to rain".'

the 'absolute' reading. It's only if we give a negative answer that we can use the Optionality Criterion to establish that quantifier domain restriction is not an instance of saturation.

Are there other criteria? According to Jason Stanley, there is one that is most helpful: the Binding Criterion. Stanley's idea is the following. Whenever a contextual ingredient is provided as a result of saturation, there is something like a free variable in logical form, which must be contextually assigned a value. If a contextual ingredient does *not* result from saturation, but is pragmatic through and through, there is no variable in logical form to which that ingredient corresponds. It is 'unarticulated' in the strongest possible sense. But that entails that no 'binding' of the relevant constituent is possible:

Since the supposed unarticulated constituent . . . is not the value of anything in the sentence uttered, there should be no reading of the relevant linguistic constructions in which the unarticulated constituent varies with the values introduced by operators in the sentence uttered. Operators in a sentence only interact with variables in the sentence that lie within their scope. But, if the constituent is unarticulated, it is not the value of any variable in the sentence. Thus, its interpretation cannot be controlled by operators in the sentence.[6]

For binding to occur, Stanley argues, there must be a bindable variable in the sentence to which the operator is prefixed; but if there is such a variable, then the contextual ingredient (when there is one) ought to be seen as the value contextually assigned to that variable in the process of saturation, rather than as an 'unarticulated constituent' corresponding to nothing in the sentence and resulting from 'free enrichment'. This, then, is the criterion Stanley uses:

Binding Criterion
A contextual ingredient in the interpretation of a sentence *S* results from saturation if it can be 'bound', that is, if it can be made to vary with the values introduced by some operator prefixed to *S*.

Using that criterion, Stanley attempts to show that quantifier domain restriction *is* an instance of saturation. For there are cases in which the domain of a quantifier may be *bound by another quantifier*, as in the following examples:

(1) In most of John's classes, he fails exactly three Frenchmen.
(2) In every room in John's house, every bottle is in the corner.
(3) Whatever John does, most of the class falls asleep.

'In each of these examples', Stanley and Szabó say,

the domain of the second quantifier expression varies with the values of the first quantifier expression. For example, the proposition intuitively expressed by an utterance of (1) is the proposition that, for most *x* such that *x* is a class of John's, John failed three Frenchmen

---

[6] Stanley, 'Context and Logical Form', pp. 410–11.

in *x*. Thus the domain of the quantifier expression 'three Frenchmen' varies with the value of the variable introduced by the quantifier 'most'.[7]

Since there is no binding without a bindable variable, Stanley and Szabó conclude that 'in the logical form of quantified sentences, there are variables whose values, relative to a context, are (often restricted) quantifier domains'.[8] It follows that the contextual provision of a restricted domain of quantification is an instance of saturation.

7.3   The indexicalist challenge

Sometimes the Binding Criterion and the Optionality Criterion converge and give the same verdict. Take parametric predicates such as 'small', or verbs subject to Definite Null Instantiation, such as 'notice':

(4) John is small <for a basketball player>.
(5) John noticed <the mistake>.

The Optionality Criterion tells us that the contextual provision of the comparison class (for 'small') or of the thing noticed (for intransive uses of 'notice') is in both cases an instance of saturation because there is no possible context of utterance for (4) or (5) in which no such ingredient would be provided yet the sentence would still express a complete proposition. Using the Binding Criterion we reach the same conclusion, for binding can occur in both cases. Stanley gives the following example:

(6) Most species have members that are small.

Here, instead of being contextually specified, the comparison class varies with the values introduced by 'most species': each species in turn serves as comparison class for smallness. Likewise, Partee points out that we can bind the 'object' of 'notice' even though it is unarticulated in surface syntax:[9]

(7) Every secretary made a mistake in his final draft. The good secretary corrected his mistake. *Every other secretary did not even notice.*

The two criteria converge also with respect to examples like

(8) John is home.

No proposition is expressed unless it is determined whose home is in question (John's home, or the speaker's home – not to mention other possibilities). Moreover, there is no possible context of utterance for that sentence where it means that John is at someone or other's home. Saturation is required. The Binding

---

[7] Stanley and Szabó, 'On Quantifier Domain Restriction', p. 243.   [8] *Ibid.*, p. 258.
[9] See Barbara Partee, 'Binding Implicit Variables in Quantified Contexts', *CLS* 25 (1989), 342–65.

Criterion confirms this verdict. We can say

(9) Everybody went home.

and mean that each of the persons in question went to his or her home. On that interpretation the implicit argument varies with the values introduced by 'everybody'. According to the Binding Argument, this shows that there is a variable in logical form, which can be bound or contextually assigned a value, as the case may be. When a value is contextually assigned, as in (8), this is an instance of saturation.

Life is not as simple as that, however. There are also cases in which the two criteria yield conflicting results. By the Optionality Criterion, as we have seen, the location of rain which is implicit in 'It's raining' is provided through an optional process of free enrichment; yet, Stanley points out, it can be bound:

(10) Everywhere I go, it rains.

In such a statement the location of rain is undertood as varying with the places introduced by the quantifier 'Everywhere I go'. The statement means that:

For every location l such that I go to l, it rains in l (when I am there).

For such binding to occur, Stanley says, there must be a free variable l in the sentence 'it rains'. That variable can either be bound (as in (10)), or be contextually given a value. Whatever location may be contextually provided for the rain is therefore not a genuine 'optional' ingredient, but the contextual value of a free variable in logical form. The contextual provision of a specific location therefore counts as an instance of saturation, contrary to the verdict delivered by the Optionality Criterion.

Similarly, the temporal location of the breakfast event in Sperber and Wilson's example ('I've had breakfast') seems to result from enrichment according to the Optionality Criterion; yet it can be bound by a quantifier.[10] We can say:

(11) No luck. Each time you offer me lunch, I've had a very large breakfast.

The temporal location of the breakfast event now systematically varies with the temporal values introduced by 'each time you offer me lunch'. It follows that there is a variable in logical form. But if there is, then the alleged instance of enrichment is an instance of saturation after all. So the argument goes.

Unsurprisingly, Stanley uses the Binding Criterion in arguing for Indexicalism. He appeals to data of the sort originally collected by Barbara Partee[11] to show that, *whenever* an 'optional' ingredient has been postulated to account for

---

[10] Stanley does not actually discuss that example, but his general argument applies nonetheless.

[11] *Ibid.* See also Jonathan Mitchell, *The Formal Semantics of Point of View* (PhD dissertation, University of Massachusetts, Amherst, 1986), where some of Partee's examples originate. An early discussion of the quantification of implicit variables can be found in Östen Dahl, 'On Points of Reference', in *Semantikos* 1 (1975), pp. 58–60. Dahl refers the reader to an unpublished manuscript by George Lakoff, dated 1970.

the intuitive meaning of an utterance, one can intuitively 'bind' it, that is, make it vary according to the values introduced by some operator. It follows that 'we have been given no reason to abandon the thesis that the only truth-conditional role of context is the resolution of indexicality, broadly construed'.[12] Stanley therefore maintains that 'all truth-conditional context-dependence results from fixing the values of contextually sensitive elements in the real structure of natural language sentences'.[13] There are no 'optional' contextual ingredients in truth-conditional content.

7.4   Is the Binding Criterion reliable?

For the 'breakfast' example, we could perhaps accept Stanley's conclusion. For that example is very similar to cases of quantifier domain restriction (§6.2); and for such cases it is not easy to apply the Optionality Criterion in a non-question-begging manner. When the Optionality Criterion is not reliable, it seems reasonable to appeal to the other criterion. Still, the conflict between the criteria (in cases such as 'It is raining') creates an obvious problem, and should make us cautious; especially in view of the use which Stanley makes of the Binding Criterion. Stanley uses it to deny the very existence of optional ingredients in truth-conditional content. Before accepting such an extreme conclusion, we must assure ourselves that the Binding Criterion is reliable. Is it really?

I think it is not, for it works too well. It obliges us to treat as provided through saturation not only contextual elements which can plausibly be regarded as values of variables in logical form, as well as elements for which at least the question arises, but also many contextual elements for which that sort of treatment is simply out of question. This is a serious weakness which should lead one to doubt the reliability of the Binding Criterion. Let me give two striking examples.

The first example, which I already mentioned in chapter 5, is adapted from David Rumelhart:[14]

(12) The policeman stopped the car.

In interpreting this utterance we make certain assumptions concerning the way the car was stopped by the policeman. On the most natural interpretation we assume that the policeman issued appropriate signals to the driver, who stopped the car accordingly. But if we know, or suppose, that the policeman was actually *driving* the car in the reported scene, we will understand his stopping of the car very differently from the way we understand it when we assume that he was regulating the traffic. Quite different 'manners of stopping' are involved in the two cases. Those implied manners of stopping are part of the way we understand the utterance but they are *additional* aspects of the interpretation,

---

[12] Stanley, 'Context and Logical Form', p. 401.
[13] *Ibid.*, p. 392.   [14] Rumelhart, 'Problems with Literal Meanings', p. 78.

linguistically optional hence external to what is said by minimalist standards. What is said in the minimal sense is only that the policeman stopped the car *in some way or other.*

Here, as in the case of 'It's raining', the Optionality Criterion tells us that the contextually provided manner of stopping is provided through free enrichment. For we have no trouble imagining a context in which no such manner of stopping would be contextually specified. Moreover, in contrast to the 'rain' case, there is a wide consensus among theorists that the contextually provided manner of stopping in such an example is a pragmatic embellishment of the interpretation which is of no more concern to semantics than our tendency, as interpreters, to imagine the policeman dressed in a certain way. Indeed I think that *everybody*, including Stanley, would agree that in the policeman case the contextually provided constituent is pragmatic through and through. It is not part of the proposition literally expressed in the minimalist sense (what is said$_{min}$). Yet the argument from binding shows that, *even in that case*, the contextually provided constituent is linguistically articulated by a variable. For we can say things like

(13) However he did it, the policeman stopped the car.
(14) In some way or other, the policeman stopped the car.

meaning:

For some manner of stopping *m*, the policeman stopped the car in manner *m*.

If we apply the Binding Criterion, we shall have to conclude that the contextually provided manner of stopping is articulated and determined through a bottom-up process of saturation, like the reference of indexicals. The absurdity of this conclusion argues against the Binding Criterion.

The other example is even more striking. Remember the utterance: 'Look! He is eating!' We imagined a context in which a salient mushroom was understood as being the thing eaten. That the contextually provided constituent results from free enrichment follows from the fact that intransitive 'eat', as Stanley himself accepts,[15] denotes the property of eating, abstracted from the relation of eating-something by suppressing the second argument role. That is a case of 'indefinite null instantiation' in which no contextual specification of the thing eaten is required in virtue of the semantics of the verb (in contrast to what happens in cases of 'definite null instantiation', such as 'I noticed' or 'I heard'). *Still, intuitively, binding is possible.* We can say:

(15) John is anorexic, but whenever his father cooks mushrooms, he eats.

On a natural interpretation, we understand that John eats *the mushrooms his father has cooked.* Intuitively, a form of binding is operative here; for the food eaten by John covaries with the food cooked by his father. Such examples show that intuitive binding, per se, does not entail the existence of a free variable in

---

[15] See Stanley, 'Context and Logical Form', p. 401, fn. 14.

logical form. The Binding Criterion, on which Stanley's argument rests, must be rejected.

It remains to be shown what exactly is wrong with the Binding Criterion, and with Stanley's argument in support of Indexicalism. I will provide a detailed analysis of what I call the 'Binding Fallacy' in §7.6. First, however, we need a bit of stage-setting, which the next section will provide.

7.5   Variadic functions

When someone says 'It's raining', there often is a tacitly understood location, such that the utterance is true if and only if it's raining at that location. The location can also be made explicit, by means of modifiers such as 'in Paris', 'here', or 'everywhere I go'. Looking at those modifiers can help us understand the status of the contextually provided ingredient in the cases in which the location remains implicit.

The modifiers in question are syntactically optional. They make a predicate out of a predicate. If we start with a simple predicate, say 'rain', we can make a different predicate out of it by ajoining an adverb such as 'heavily' or a prepositional phrase such as 'in Paris'. Thus we go from 'It's raining' to 'It's raining heavily' to 'It's raining heavily in Paris.' Semantically, I suggest that we construe the modifier as contributing a certain sort of function which I call a *variadic function*. A variadic function is a function from relations to relations, where the output relation differs from the input relation only by its decreased or increased adicity. Adding a predicate modifier (adverb or a prepositional phrase) to a predicate expressing a n-ary relation R^n thus results in a complex predicate expressing an $n + 1$-ary relation, in which the $n + 1^{th}$ argument is a *circumstance*: a time, a location, a manner, or what not.

A relation can be represented as a set of interconnected argument-roles, as in frame semantics. Thus the EAT relation contains two argument-roles: the EATER and the FOOD. The effect of an 'expansive' variadic function of the sort contributed by adverbial modifiers is to add an argument-role. The output relation therefore contains *the same argument-roles* as the input relation, plus the extra argument-role provided by the variadic function. For example, in the statement 'John eats in Paris' the prepositional phrase 'in Paris' contributes a variadic function which maps the property of eating, ascribed to John in the simpler statement 'John eats', onto the dyadic relation Eat_in (x, l) between an individual and a location. *That* relation is predicated of the pair $<$John, Paris$>$ in the more complex statement. Note that the prepositional phrase 'in Paris' contributes not only the variadic function, but also the argument (Paris) which fills the extra argument-role.[16]

---

[16] As Sally McConnell-Ginet puts it, such phrases 'have a dual role of augmenting the predicate to which they attach and of providing an argument for the augmented predicate' ('Adverbs and Logical Form', in *Language* 58 (1982), p. 171).

There are also 'recessive' variadic functions that decrease the valence of the input relation by suppressing an argument-role.[17] In English, various alternations such as the *passive alternation* and the *intransitive alternation*[18] can be analysed in such terms. The operation of passivation ('John kisses Mary' → 'Mary is kissed') suppresses the argument-role corresponding to the subject of the active sentence, whereas intransitivation ('John eats the apple' → 'John eats') has the effect of suppressing the argument-role corresponding to the direct object of the verb. Quine's 'Der' operator, which I mentioned earlier, does something similar: it decreases the adicity of the input relation R^n by existentially quantifying the nth argument. But I think recessive variadic functions do not, by themselves, involve existentially quantifying the suppressed argument-role. Thus if we start with 'John spoke to Mary', we can suppress the argument-role of ADDRESSEE and generate 'John spoke'. This does not entail that John spoke to someone. Whether or not the suppression of an argument-role, effected through a recessive variadic function, amounts to existentially quantifying that argument-role depends upon the nature of the argument-roles that remain unsuppressed. To fill the SPEAKER argument-role one need not have an addressee. One can speak without speaking to anyone. But to fill the EATER argument-role, arguably, there must be something (edible) that one eats: NO EATER without an EATEE. The suppressed argument-role therefore remains in the background via the EATER argument-role which, for metaphysical reasons, cannot be entirely dissociated from it. That is why 'John is eating something' can be inferred from 'John is eating.' That, according to me, is a non-formal, 'metaphysical' inference similar to that from 'Mary is dancing' to 'Mary is dancing somewhere.'[19]

---

[17] 'Recessive' comes from Lucien Tesnière, a pioneer in that area (*Eléments de Syntaxe Structurale*, 2nd edn, Klincksieck, 1969). 'Expansive' comes from Dowty (cited in McConnell-Ginet, 'Adverbs and Logical Form', p. 168), and is also reminiscent of Bach's 'expansion'.

[18] See Beth Levin, *English Verb Classes and Alternations* (University of Chicago Press, 1993), for a detailed description.

[19] It is arguably for the same sort of reasons that the agent remains lurking in the background even after the AGENT argument-role has been suppressed through passivation. The fact that 'The ship was sunk voluntarily / to collect the insurance' is possible, while 'The ship sank voluntarily / to collect the insurance' is not, is sometimes taken to show that in the passive sentence the AGENT argument-role has not been suppressed but remains covertly present at some level of syntactic structure (Jason Stanley, 'Making it Articulated', in *Mind and Language* 17 (2002), pp. 152–3). Chomsky argues that the argument-role is present lexically (in the valence of the verb) even though, syntactically, it is not (Noam Chomsky, 'Changing Perspectives on Knowledge and Use of Language', in Myles Brand and Mike Harnish (eds.), *The Representation of Knowledge and Belief* (University of Arizona Press, 1986), pp. 32–5). As far as I am concerned, I favour the hypothesis that the argument-role is metaphysically implied rather than linguistically realized. A passive sentence such as 'The ship was sunk' results from passivation of the *transitive* 'sink', as in 'John sank the ship.' Now the ship plays two roles in (the relations described by) sentences such as 'The ship was sunk' or 'John sank the ship': the P-role (PATIENT or THING_ACTED_UPON), and the U-role (UNDERGOER_OF_CHANGE_OF_STATE). 'John sank the ship' means *John did*

The variadic functions that increase the valence of the input relation through the addition of a circumstance to the set of its argument-roles can be represented by means of an operator (or rather, a family of operators) 'Circ'. When applied to an n-place predicate P, 'Circ' produces an $n + 1$ place predicate ('Circ P'). There will be as many Circ-operators as there are argument-roles which can be added to the set of argument-roles of the input relation. There will be a temporal Circ-operator, a locational Circ-operator, etc., depending on the nature of the extra argument-role. Which Circ-operator is at issue will be indicated by means of a subscript. For example, the operator 'Circ$_{location}$' contributed by locative modifiers (such as the prepositional phrase 'in Paris') will map, for example, the E A T relation to the E A T_I N relation by adding a Location argument-role:

$$\text{Circ}_{location} \ (\text{Eats} \ (x)) = \text{Eats\_in} \ (x, l)$$

As I pointed out, a modifier such as 'in Paris' does not merely increase the valence of the input relation by adding a new argument-role; it also provides the extra argument needed to fill that argument-role. 'John eats in Paris' should therefore be represented as follows:

$$\text{Circ}_{location: \ Paris} \ (\text{Eats} \ (\text{John})) = \text{Eats\_in} \ (\text{John, Paris})$$

Like the prepositional phrase 'in Paris', the Circ-operator thus completed does two things: map the E A T relation to the E A T_I N relation by adding a L O C A - T I O N argument-role; and supply a particular value (Paris) for that role.[20]

7.6   The Binding Fallacy

In 'Everywhere I go, it rains' a variable is bound by the quantifier 'everywhere I go'. The sentence says that, for every place l such that I go to l, it rains

something to the ship that resulted in the ship's sinking, where the two tokens of 'the ship' correspond to the P-role and the U-role respectively. In 'The ship sank', the ship plays only the U-role. Now nothing can fill the P-role unless there is an agent doing something. Hence expressions like 'voluntarily' or 'to collect the insurance', which qualify the manner of acting or the goal of an agent, can be adjoined to sentences like 'The ship was sunk', since the P-role which occurs in the denoted relation is metaphysically tied to the (linguistically unrealized) A G E N T role. In contrast, the expression cannot be adjoined to sentences like 'The ship sank', because no action is denoted and no agent is even 'lurking in the background'. (The explanation I have just offered is very tentative, of course. There may be decisive syntactic evidence that the argument-role has not really been suppressed through passivation. But the mere fact that 'The ship was sunk to collect the insurance' is good while 'The ship sank to collect the insurance' is bad is not sufficient to establish such a conclusion, contrary to what Stanley suggests.)

[20] According to McConnell-Ginet, who puts forward a similar proposal in her paper 'Adverbs and Logical Form', adverbs such as 'slowly' do not contribute an argument filling the extra argument-role, but they existentially quantify the new argument-role while contributing a property of its values. If we accept McConnell-Ginet's idea, 'John eats slowly' will be analysed as follows: $\text{Circ}_{rate: \ slow} \ (\text{Eats} \ (\text{John})) = (\exists r) \ (\text{Slow} \ (r) \ \& \ \text{Eats\_at\_rate} \ (\text{John}, r))$. That is, there is a rate r which is slow, such that John eats at that rate.

in *l*. Stanley concludes that, when 'It rains' is understood with respect to a contextually provided location, that location is provided through saturation. The sentence 'It rains' really is the sentence 'It rains in *l*', where the unpronounced location variable can either be bound or be contextually assigned a value. Fully spelled out, Stanley's indexicalist argument against optional ingredients runs as follows:

(1) Contextualists say that in the simple statement 'It rains', the tacitly understood location of rain is unarticulated and results from an optional pragmatic process of free enrichment.

(2) In 'Everywhere I go it rains', binding occurs: the location of rain varies with the values introduced by the quantifier 'everywhere I go'.

(3) There is no binding without a bindable variable.

(4) Therefore, 'It rains' involves a variable for the location of rain.

(5) It follows that the contextualist is mistaken: in the simple statement 'It rains', the location of rain *is* articulated. It is the (contextually assigned) value of a free variable in logical form, which variable can also be bound (as in the complex sentence 'Everywhere I go, it rains').

The argument is fallacious because of a crucial ambiguity at stage 4. When it is said that 'It rains' involves a variable (because binding occurs), which sentence 'It rains' is at issue? One may well accept that in the complex sentence 'Everywhere I go it rains', *the (open) sentence on which the quantifier operates* involves a location variable which the quantifier binds: 'For every place *l* such that I go to *l*, it rains in *l*'. That indeed follows from step 3. But in order to reach the conclusion at step 5, we need something stronger: 4 must be understood as claiming that the location variable is also involved *when the sentence 'It rains' is uttered in isolation*. Stanley's argument therefore relies upon an unstated premiss, namely the following:

(SUP)
In 'Everywhere I go it rains', the sentence on which the quantifier 'everywhere I go' operates is the very sentence 'It rains' which can also be uttered in isolation (and whose usual interpretation involves a contextually provided ingredient).

If we accept (SUP) it follows that the variable which is bound in the complex sentence has got to be present also, unbound, in the simple sentence 'It rains.' Whoever accepts the analysis of adverbial modification in terms of variadic functions must reject (SUP), however.

According to the variadic analysis, the phrase 'everywhere I go' does not merely contribute what binds the variable, it also contributes the variable itself, that is, the extra argument-role for a location. The phrase 'everywhere I go' has a dual role exactly like that of any prepositional phrase. Consider 'in Paris'. In 'In Paris it rains', the prepositional phrase 'in Paris' contributes both (a) a variadic function which adds an extra argument-role to the set of argument-roles of the input predicate 'rain', and (b) an argument which fills the role. This duality is quite transparent since the prepositional phrase consists of two items: a preposition which determines the type of the extra argument-role, and a name which specifies what fills the role. When the prepositional phrase is an 'intransitive preposition' like 'here', it is less obvious that it plays two semantic roles, but it does so nonetheless. In 'It rains here', the locative adverb 'here' contributes a variadic function which increases the valence of the expressed relation, and it also contributes a specific location which fills the extra argument-role. We find the same duality when the phrase is quantificational instead of being singular. In 'Everywhere I go, it rains', the phrase 'everywhere I go' contributes both the expansive (adicity-increasing) variadic function *and* the operator which binds the extra argument-role. From the point of view of the variadic analysis, therefore, the proper representation of 'Everywhere I go it rains' is:

[For every place l such that I go to l] (in l (it rains))

What the quantifier operates on here is the sub-formula 'in l (it rains)', whose free variable it binds. In that sub-formula we do find a variable for a location. The simple sentence 'It rains' does not correspond to that sub-formula, however, but to the sub-sub-formula 'it rains', which does *not* contain a free variable for a location. Stanley's argument goes through only if we conflate two different things: the open sentence on which the quantifier operates, and the simple sentence 'It rains' to which the phrase 'everywhere I go' has been adjoined. On the variadic analysis, they are clearly distinguished.

7.7   Conclusion: the failure of Indexicalism

Stanley uses the Binding Criterion in attempting to establish that, in examples like 'It rains', the contextually provided location is not an optional ingredient of truth-conditional content, as the contextualists claim, but results from contextually assigning a value to a free variable. The same argument can be used in indefinitely many cases to show that what was thought to be an optional ingredient of truth-conditional content is not really. Indeed, the Binding Argument is the major weapon Stanley uses in his indexicalist assault on Contextualism. It is this argument which Stanley and Szabó use to show that quantifier domain restriction is an instance of saturation.

In this chapter we have seen that Stanley's attempt fails. It fails because the Binding Argument rests on a fallacy. The construction 'rain + locative prepositional phrase' expresses a relation in which there is indeed an empty argument-slot for a location. When the prepositional phrase is quantified, as in 'Everywhere I go it rains', the variable representing that empty slot is indeed bound. But in the simple construction, without prepositional phrase, there is neither an empty argument-slot for a location nor a free variable. That is so because the quantified prepositional phrase (QPP) does more than bind the variable; it also contributes the variadic function 'in *l*' which maps the relation R A I N to R A I N_I N_*l*. If we disregard the prepositional phrase and abstract from its contribution, we suppress the variadic function and the free variable that goes with it.

I conclude that 'It rains' no more contains a free variable for a location than 'He is eating' (with intransitive 'eat') contains a free variable for the thing eaten. When, in context, an implicit location is contextually supplied, or when some specific piece of food (for example, the dangerous mushroom) is tacitly understood as being the thing eaten, the contextual ingredient thus provided is not assigned to a free variable; it does not come to fill a pre-existing gap in semantic structure, but enriches the interpretation of the utterance, in a typical top-down manner. This is similar to the sort of enrichment that takes place in (12) (Rumelhart's policeman example).

With quantifier domain restriction the Binding Argument also fails. As Stanley and Szabó themselves mention,

one might respond [to the argument] by conceding that in sentences such as (1)–(3) there is a quantifier domain variable that is bound by the initial quantifier, but deny that in an 'unembedded' sentence such as

(16) John failed exactly three students

there is a quantifier domain variable present. According to this response, a variable is associated with quantifier expressions only in the special case of bound readings such as (1)–(3).[21]

This exactly parallels the response I made to the Binding Argument as applied to the 'rain' example. Now Stanley and Szabó think they can dispose of this response, in the quantifier domain case. They write:

Consideration of facts from ellipsis serves to dispose of this response. Consider the discourse:

(17) John has failed exactly three Frenchmen. In fact, in most classes John has taught, he has.

The natural reading of the second sentence in (17) is that in most classes *x* such that John has taught *x*, he has failed exactly three Frenchmen in *x*. However, if there is no quantifier domain variable present in the initial sentence in (17), then there is no way of deriving the natural reading of the second sentence.

The second sentence of (17) is a standard case of syntactic ellipsis (verb phrase ellipsis). According to standard theories of such ellipsis, the predicate 'failed exactly three Frenchmen' in the first sentence is copied or reconstructed in the final syntactic structure of the second sentence. If there is no quantifier domain variable available for binding in the predicate 'failed exactly three Frenchmen' in the first sentence of (17), then the result of copying or reconstructing it in the logical form of the second sentence

---

[21] Stanley and Szabó, 'On Quantifier Domain Restriction', p. 244.

will also not contain a bindable variable, in which case there will be no way to derive its natural reading . . . Therefore, on the assumption that standard theories of syntactic ellipsis are correct, there is a bindable variable for quantifier domains present even in sentences such as (16).[22]

In this passage, however, Stanley and Szabó commit the Binding Fallacy once again. Let us see why.

I suggested that the quantified prepositional phrase 'everywhere I go' in 'Everywhere I go, it rains' has a dual role. It does not merely contribute what binds the variable, it also contributes the variable itself, that is, the extra argument-role for a location. From this point of view the proper representation of 'Everywhere I go it rains' is:

[For every place l such that I go to l] (in l (it rains)).

What the quantifier operates on here is the sub-formula 'in l (it rains)', whose free variable it binds. The simple sentence 'It rains' does not correspond to that sub-formula, but to the sub-sub-formula 'it rains', which does *not* contain a free variable for a location.

The same analysis can be applied to the case of quantifier domain restriction. On this analysis the second sentence of (17) will be represented as:

[For most classes x such that John has taught x] (in x (John has failed exactly three Frenchmen)).

What the quantifier operates on here is the sub-formula 'in x (John has failed exactly three Frenchmen)', whose free variable it binds. The first sentence of (17) does not correspond to that sub-formula, however, but to the sub-sub-formula occurring within the rightmost parentheses. In other words, the quantified prepositional phrase 'In most classes he has taught' contributes not only the quantifier 'for most classes x such that John has taught x', it also contributes the variadic function 'in x' with its free variable. *All the material that is underlined in the above formula, including the domain variable, corresponds to what the QPP contributes.* So it is a fallacy to conclude, as Stanley and Szabó do, that 'if there is no quantifier domain variable present in the initial sentence in (17), then there is no way of deriving the natural reading of the second sentence'. There is an easy way of deriving that reading: one has merely to assume that the QPP contributes the variable as well as the quantifier which binds it. On this analysis, the result of copying or reconstructing the first sentence of (17) in the logical form of the second sentence will not contain a bindable variable, but that's fine since the bindable variable is contributed independently by the QPP.

---

[22] *Ibid.*, pp. 244–5.

Of course, it does not follow that quantifier domain restriction is *not* an instance of saturation. The only thing that follows is that Stanley's and Szabó's argument in favour of an indexicalist treatment in terms of saturation is fallacious and must be disregarded. Contrary to what they claim, they have not 'demonstrated the existence of quantifier domain variables'.[23] It remains an open question whether quantifier domain restriction is best treated as an instance of enrichment or as an instance of saturation. The Optionality Criterion does not settle the issue because, as we have seen, it gives no clear result in that sort of case. In other cases, however, the Optionality Criterion works reasonably well; well enough for us to conclude (*pace* Stanley) that *there are* cases in which some ingredient of truth-conditional content results from a pragmatic process of the optional variety.

---

[23] *Ibid.*, p. 245.

8   Circumstances of evaluation

In this book we have been concerned with the contribution context makes to truth-conditional content. How essential is that contribution, and how much controlled by linguistic conventions? These are two of the main questions we have dealt with, in an attempt to revive the debate between Literalism and Contextualism. In this chapter we will consider a fundamental dimension under which context contributes to truth-conditional content: the so-called 'circumstance of evaluation'.

Truth-evaluation (or semantic evaluation more generally) requires not merely a content to evaluate, but also a 'circumstance' against which to evaluate that content. As Austin once put it, 'it takes two to make a truth'.[1] The circumstance of evaluation is not an aspect of the content to be evaluated, but an entity with respect to which that content is evaluated. Still, according to the theory of situations to be introduced in this chapter, the circumstance of evaluation is an aspect of content in a broader sense of 'content'. And that aspect of content is irreducibly contextual.

8.1   Modality

The notion of circumstance of evaluation is familiar from modal logic. In modal logic, propositions are evaluated relative to 'possible worlds'. The possible worlds are necessary to truth-evaluation, but they are not themselves represented in the propositions that we evaluate. Thus 'I am French' (said by me) is true, with respect to a world w, iff I am French in w; but the sentence 'I am French' only talks about me and the property of being French. The world of evaluation is not a constituent of the content to be evaluated.

One can bring the world into the content by making the statement more complex. The complex sentence 'Possibly, I am French' tells us that *in some possible world* I am French. The modal statement I make by uttering that sentence is about possible worlds, not merely about me and the property of being French.

---

[1] John Austin, 'Truth', in his *Philosophical Papers* (2nd edn, Oxford University Press, 1970), p. 124 n.

In hybrid logic (a variety of modal logic), one can even make statements 'referring' to specific possible worlds: 'In w, I am French.'[2] But the worlds that are thus introduced into the content of the complex statement (via modal operators such as 'Possibly' or 'in w') are used in evaluating the *simple* statement 'I am French', that is the statement that is embedded within the modal statement. The modal statement itself is evaluated with respect to possible worlds, and it shares with the simple statement the property that *the world with respect to which it is evaluated is not itself represented in the statement under evaluation.*[3]

To appreciate the unarticulated character of the circumstance of evaluation in the modal framework, it is worth looking at what happens when we (standardly) translate a modal statement into first-order logic, by explicitly quantifying over possible worlds. Thus translated 'Necessarily p' becomes '$\forall w\, p(w)$', 'Possibly p' becomes '$\exists w\, p(w)$', etc. All complete sentences are transformed into predicates (of worlds). A simple categoric statement such as 'Rain is wet' will be represented as '$p(w)$', where 'p' is the proposition that rain is wet transformed into a predicate of worlds, and 'w' is a free variable to which the actual world is contextually assigned as default value.

The big difference between the modal statement and its standard extensional translation is that, in the extensional framework, the circumstance of evaluation (the world) becomes a constituent of content. The contrast between content and circumstance is lost. This is too bad, for that contrast makes a lot of sense. To evaluate a sentence, we determine whether the state of affairs it describes obtains in some 'reality' which serves as circumstance of evaluation. But that reality – the actual world, say – is not itself, or at least doesn't have to be, among the constituents of the state of affairs in question, that is, among the entities that are talked about and articulated in the content of the proposition. The world comes into the picture for purposes of evaluation, but the thoughts that are evaluated need not be metaphysically elaborated thoughts *about* the world. Indeed the users of the language need not even have the ability to entertain such thoughts. Only the theorist needs to be able to talk about the world of evaluation, in her metalanguage. The thoughts that are evaluated 'concern' the world, but they need not be 'about' it in the sense in which they are about the entities which they represent.[4]

Let us consider a simple language without modal operators or other means of talking about worlds; let us go further and assume that the users of the language don't possess the reflective abilities necessary for thinking about modal issues. They entertain only non-modal thoughts such as 'Rain is wet.' The

---

[2] See Patrick Blackburn, Maarten de Rijke and Yde Venema, *Modal Logic* (Cambridge University Press, 2001), pp. 434–45.

[3] The possible worlds which the modal statement talks about are themselves *possible with respect to* (that is, accessible from) the world relative to which the modal statement happens to be evaluated.

[4] See Perry, 'Thought Without Representation', for the distinction between 'concerning' and 'being about'.

possible-worlds semanticist who studies their language will still need to think and talk about the possible worlds relative to which the sentences of the language are evaluated; but, contrary to what the standard extensional translation suggests, mention of the possible worlds in question will be confined to the theorist's metalanguage.

Now suppose the users of the object-language become sophisticated and start thinking about metaphysical issues. Suppose they come to talk and think about what is *actually* the case as opposed to what *might be* the case. Such modal talk can be formally represented in two ways, as we have seen: by using sentence operators, or by explicitly quantifying world variables in the object-language. If we use the modal framework and introduce modal operators such as 'actually' or 'possibly', *nothing will be changed for the fragment of the language that does not involve those operators*. The sentence 'Rain is wet' will still be a simple, modally innocent sentence. The language will simply have been enriched by the introduction of new resources enabling us to construct more complex sentences. But if we use the standard extensional framework and represent modal sentences ('It might be that . . .', 'Actually . . .') by means of explicit quantification over possible worlds, as suggested above, then, unless special precautions are taken to avoid that consequence, *a change of language takes place,* not merely an enrichment. In the new language, *all* sentences (including simple sentences) now contain a hidden argument-place for a world. Modal innocence is lost.

I think this move is (almost) as damaging as the previous one – the ascription of thought and talk about possible worlds to modally innocent subjects. Even if the users of the language are sophisticated enough and can think about modal issues, it is misleading to suggest that they *always* think and talk about such issues even when they entertain simple thoughts or utter simple sentences such as 'Rain is wet.' By forcing us to construe for example the assertion that rain is wet as involving a covert argument-place which the actual world fills, the extensional translation blurs the cognitively important distinction between the simple, modally innocent assertion 'Rain is wet' and the modal assertion 'Actually, rain is wet.' To maintain that distinction, we have to see modal sentences as *constructed from* simple sentences by the application of modal operators to them. In this way we can analyse the ability to use and understand modal sentences as resting on two distinct abilities: the ability to use and understand simple sentences; and the ability to imagine other possible worlds and to contrast the actual world with them. The first ability is independent of the second: we can use and understand simple sentences (for example, 'Rain is wet') even if we lack the ability to think thoughts about the actual world (in Perry's sense of 'about').[5]

---

[5] The important thing, I said, is to see modal sentences as constructed from simple sentences by means of operators. Now this is something we can do *even if we want to represent modal talk extensionally.* The apparatus of variadic functions enables us to do just that. In §7.6 I analysed

8.2   Time and tense

The difference we have found between two ways of representing modality can be found also between two ways of representing tense, one which preserves temporal innocence in simple sentences and one which does not.

In tense logic, tense is represented by means of sentence operators.[6] Alternatively, tenses can be represented by adding extra argument-places for times.[7] If we choose the latter course, it is no longer possible to consider adjectives such as 'warm' or 'yellow' as denoting properties; they have to be considered as denoting relations – relations between the objects which have the alleged properties and the times at which they have them. As Michael Dummett has pointed out, this relational approach significantly departs from our habitual way of thinking:

We think of adjectives such as 'warm', 'smooth', 'slender' and so on as denoting *properties*; properties that a thing may have at one time, and not at another, but nevertheless properties rather than relations between objects and times. And this goes with the way in which we come to understand such adjectives. To know what it is for someone to be my nephew, I have first to learn what it is for anyone to be the nephew of any given person. But we do not begin by learning in what relation an object must stand to an arbitrary time for it to be warm or wet at that time, and then, having learned what time is referred to by the adverb 'now', derive from this a grasp of what it is for it to be warm now. Rather, we first learn what it is for something to be warm, wet, smooth or slender, that is to say, for the predicate '*is* warm (wet, smooth, slender)' to be applicable to it, where the verb 'is' is in the true present tense. From this we advance to an understanding of what is meant by saying of an object that it was or will be warm, etc., at some other time. The

'Everywhere I go it rains' as resulting from the application of a locative variadic operator to the sentence 'It rains.' That operator does two things. First, it modifies the adicity of the predicate in the sentence it applies to: it adds an extra argument-place for a location, which can be represented by a free variable. Second, it introduces a restricted quantifier which binds that variable. The operator can be paraphrased as 'for every location l such that I go to l, in l it is the case that'. 'Necessarily it rains' can be represented in the same hybrid way, by applying to the sentence 'It rains' a sentence operator which can be rendered as: 'for every world w, in w it is the case that'. Since the variable w is introduced by the variadic operator, we don't have to treat the emergence of modalities as a radical change in the language, but simply as an enrichment of it; an enrichment which does not affect the simple (non-modal) sentences, hence preserves modal innocence.

[6] In 'Structural Analogies Between Tenses and Pronouns', Barbara Partee says that examples like 'I did not turn off the stove' (in which reference is made to a specific time) speak against a treatment in terms of operators, because modal operators can't capture the referential nature of (some uses of) tenses. But the referential/quantificational issue is orthogonal to the question, whether or not we should use operators. Even if standard modal operators are quantificational rather than referential, nothing prevents the introduction of 'referential' operators in the modal framework. See Arthur Prior, *Past, Present, and Future* (Clarendon Press, 1967) and 'Now' in *Noûs* 1(1968), 101–19; and Patrick Blackburn, 'Tense, Temporal Reference and Tense Logic', in *Journal of Semantics* 11(1994), 83–101.

[7] There is a third option: tenses can be represented as temporal predicates of events. If we like Davidson's analysis of adverbial modification better than the variadic analysis, that is a natural move to make.

advance is made by our acquiring a general grasp of the past and future tenses. That is to say, to understand 'was warm' or 'will be warm', we apply to our prior understanding of what is meant by saying that something is warm our general comprehension of what it is to speak of how things were or will be at another time. In so doing, we are in effect treating the tenses (and other indications of time) as operators applied to sentences in the present tense of which we have previously acquired an understanding, just as the tense-logical semantics treats them. We could not learn the language in any other way.[8]

Dummett's complaint about the relational treatment of tenses parallels my complaint about the extensional rendering of modal talk. The relational treatment threatens temporal innocence, just as overt quantification over world variables (without variadic functions) threatens modal innocence.

In the temporal case there is a possible objection, due to the fact that tense is (to put it crudely) obligatory in English. Since it is, one might argue that there is no such thing as non-temporal talk, hence no such thing as temporal innocence. According to that line of argument, there is a contrast between time and modality: there are simple, non-modal sentences, whose characteristics must admittedly be preserved and captured; but there are no simple, non-temporal sentences in our language.

From the tense-logical point of view, that objection is misguided. The present tense is not a tense like the past or the future. It is more primitive and, in a sense, temporally neutral. Someone can think 'It is hot in here' even if she has no notion of time whatsoever, hence no mastery of the past and the future. If this is right, mastery of genuine temporal talk rests on two distinct abilities: the ability to use and understand simple sentences (that is, sentences in the present) and the ability to think about times and to contrast the past and the future with the present. As in the case of modality, the first ability is independent of the second.

It is true that, when we say or think 'It is hot in here', we talk (or think) about what is presently the case; we characterize the situation *at the time of utterance*. Yet this is not part of what the sentence itself expresses. The content of the sentence, from the tense-logical point of view, is a function from times to truth-values. When the sentence is uttered, the function is applied to the time of utterance. That is so *whether the sentence is in the present or any other tense*. Even if I say 'It has been hot' or 'It will be hot', I characterize the time of utterance (and, in relation to it, some earlier or later time). The time of utterance, which the sentence is used to characterize, is the time with respect to which we *evaluate* the sentence. The best thing I can do here is to quote Prior:

> If tenses are formed by attaching prefixes like 'It has been the case that' to the present tense, or to a complex with a present tense 'kernel', it is not always true to say that what is in the present tense is understood as a characterisation of the time of utterance; rather, it characterises whatever time we are taken to by the series of prefixes. The *presentness*

---

[8] Michael Dummett, 'Existence, Possibility, and Time' (typescript, Oxford University), pp. 16–17.

of an event, we may say, is simply the *occurrence* of the event, and that is simply the event itself. But every complete tensed sentence characterises the time of utterance in some way or other, and other times only through their relation to that one.[9]

To sum up, the time of utterance is not represented, it does not feature in the content of tensed sentences; it only comes into the picture as the circumstance with respect to which the content of a tensed sentence is evaluated.

Another objection, voiced by Evans,[10] concerns the fact that a tensed sentence like 'It is hot', 'It has been hot' or 'It will be hot' is not evaluable as true or false, unless we are given a particular time. In the absence of a time specification, the sentence is only 'true-at' certain times and 'false-at' others. Such a sentence, therefore, is *semantically incomplete* by Frege's lights:

A thought is not true at one time and false at another, but it is either true or false, *tertium non datur*. The false appearance that a thought can be true at one time and false at another arises from an incomplete expression. A complete proposition or expression of a thought must also contain a time datum.[11]

As Evans points out, the problem of semantic incompleteness does not arise in the modal case. Even if a thought is said to be 'true at' one world and 'false at' another, as in modal logic, this does not prevent it from being true (or false) *tout court*. It is true *tout court* iff it is true-at the actual world. But the 'thought' that it is hot cannot be evaluated as true or false *tout court*. In the absence of a contextually supplied time it can *only* be ascribed relative, 'truth-at'-conditions. Only a particular, dated utterance of such a sentence can be endowed with genuine truth-conditions. What this shows is that the time of utterance is part of the (complete) content of the utterance;[12] hence it cannot be expelled out of the content and treated like the world of evaluation. So the objection goes.

According to Dummett, Evans's objection to Prior is based on a misunderstanding. Prior was concerned only with *sentence-types* and *their* contents. The content of a sentence-type is a function from times to truth-values, hence a sentence-type has only relative truth-conditions: it is true at some times and false at other times. To introduce a notion of absolute truth, one thing we can say (though not, according to Dummett, what Prior himself would say)[13] is

---

[9] Arthur Prior, 'Egocentric Logic', in Arthur Prior and Kit Fine, *Worlds, Times and Selves* (Duckworth, 1977), p. 30.

[10] See Gareth Evans, 'Does Tense Logic Rest on a Mistake?', in his *Collected Papers* (Clarendon Press, 1995), pp. 350–3.

[11] Gottlob Frege, *Kleine Schriften* (Olms, 1967), p. 338, quoted in Evans, 'Does Tense Logic Rest on a Mistake?', p. 350.

[12] Or, in a Fregean framework, part of the expression of such a content.

[13] 'The simplest way to introduce a notion of absolute truth', Dummett writes, 'is to follow the analogy with possible worlds semantics and stipulate a type sentence to be true simpliciter just in case it is true-now. Tense-logic, in the hands of its inventor, could be regarded, without violation of its principles, as a semantics exclusively of statements uttered at one particular time' ('Existence, Possibility, and Time', p. 19).

that, when a sentence is uttered, the function which is its content is applied to some contextually provided time (typically, the time of utterance). The time in question serves as circumstance of evaluation for the utterance: the utterance is true *tout court* iff the sentence is 'true-at' the contextually provided time. As Dummett points out,

The variable truth-value and the absolute truth-value attach to different things; it is the type sentence that is true at one time, false at another, but the utterance that is true or false simpliciter.[14]

Since there are two distinct levels, corresponding to the sentence-type and the utterance, there is no harm in taking the utterance to possess a 'content' also (content$_u$), distinct from that of the sentence (content$_s$). For example, we can treat the utterance as expressing a structured proposition consisting of (i) the contextually provided time as subject, and (ii) the content of the sentence-type, predicated of that time. But if we do so, we must acknowledge the unarticulated nature of the 'subject' in the content$_u$ of tensed utterances. As Prior says, 'tensed propositions are understood as directly or indirectly characterizing the *un*mentioned time of utterance'.[15] Hence there is a trade-off: if we want to restrict ourselves to what is linguistically articulated, we must focus on the content$_s$, which is 'semantically incomplete' by Frege's lights – it corresponds to the content of a predicate rather than to that of a complete sentence in a logically perfect language. If, following Frege, we want to focus on the complete content of the utterance, that which makes it truth-evaluable in absolute terms, we must acknowledge the role played in that content (content$_u$) by unarticulated constituents corresponding to the circumstances in which the content$_s$ is evaluated.

8.3   Situations

Let us take stock. For purposes of semantic evaluation we need a circumstance as well as a content. Even Frege, who was unconcerned with modalities and thought of the actual world as the only world there is, was aware of that fact. He took fictional sentences to be unevaluable, for the following reason: since the author of a fictional statement does not attempt to characterize the actual world, we are given a content without any circumstance of evaluation for it. The obvious conclusion to draw from Frege's remarks on fiction is that, to get a truth-value, a content is not sufficient; we need to connect that content with the actual world, via the assertive force of the utterance, in virtue of which the content is presented as characterizing that world. Frege was aware not only that we need a circumstance in addition to a content, but also that the circumstance is not, and cannot be, an aspect of the content articulated in the sentence. If a sentence

---

[14] *Ibid.*, p. 44.   [15] Prior, 'Egocentric Logic', p. 30.

lacks the force of a serious assertion, because the speaker does not attempt to characterize the actual world but is engaged in a different enterprise (for example poetry), making the content of the sentence more complex by means of an additional phrase such as 'it is true that' will not change the situation. Whether or not an utterance is serious and characterizes the actual world is a pragmatic matter – a matter of 'force', not a matter of content (in the narrow sense of 'content').[16]

Once it is admitted that we need a circumstance over and above the content to be evaluated, we can part from Frege and, following Prior, tolerate contents that are not 'semantically complete' in Frege's sense, that is, endowed with absolute truth-conditions. We can, because the circumstance is there which enables the content to be suitably completed. Thus the content of tensed sentences is semantically incomplete, yet the circumstance (the time) relative to which such a sentence is evaluated is sufficient to complete it. It follows that we must distinguish two levels of content. The content we evaluate with respect to the circumstance is the content$_s$; it may, but need not be, semantically complete by Frege's lights. What is semantically complete in any case is the content$_u$. It consists of the content$_s$ *and* the circumstance with respect to which the content$_s$ is evaluated.

Situation theory as I understand it[17] follows those ideas to their consequences. It generalizes and systematizes them, in two main directions:

(1) There is no reason why only times and worlds should be accepted as features of the circumstance of evaluation. Why not also, for example, *locations*? If I say 'It's raining', the location is unarticulated, but it is relevant *qua* feature of the circumstance of evaluation: what I say (or think) is true iff it's raining *at the contextually provided location*. Why not also consider the *agent* of the speech act (the speaker) or the thought act (the thinker) as (part of) the circumstance of evaluation, to handle the cases in which the content to be evaluated is a property of agents which the speaker or thinker self-attributes?[18] Why not extend the notion also to ordinary objects? If, talking about my car, the mechanic tells me, 'The carburettor is in good condition but there is a problem with the front

---

[16] See Gottlob Frege, 'Thought', in Michael Beaney (ed.), *The Frege Reader* (Blackwell, 1997), p. 330.

[17] By 'situation theory' here I do not mean the official doctrine expounded in Barwise's and Perry's *Situations and Attitudes* (MIT Press, 1983), but a later doctrine, influenced by Perry's 'Thought Without Representation' and centred around the notion of Austinian proposition. See Jon Barwise and John Etchemendy, *The Liar: An Essay on Truth and Circularity* (Oxford University Press, 1987); Jon Barwise, 'Situations, Facts, and True Propositions', in his collection *The Situation in Logic* (CSLI Publications, 1989), 221–54; François Recanati, 'The Dynamics of Situations', in *European Review of Philosophy* 2 (1997), 41–75, 'Situations and the Structure of Content', and *Oratio Obliqua, Oratio Recta. An Essay on Metarepresentation* (MIT Press, 2000), chapters 5 to 7; and Jérôme Dokic, 'Steps Toward a Theory of Situated Representations' (typescript, Institut Jean Nicod).

[18] See David Lewis, 'Attitudes *de dicto* and *de se*', reprinted (with a postscript) in his *Philosophical Papers* vol. 1 (Oxford University Press, 1983), pp. 133–59.

wheels', my car is a crucial feature of the circumstance of evaluation. It is true (or false) *of my car* that the carburettor is in good condition, and so on. The same thing could have been said of another car, but as things turn out it is my car which figures in the content$_u$ of the mechanic's utterance.

Rather than list all the features which may figure in a circumstance of evaluation, let us use the word 'situation' to denote any entity or complex of entities which can play that role. Anything counts as a situation provided, for some sentence S, it makes sense to ask whether or not what S expresses is true *in it* (or 'of it' or 'at it' or 'with respect to it'). Ordinary situations – restricted portions of the actual world – are, of course, the paradigmatic case of a situation in this generalized sense.

(2) When the content of the sentence is semantically incomplete, it is the utterance which is the proper bearer of (absolute) truth-value. Thus tensed sentences only have relative truth-values, they express 'relativized propositions',[19] and we need to shift to utterances to get absolute truth-values and absolute propositions. Traditional theorists think that *with sentences that are not relevantly context-sensitive and whose content is not semantically incomplete*, there is no need to invoke a double layer of content. The content of the sentence, insofar as it has an absolute truth-value, is the only thing we need.

Situation theory rejects that viewpoint. In situation theory, the content of a sentence (whatever the sentence) is a function from situations to truth-values. Hence the relativity of truth, construed as a property of sentences: the same sentence may be true relative to a situation and false relative to another one. That is so *even if the sentence itself is not relevantly context-sensitive or semantically incomplete*. Even when the sentence *is* truth-evaluable in the absolute sense – when it is 'semantically complete' by Frege's lights – situation theory says there is a principled distinction between the content$_s$ of the sentence and the content$_u$ of the utterance.[20] In such a case, the content$_s$ will be a 'classical' proposition (a function from possible worlds to truth-values), and the content$_u$ will contain a situation in addition to that proposition. What the utterance 'says' is that *the situation in question supports the proposition in question*. It follows that two distinct evaluations are possible, in such cases. We can evaluate the sentence itself (that is, evaluate the proposition with respect to the actual world), or we can evaluate the utterance, that is, evaluate the proposition *with respect to the situation figuring in the content$_u$*.

I can't refrain from quoting my favourite example here (from Barwise and Etchemendy, *The Liar*, p. 29). Commenting upon a poker game I am watching,

[19] See John Perry, *The Problem of the Essential Indexical*, pp. 42–3.

[20] When I introduced the distinction between the two levels of content, I said, following Dummett, that the first level or 'content$_s$' corresponds to the content of the sentence-*type*. That is too restrictive. In the situation-theoretic framework the first level of content may itself be construed as context-dependent (that is, as a property of the sentence-*token*), without blurring the distinction between that content and the complete, Austinian content of the utterance (content$_u$). See below, §8.6.

I say: 'Claire has a good hand.' What I say is true, iff Claire has a good hand in the poker game I am watching (at the time of utterance). But suppose I made a mistake and Claire is not among the players in that game. Suppose further that, by coincidence, she happens to be playing poker in some other part of town and has a good hand there. Still, my utterance is not intuitively true, because the situation it concerns (the poker game I am watching) is not one in which Claire has a good hand. But we can say that the *sentence* is true, or at least true at the time of utterance: for it says that Claire has a good hand, and Claire *has* a good hand (somewhere). The unarticulated constituent which distinguishes the content$_u$ from the content$_s$ makes all the difference here, and it accounts for our intuitive classification of the utterance as non-true.

8.4   Saturation or enrichment?

The situation-theoretic framework I have sketched can, hopefully, be used to handle some of the examples of enrichment discussed in previous chapters:

(1) I've had breakfast <this morning>.
(2) You're not going to die <from that cut>.
(3) It's raining <here>.

We may construe the content$_u$ of (2) as involving as unarticulated subject the cut-finger situation in which the child finds himself. The utterance is true, because that situation is not one in which the child is going to die. (That is: it is not the case that, in that situation, there is a time t posterior to the time of utterance t^* such that the addressee dies at t. There is bound to be a time t posterior to t^* at which the addressee dies, but it is presumably not to be found in that particular, temporally restricted situation, corresponding to the cutting event and its immediate consequences.) Similarly, (1) posits the past existence of a breakfast event, and is evaluated with respect to a certain day. It is therefore true iff, *on that day*, there is a time t anterior to the time of utterance t^* such that the speaker has breakfast at t.[21]

I keep assuming that the above examples are instances of free enrichment (rather than instances of saturation), but this still is an open question. Contrary to what one might think, the situation-theoretic framework can accommodate both options. It all depends on whether we think that the relevant circumstantial constituent is necessary for the utterance to express a complete proposition, that is, a function from possible worlds to truth-values.

Consider (3). If we take the sentence 'It is raining' to express a complete proposition once a time has been contextually provided, then the provision of the

---

[21] Admittedly, that is not even a sketch of an analysis. Detailed work is needed to substantiate the claim that (1) and (2) can be appropriately handled in this sort of way. In particular, the relations between the various 'coordinates' of the circumstance of evaluation must be exactly specified.

unarticulated location is an instance of enrichment. The sentence expresses the proposition that there is rain (at the relevant time) and this is evaluated relative to a specific location. Insofar as the sentence expresses a complete proposition (with respect to a given time), that proposition can also be evaluated 'directly', that is, it can be evaluated with respect to the actual world. Thus evaluated the proposition comes out true, since there is rain (at the present time) in the actual world. So we find the two levels of truth-conditions talked about earlier, corresponding to the content$_u$ and the content$_s$. On the other hand, if we think that we need to be contextually given a place and not merely a time in order to get a function from possible worlds to truth-values, then we hold that the contextual provision of a location is a matter of saturation. The content$_s$ is now taken to be semantically incomplete even after a time has been contextually provided: with respect to a given world-time pair, 'It's raining' only expresses a function from places to truth-values. This is like the case of tensed sentences, whose contents, as we have seen, are semantically incomplete. The distinction between the two levels of content – the content$_s$ and the content$_u$ – still holds, whether or not the content$_s$ is semantically complete. The provision of the relevant circumstantial constituent is an instance of saturation when the content$_s$ is incomplete, and it is an instance of enrichment when it is complete. The same two options are presumably available for (1) and (2), in the situation-theoretic framework.

The contextual restriction of the domain of quantification can also be handled as the provision of a circumstance of evaluation, without begging the question whether this is an instance of enrichment or saturation. First option: we take a sentence such as 'Everybody is tired' to determine a function from possible worlds to truth-values (again, after a time has been contextually provided) – a function that yields truth with respect to all worlds in which everybody is tired. That function can then be evaluated with respect to a particular situation, in which case it will yield truth iff everybody in that situation is tired. Second option: we decide that the contextual provision of a time is not sufficient – an appropriate domain for the quantifier, that is, a particular set of people, must also be contextually provided for the sentence to express a complete proposition. Whether we take the first or the second option, in both cases a particular set of people can be contextually provided via the situation of evaluation and serve as domain for the quantifier. But its contextual provision will be considered as an instance of enrichment if we take the first option, and as an instance of saturation if we take the second option.

8.5 Sub-sentential circumstances

A well-known objection to the situation-theoretic treatment of quantifier domain restriction concerns cases in which there is more than one quantifier, and possibly more than one contextual domain, in a given sentence. The sentence 'Every sailor waved to every sailor' can be used to say that every sailor on the ship waved to every sailor on the shore.[22] Since we can have only one circumstance of evaluation for that sentence, how can we deal with this multiplicity of contextual domains? This is also the objection raised by Scott Soames to the situation-theoretic treatment of incomplete definite descriptions.[23] As I pointed out in the third section of 'Domains of Discourse',[24] the answer to this difficulty consists in multiplying situations of evaluation. This can be done by extending the notion of a circumstance of evaluation to sub-sentential expressions. Thus, following Kuroda, I have argued that every *predicate* requires a situation of evaluation.[25] Let me briefly sketch a treatment of quantifier domain restriction within that framework.

In a standard conception, predicates denote sets of objects, and quantifiers denote relations between sets of objects. In 'Every *F* is *G*', 'every' denotes that relation which holds between the set of *F*s and the set of *G*s just in case the former is included in the latter. Now predicates denote sets of objects only relative to situations. It follows that, before we can evaluate a quantificational statement, we must evaluate the predicates with respect to situations so as to determine the sets of objects which serve as arguments to the quantifier.

When I say that predicates denote sets of objects only relative to situations, I intend this as a rather trivial point. Some objects are red in a given situation, which may no longer be red in a different (say, temporally posterior) situation. So the set of red objects is variable and depends upon the situation at stake, even if we do not vary the domain from one situation to the next. There may be properties which stick to their objects in the sense that, if an object has them in a situation, it must have them in any situation to the domain of which that object belongs. Even if there are such sticking properties, still the predicates which correspond to them will possibly denote different sets of objects in different situations because the domain of objects itself can vary from one situation to the next.

So predicates require situations for their evaluation. The same thing holds for sentences, as we have seen. Whether a sentence is true or false depends upon how

---

[22] This example comes from Jason Stanley and Tim Williamson, 'Quantifiers and Context-Dependence', in *Analysis* 55 (1995), 291–5.

[23] Scott Soames, 'Incomplete Definite Descriptions', in *Notre Dame Journal of Formal Logic* 27 (1986), 349–75.

[24] François Recanati, 'Domains of Discourse', in *Linguistics and Philosophy* 19 (1996), pp. 445–75.

[25] Yuki Kuroda, 'Indexed Predicate Calculus', in *Journal of Semantics* 1 (1982), 43–59; François Recanati, 'Contextual Dependence and Definite Descriptions', in *Proceedings of the Aristotelian Society* 87 (1987), 57–73, and 'Descriptions and Situations', in Anne Bezuidenhout and Marga Reimer (eds.), *Descriptions and Beyond* (Oxford University Press, forthcoming).

things are in the relevant situation of evaluation. Now the main predicate in that sentence – the predicate which corresponds to the topmost verb-phrase – will always be evaluated with respect to the situation of evaluation for the sentence in question. But the other predicates in the sentence will possibly involve distinct situations of evaluation ('resource situations', in the terminology of Barwise and Perry, *Situations and Attitudes*).

Consider the sentence: 'Every student laughs.' There is no possibility of a divergence between the situation with respect to which the sentence is evaluated and the situation with respect to which the main predicate, 'laughs', is evaluated. That means that, if the sentence is evaluated with respect to some situation s, the set of laughers which serves as second argument to the quantifier 'every' will be the set of laughers-in-s. In contrast, the predicate which occurs as part of the noun-phrase, 'student', can be evaluated with respect to *any* situation: it may be the situation of evaluation s (in which case every student-in-s is said to be among the laughers-in-s), it may be the situation of utterance c (in which case every student-in-c is said to be among the laughers-in-s), or it may be any auxiliary situation which happens to be sufficiently salient for either linguistic or extra-linguistic reasons.

In this framework, we can handle the problem of quantifier domain restriction (and the analogous problem of incomplete definite descriptions) via the provision of a situation of evaluation, *or of a sequence of such situations*. Again, this does not settle the issue, whether the provision of a situation for the evaluation of a given predicate is an instance of enrichment or of saturation. It's an instance of saturation if, like Stanley and Szabó, we take a situation variable (or something like that) to be associated with every common noun in logical form. But we may also consider that the provision of a situation of evaluation is not the assignment of a value to a variable in logical form, but an optional process which may or may not take place. Whenever that process does *not* take place, the situation of evaluation for the predicate can only be the situation of evaluation for the sentence. That means that if the sentence is semantically complete and we evaluate it directly relative to the actual world, the set of objects denoted by the predicate will be the set of objects which satisfy the predicate in the actual world.

8.6   Conclusion

As we have seen at the beginning of this chapter, the possible worlds relative to which, in modal logic, sentences are evaluated are not aspects of the contents to be evaluated, but remain external to those contents. The same thing holds when time is the relevant circumstance of evaluation. Yet there is a difference between time and modality: the type of content that is evaluated with respect to a time in tense logic is not semantically complete in the sense in which the content which is evaluated with respect to a possible world is. This difference was emphasized by Evans in his attack on tense logic. But the proper response to make, on behalf of tense logic, is the drawing of a distinction between two levels of content. The content which a sentence articulates is one thing; the content of an utterance of that sentence, with respect to a given circumstance of evaluation, is another thing. Only the second, richer type of content is a legitimate bearer of truth-value, by Fregean lights. It follows that the truth-conditions of a tensed utterance crucially involve the circumstance of evaluation, which is not an aspect of the content articulated in the sentence. Hence there is a fundamental aspect of truth-conditional content that is not articulated in the uttered sentence.

The theory of situations I briefly introduced generalizes the lessons from tense logic. In this theory every utterance articulates a certain content and expresses a richer type of content (an 'Austinian proposition') consisting of the articulated content *and* the situation with respect to which that content is (intended to be) evaluated. The complete, Austinian proposition expressed by an utterance is true iff the situation of evaluation supports the articulated content. That content is typically not a classical proposition but a relativized proposition – a function from rich circumstances to truth-values.

In this framework there is an 'unarticulated constituent' in the (complete) content of every utterance, namely the circumstance of evaluation. Admittedly, there are different types of unarticulated constituent.[26] In many cases a circumstantial constituent counts as 'unarticulated' only in a weak sense. That is so whenever the constituent, without being explicitly represented in the articulated content, is nevertheless mandatory because that content is not semantically complete by Frege's lights. Thus the time of evaluation (that is, the time relative to which an utterance is evaluated) is unarticulated because, as Prior says, it is 'unmentioned' in the utterance, yet its contextual provision results from a form of saturation: such a constituent must be provided in order to get a complete proposition, that is, a function from possible worlds to truth-values. In situation theory, however, the necessity to provide the relevant circumstantial constituent is exactly like the necessity to provide a possible world in order to determine a truth-value. In general, *contents need circumstances for their evaluation*. Once this is acknowledged, the door is open to relativized contents of all sorts, and the privilege given to classical propositions (functions from possible worlds to truth-values) over relativized propositions (functions from rich circumstances to truth-values) looks somewhat arbitrary.[27] Be that as it may, a distinction must

---

[26] See footnote 4, p. 99.
[27] Classical propositions fulfil two functions: they are the bearers of absolute truth-values, and they are the object of the attitudes. In the situation theoretic framework, the Austinian proposition

be drawn in all cases between the articulated content ($content_s$) and the complete content of the utterance ($content_u$); and the irreducibly contextual nature of the circumstance that features in the $content_u$ must be acknowledged. Insofar as this position generalizes the context-dependence of truth-conditional content, it can be categorized as 'contextualist'.

Still, one might argue, the theory I have sketched posits a level of content that is very close to the linguistic meaning of the sentence: the $content_s$. Insofar as it posits such a level, the theory of situations sounds more similar to the Syncretic View than to Contextualism or even Quasi-Contextualism. I find this reaction natural, yet I maintain that the theory of situations stands on the contextualist side. I concede that there are similarities with the Syncretic View, but they are more superficial than they seem.

The main analogy consists in the fact that, in both cases, we find two levels of content: the proposition expressed by the sentence, and a richer proposition containing unarticulated constituents.[28] Taken literally, 'You're not going to die' is true iff the addressee is not going to die. This corresponds to the minimal proposition of the Syncretic View (what is strictly and literally said), and to the $content_s$ of situation theory. That content yields falsity in all possible worlds in which the addressee is not immortal. So the utterance counts as false ('literally false') if we evaluate the $content_s$ directly with respect to the actual world. If we take the intended situation of evaluation into account and evaluate the complete Austinian proposition ($content_u$), the utterance counts as true iff the addressee is not going to die *in that particular situation* (resulting from the cut). This truth-condition corresponds to the intuitive truth-conditions of the Syncretic View.

Despite this convergence between the two views, there are important differences. The articulated content (right-hand-side of the Austinian proposition) is unlike the minimal proposition of the syncretist in two respects:

(1) As we have seen, the articulated content of the situation theorist need not be a complete proposition; it may be a relativized proposition. In contrast, the minimal proposition must be a complete proposition, because the 'minimalist' criterion that is used in individuating it involves truth-evaluability.[29]

---

fulfils the first function, and the articulated content (relativized proposition) fulfils the second function, for which classical propositions are in any case ill-suited. So it is unclear that we need classical propositions.

[28] I stressed that analogy in 'Situations and the Structure of Content', pp. 121–2.

[29] Note, however, that some syncretists use a different criterion, and can therefore accommodate relativized propositions. Thus for Bach (who uses the 'IQ test' as criterion), what is literally said need not be a complete proposition, it may be a 'propositional radical'. Soames has recently come to endorse a similar view. See his 'Naming and Asserting', in Zoltán Szabó (ed.), *Semantics and Pragmatics* (Oxford University Press, forthcoming).

(2) More important in the context of the present discussion, there is abso-
lutely no reason why the articulated content (content$_s$) of the situation theorist
should not be affected by primary pragmatic processes of the optional variety.[30]
Typically, the situation that is contextually provided for the evaluation of an utterance will contribute to shaping the content that is evaluated with respect to
that situation: the meaning of words will naturally be enriched and adjusted to
fit the intended situation of evaluation. So the articulated content of the situation
theorist is definitely not the minimal proposition posited by the Syncretic View.

---

[30] Hence it would be misleading to keep describing this content as 'the content of the type sentence',
to use Dummett's words. The content$_s$ is as much a property of the utterance as the content$_u$. The
content$_s$ is the *articulated* content of the utterance, while the content$_u$ is the *complete* content
of the utterance (including the intended circumstance of evaluation).

9 Contextualism: how far can we go?

9.1 The modulation of sense

In context the meaning of words is adjusted or 'modulated' so as to fit what is being talked about.[1] Sense modulation is essential to speech, because we use a (more or less) fixed stock of lexemes to talk about an indefinite variety of things, situations and experiences.[2] Through the interaction between the context-independent meanings of our words and the particulars of the situation talked about, contextualized, modulated senses emerge, appropriate to the situation at hand. The meaning of a word can thus be made contextually more specific, or it may, on the contrary, be loosened and suitably extended, as in metaphor. It may also undergo 'semantic transfer', etc.

According to many authors among those who have studied the phenomenon, modulation is the process whereby the meaning of a given word is affected by *the meanings of other words in the same sentence*.[3] Thus the meaning of the adjective 'light' is affected by the meaning of the noun it modifies: a light lunch is not light in quite the same sense in which a piece of luggage is said to be light.[4] According to Jonathan Cohen, this is one of the big differences between natural language and formal languages: 'artificial languages

---

[1] 'Modulation' is the term used by Alan Cruse, *Lexical Semantics* (Cambridge University Press, 1986), pp. 50–3, and by Ruhl, *On Monosemy*, pp. 85–95 and elsewhere. James Ross, in his *Portraying Analogy* (Cambridge University Press, 1981), occasionally speaks of 'meaning adjustment' (for example on p. 50), though his official phrase is 'meaning differentiation'.

[2] See Dwight Bolinger, *Aspects of Language* (Harcourt, Brace and World, 1968), p. 230: 'Since the universe never repeats itself exactly, every time we speak we metaphorize'; and Peter Strawson, *Introduction to Logical Theory* (Methuen, 1952), also p. 230: 'In the effort to describe our experience we are continually putting words to new uses, connected with, but not identical with, their familiar uses; applying them to states of affairs which are both like and unlike those to which the words are most familiarly applied. Hence . . . it is . . . hard to frame a grammatical sentence to which it is impossible to imagine some sense being given; and given, not by arbitrary *fiat*, but by an intelligible, though probably figurative, extension of the familiar senses of the words and phrases concerned.'

[3] See for example Ross, *Portraying Analogy*; Jonathan Cohen, 'How is Conceptual Innovation Possible?', in *Erkenntnis* 25 (1986), 221–38; Ron Lahav, 'Against Compositionality: The Case of Adjectives', in *Philosophical Studies* 57 (1989), 261–79; and Pustejovsky, *The Generative Lexicon*.

[4] On this example, see Michael Pelczar, 'Wittgensteinian Semantics', in *Noûs* 34 (2000), 483–516.

satisfy an insulationist account whereas natural languages require an interactionist one'.[5] Cohen characterizes insulationist and interactionist accounts as follows:

According to the insulationist account the meaning of any one word that occurs in a particular sentence is insulated against interference from the meaning of any other word in the same sentence. On this view the composition of a sentence resembles the construction of a wall from bricks of different shapes. The result depends on the properties of the parts and the pattern of their combination. But just as each brick has exactly the same shape in every wall or part of a wall to which it is moved, so too each standard sense of a word or phrase is exactly the same in every sentence or part of a sentence in which it occurs . . .

Interactionism makes the contradictory assertion: in some sentences in some languages the meaning of a word in a sentence may be determined in part by the word's verbal context in that sentence . . . On this view the composition of a sentence is more like the construction of a wall from sand-bags of different kinds. Though the size, structure, texture and contents of a sand-bag restrict the range of shapes it can take on, the actual shape it adopts in a particular situation depends to a greater or lesser extent on the shapes adopted by other sand-bags in the wall, and the same sand-bag might take on a somewhat different shape in another wall or in a different position in the same wall. By exploiting local context in this way a language can be much more prolific of semantic variety than insulationalism can give it credit for being.[6]

I agree with Cohen that the semantics of natural language is not insulationist. As I have been at pains to emphasize, the meaning of the whole is *not* constructed in a purely bottom-up manner from the meanings of the parts. The meaning of the whole is influenced by top-down, pragmatic factors, and through the meaning of the whole the meanings of the parts are also affected. So we need a more 'interactionist' or even 'Gestaltist' approach to compositionality.[7] But I think Cohen takes too narrow a view of the sort of interaction that sense modulation results from.

Let us go back to the example discussed by Michael Pelczar:

In these sentences:
'There was a light breeze from the south.'
'This is a light package.'
'The fire won't last with such light fuel.'

– 'light' expresses a content having to do with intensity, weight, and density, respectively. And this clearly results from the fact that in the first sentence 'light' is used to speak of a breeze, whereas in the second it is applied to describe a package, and in the third, to some fuel for a fire.[8]

---

[5] Cohen, 'Conceptual Innovation', p. 224.   [6] *Ibid.*, pp. 223–4.
[7] The idea of 'Gestaltist compositionality' comes from Bernard Victorri and Catherine Fuchs, *La Polysémie* (Hermès, 1996).
[8] Pelczar, 'Wittgensteinian Semantics', p. 488.

According to Cohen, Ross and many others, the sense of 'light' is modulated through its interaction with the meaning of the head noun ('breeze', 'package', 'fuel').[9] I think this is not quite right. The meaning of the head-noun is not what matters most. It is, as Pelczar emphasizes, what the word 'is used to speak of', what it 'is applied to describe', that matters. Nothing prevents us from using 'light', *in the same phrase 'light fuel'*, to characterize the weight of the fuel rather than its density, if this is what is relevant to us in the context at hand. We can even imagine a context in which 'light', as applied to a package, would characterize the intensity of the sound it emits.

To take another example from Pelczar's study, the word 'get' takes on different senses – denotes different relations – depending on what fills the second argument-place of the relation. Thus 'Smith has got the virus' means that he has *contracted* the virus, while in 'I need to get some eggs' 'get' has what Pelczar calls the *acquisitional* sense. Yet, as Pelczar points out, we can easily imagine a context in which 'Smith has got the virus' means that Smith has acquired, that is, successfully collected a sample of, the virus. The same remarks can be made with respect to the word 'cut', whose meaning is modulated differently in 'John cut the grass' and 'John cut the cake.' As Searle points out, if I ask John to cut the grass, and he cuts it the way one cuts a cake (or if I ask him to cut the cake, and he cuts it the way one cuts grass), he has not complied with my request; he has not done what I asked him to do. Still, we can imagine a context in which in asking John to cut the grass, I would mean that he is to cut it the way one cuts a cake:

Suppose you and I run a sod farm where we sell strips of grass turf to people who want a lawn in a hurry . . . Suppose I say to you, 'Cut half an acre of grass for this customer'; I might mean not that you should *mow* it, but that you should slice it into strips as you could cut a cake or a loaf of bread.[10]

So it's not just the interaction of the meaning of the word with the linguistic context that is relevant. The really important factor is the discourse topic. The 'internal' interaction of word-meanings within the same sentence or discourse is only a reflection of the more general phenomenon: the interaction between word meaning and the situation the words are used to talk about.

9.2   The semantic relevance of modulation

As the virus example shows, modulation is not just the post-semantic addition of a truth-conditionally irrelevant 'shade of meaning' to the core meaning of

---

[9] This is what Lahav calls the 'noun-dependence' of adjectives and verbs – a feature that, according to him, threatens the Principle of Compositionality.

[10] Searle, 'The Background of Meaning', pp. 224–5.

words. Modulation *is* truth-conditionally relevant, because the words' contribution to truth-conditional content (or to satisfaction-conditions more generally) is not their pre-modulation meaning but their modulated senses.[11] Thus different truth-conditions correspond to the two senses which 'get' may take on through modulation: the sense of 'acquire' or that of 'contract'. In the acquisitional sense 'Smith has got the virus' will be true if Smith has collected a sample of the virus, *even if Smith has not thereby contracted the virus in question.* But unless he has contracted the virus, it will be false that he has 'got the virus', in the other sense. So modulation results in a truth-conditional difference. Thanks to that difference, it is possible to say 'He has got the virus, without getting the virus', consistently – provided the sense of 'get' is modulated differently on its two occurrences.

Since modulation has an impact on truth-conditions, it cannot be relegated to the 'post-semantic' periphery. But there is another way of denying modulation semantic relevance: we can relegate it to the 'pre-semantic' limbo by construing it as a variety of disambiguation. The word 'get', one might argue, has several senses, one of which must be contextually selected on any particular use. Since disambiguation is not a semantic but a pragmatic process, there is no reason why modulation (a variety of disambiguation) should matter to semantics.

Like the post-semantic dismissal, this strategy fails. For there to be the sort of disambiguation that would support the pre-semantic dismissal, a pre-established list of discrete senses for 'get' must be somehow given, from which the contextually relevant sense can be selected. But, as Herb Clark and many others following him have stressed, modulated senses result from a process of 'generation' or 'creation' rather than of selection.[12] The fundamental difference between sense generation and sense selection is that generation is productive: new senses can be generated, in a creative manner. As a result words can take on an indefinite variety of possible senses. (Another important difference between straightforward ambiguity and modulation is the non-discrete nature of the senses generated through modulation: as several authors point out, there is a *continuum* of possible semantic values for a polysemous word such as 'get'.)[13]

---

[11] This can be established by appealing to examples like 'Mary is wearing a light coat; so is Jane.' For that to be true, Jane's coat must be light *in the same modulated sense* as that in which Mary's coat is said to be light. (I have borrowed this example from Alan Cruse, *Meaning in Language: An Introduction to Semantics and Pragmatics* (Oxford University Press, 2000), p. 106.)

[12] See for example 'Making Sense of Nonce Sense' and 'Understanding Old Words with New Meanings', two papers published by Herb Clark in 1983 (the second one co-authored by Richard Gerrig) and reprinted respectively as chapter 10 and chapter 11 in his *Arenas of Language Use* (The University of Chicago Press, 1992). See also Jay Atlas, *Philosophy without Ambiguity* (Clarendon Press, 1989), pp. 29–31, and Pustejovsky, *The Generative Lexicon*, chapter 4.

[13] See Catherine Fuchs, 'Polysémie, Interprétation et Typicalité', in Danièle Dubois (ed.), *Sémantique et Cognition: Catégories, Prototypes, Typicalité* (Editions du CNRS, 1991),

Can we say at least that the phenomenon of modulation only concerns a re-stricted class of words, namely those that are 'polysemous' and possess a family of related senses? No. First, as Cohen points out, polysemy is the norm rather than the exception.[14] To be sure, not all polysemous words are *as* polysemous as ultrafrequent words such as 'get'. Polysemy comes in grades, and it could be argued that modulation is associated with a high degree of polysemy: highly polysemous words, it may be said, have an abstract core meaning which calls for elaboration or modulation, and from which the various senses of the poly-semous expression are generated.[15] This does not entail that non-polysemous words are not subject to modulation, however. Polysemy arguably proceeds from modulation (since the array of senses of a polysemous expression re-flects conventionalized patterns of modulation), not the other way round.[16] So the proper response to make is that modulation *can* affect any ordinary word, whether or not it is (highly) polysemous.

A paradigm example of modulation is the use of colour terms such as 'red'.[17] The conditions of application for 'red' depend upon (inter alia) what sort of thing the colour adjective is applied to. As Lahav puts it, the conditions that a table has to meet in order to be describable by 'red table' are not the same conditions that a house or a book or a bird has to meet in order to be describable by 'red house' or 'red book' or 'red bird'.[18] Yet 'red' is not especially polysemous; it is just an

pp. 165–7, on French *'pouvoir'*; Sue Atkins, 'The Contribution of Lexicography', in Madeleine Bates and Ralph Weischedel (eds.), *Challenges in Natural Language Processing* (Cambridge University Press, 1993), pp. 39–43, on *'safety'*; and Richard Grandy, 'Understanding and the Principle of Compositionality', in *Philosophical Perspectives* 4 (1990), p. 571, on *'prime'*.

[14] Jonathan Cohen, 'A Problem About Ambiguity in Truth-Conditional Semantics', in *Analysis* 45 (1985), p. 131.

[15] See Alfonso Caramazza and Ellen Grober, 'Polysemy and the Structure of the Subjective Lex-icon', in Clea Rameh (ed.), *Semantics: Theory and Application* (Georgetown University Press, 1976), 181–207.

[16] 'Ce que l'on appelle la polysémie n'est que la somme institutionnalisée, si l'on peut dire, de ces valeurs contextuelles, toujours instantanées, aptes continuellement à s'enrichir, à disparaître, bref, sans permanence, sans valeur constante' (Emile Benveniste, 'La Forme et le Sens dans le Langage', in his *Problèmes de Linguistique Générale* II (Gallimard, 1974), p. 227).

[17] See for example Charles Travis, *The True and the False* (Benjamins, 1981), p. 16, and Lahav, 'Against Compositionality', p. 264.

[18] 'For a bird to be red (in the normal case), it should have most of the surface of its body red, though not its beak, legs, eyes, and of course its inner organs. Furthermore, the red color should be the bird's natural color, since we normally regard a bird as being 'really' red even if it is painted white all over. A kitchen table, on the other hand, is red even if it is only painted red, and even if its 'natural' color underneath the paint is, say, white. Morever, for a table to be red only its upper surface needs to be red, but not necessarily its legs and its bottom surface. Similarly, a red apple, as Quine pointed out, needs to be red only on the outside, but a red hat needs to be red only in its external upper surface, a red crystal is red both inside and outside, and a red watermelon is red only inside. For a book to be red is for its cover but not necessarily for its inner pages to be mostly red, while for a newspaper to be red is for all of its pages to be red. For a house to be red is for its outside walls, but not necessarily its roof (and windows and door) to be mostly red, while a red car must be red in its external surface including its roof (but not

ordinary adjective, whose conditions of application can be varied or modulated in context, like that of any ordinary adjective. Or take the verb 'to like' which we find both in 'He likes John's sister' and in 'He likes the food John cooks.' It's not the same sort of 'liking' that is involved in both cases, and we can imagine that someone who likes John's sister in one sense (say, the culinary sense – for that you have to imagine a weird context) does not like her in the other sense. Yet 'like' is just like any other verb. So the phenomenon of modulation is not a special feature of a restricted class of expressions. *In general*, the conditions of application for words can be varied or modulated in context. That is the phenomenon a proper theory of language and communication must account for.

9.3   Four approaches

Insofar as it takes as input the conventional, linguistic meaning of an expression, and delivers as output the modulated sense that is the expression's contribution to truth-conditional content, modulation is in the same ballpark as indexicality. Cohen stresses the similarity between the two phenomena:

> It is an enormous convenience that the same word can often be uttered in one or other of several different though related senses. Instead of having to learn a very much larger number of words, each with fixed and context-independent meanings, we can learn a relatively small number of words with variable meanings . . . The economy of resources that is thus achieved by natural language is obviously comparable with the economies that are achieved by variability of reference in the case of proper nouns and other indexical expressions as an alternative to the fixed references available with the use of co-ordinate systems, individual constants, etc.[19]

There is a fundamental difference between indexicality and modulation, however. Despite its semantic relevance, modulation is a pragmatic process in the fullest possible sense: it is a *pragmatically controlled* pragmatic process, rather than a *linguistically controlled* pragmatic process (like saturation). Neither enrichment, nor loosening, nor transfer, nor any other of the mechanisms at work in modulation seems to require, on the side of the input, a 'slot' or gap in semantic structure demanding to be filled and triggering the search for an appropriate filler. In contrast to saturation, which proceeds from the bottom up, modulation seems to be fundamentally top-down.

---

its windows, wheels, bumper, etc.). A red star only needs to appear red from the earth, a red glaze needs to be red only after it is fired, and a red mist or a red powder are red not simply inside or outside. A red pen need not even have any red part (the ink may turn red only when in contact with the paper). In short, what counts for one type of thing to be red is not what counts for another' (Lahav, 'Against Compositionality', p. 264).

[19] Cohen, 'Ambiguity in Truth-Conditional Semantics', p. 132.

In this section I will introduce four types of approach to modulation, which may be placed on the scale from Literalism to Contextualism (chapter 6). Insofar as modulation is a cover term for what, in this book, I have called 'primary pragmatic processes of the optional variety', there is no account of modulation that is literalist, since the very phenomenon of modulation tells against Literalism. Still, among the possible accounts of the phenomenon, some are closer than others to the literalist pole, and some are closer than others to the contextualist pole.

The first view to be discussed is the natural view to hold for a syncretist or a quasi-contextualist. I call it the Strong Optionality view (SO). It takes the primary pragmatic processes that are involved in modulation to be optional in a strong and straightforward sense. They take place, for contingent reasons, but they might as well not take place. In a suitable context, the senses expressed by the words would be, simply, the senses they possess in virtue of the rules of the language.

Consider standard examples such as:

She took out her key and opened the door.
There is a big lion in the middle of the piazza.

The pragmatic process that enriches the meaning of the first utterance so as to convey both a sense of temporal order (giving to 'and' the sense of 'and then') and a notion of the instrument used in opening the door (giving to 'opened the door' the sense of 'opened the door with the key') – that process might also not take place. As Grice emphasized,[20] such pragmatic suggestions are always cancellable, explicitly or contextually.[21] Once the pragmatic suggestion has been cancelled, what the words contribute to truth-conditional content is their bare linguistic senses. The same thing can be said about the second example. 'Lion' can be understood in the representational sense: the 'lion' that is talked about can be a representation (for example, a statue) of a lion, not a real lion. That reading results from a primary pragmatic process that can be variously described.[22] However we describe it, its optional character is obvious: nothing

---

[20] Grice, *Way of Words*, p. 39.

[21] The speaker could cancel the suggestion explicitly by saying: 'She took out her key and opened the door – not with the key, though, and not in that order. She took out her key while opening the door (which was unlocked) with the other hand.'

[22] According to Cohen ('The Semantics of Metaphor', in Ortony, *Metaphor and Thought*, pp. 60–3), the representational sense is generated by 'cancelling' the feature + *animate* from the rich lexical meaning of 'lion'. According to Grandy ('Understanding and the Principle of Compositionality', p. 567), it is generated by enriching the structured meaning of the sentence with an unarticulated function from objects to their representations. According to yet another view, inspired by Walton's *Mimesis as Make-Believe* (Harvard University Press, 1990), the circumstance of evaluation for the predicate 'lion' is shifted from the actual world to the world of the pretence (see my *Oratio Obliqua, Oratio Recta*, p. 245).

prevents that sentence from being understood literally, as talking about a real lion.

The three other views I want to discuss are all contextualist. They all ascribe to modulation a form of necessity or ineliminability, to the point of blurring the mandatory/optional contrast. Discussing them will enable us to distinguish more or less radical varieties of Contextualism. The last view I shall consider corresponds to the most radical form: Meaning Eliminativism.

Like SO, the Pragmatic Composition view (PC) accepts that the literal, input sense undergoing modulation could, in a suitable context, be the expressed sense. So it construes the pragmatic process of modulation as optional. But it construes it as optional only *with respect to the word whose sense is modulated*. If we consider not words in isolation, but the complex expressions in which they occur, we see that the primary pragmatic processes of modulation are not always contingent and dispensable, but often essential. Even though the linguistic meaning of a given word (or the semantic value that results from saturation) could be the expressed sense, still the process of semantic composition, that is, the putting together of that sense with the semantic values for other expressions, cannot proceed unless appropriate adjustments take place so as to make the parts fit together within an appropriate whole. On this view words have meanings which could go directly into the interpretation, without modulation, but it is the composition process that forces modulation to take place, or at least invites it: often the meanings of individual words do not cohere by themselves, and can be fitted together only by undergoing a process of mutual adjustment.

Remember the examples I gave in chapter 2. If we take it as axiomatic that only sounds can be heard, then, in 'I hear the piano', either the sense of 'hear' or that of 'the piano' must be modulated for the sentence to make sense (§2.6).[23] Or remember the Gary Cooper example, 'disarm the fricassee', or Searle's example, 'Cut the sun', from §6.3. To make sense of such sentences we must imagine (or retrieve from memory) a possible scenario in which the semantic values of the words fit together.[24] That imaginative exercise involves elaborating what the meaning of the words gives us – going beyond that linguistic meaning and, for example, interpreting 'disarm' in the specific sense of: 'take the gun out of' or 'remove the gun from'.

Or consider the paradigmatic example I gave in the last section: the adjective 'red'. There is no particular incompleteness in the linguistic meaning of that

---

[23] Note that there may be no fact of the matter as to which particular word or word-meaning undergoes modulation, in examples like those of chapter 2. This is due to the holistic character of modulation.

[24] See Rumelhart, 'Problems with Literal Meanings', p. 77. See also Anthony Sandford and Simon Garrod, 'The Role of Scenario Mapping in Text Comprehension', in *Discourse Processes* 26 (1998), 159–90.

word – it means something like 'being of the colour red' or 'having the colour red'. Insofar as 'red' refers to a specific colour (and it does) this, it seems, expresses a definite property – a property that could, in principle, go into the interpretation of a sentence in which the adjective 'red' occurs. (For example: 'Imagine a red surface.') But in most cases the following question will arise: what is it for the thing talked about to count as having that colour? Unless that question is answered, the utterance ascribing redness to the thing talked about (John's car, say) will not be truth-evaluable. It is not enough to know the colour that is in question (red) and the thing to which that colour is ascribed (John's car). To fix the utterance's truth-conditions, we need to know something more – something which the meanings of the words do not and cannot give us: we need to know what it is for that thing (or for that sort of thing) to count as being that colour. What is it for a car, a bird, a house, a pen, or a pair of shoes to count as red? To answer such questions, we need to appeal to background assumptions and world knowledge. Linguistic competence does not suffice: pragmatic fine-tuning is called for.

To sum up, on the view (PC) under discussion, even if the semantic value of a word is fixed by language (and context, if saturation is necessary), composing it with the semantic values for other words often requires help from above. It is semantic composition which has a fundamentally pragmatic character.[25] So there is a sense in which modulation is necessary, but that is not quite the sense in which saturation is. With saturation there is a semantic gap and an instruction to fill the gap – both the gap and the instruction being part of the linguistic meaning of the expression. With modulation, there need be no gap and there is no instruction to search for some contextual filler. The expression means something, and that meaning could go into the interpretation – so modulation is optional – but to determine a suitable sense for complex expressions, we need to go beyond the meaning of individual words and creatively enrich or otherwise adjust what we are given in virtue purely of linguistic meaning. We must go beyond linguistic meaning, without being linguistically instructed to do so, if we are to make sense of the utterance. As Rumelhart writes, utterance understanding involves 'searching memory for a schema to account for the described event'.[26] I can't resist quoting Rumelhart's methodological comment here:

This approach is, I believe, quite different from the 'standard' approach. The standard view emphasizes the 'bottom up' process of constructing meaning from smaller component meanings. Non-linguistic knowledge comes into play *after* the set of possible

---

[25] See Benveniste, 'La Forme et le Sens', pp. 224–6, and Rumelhart, 'Problems with Literal Meanings', p. 76. In *The Architecture of the Language Faculty* (MIT Press, 1997), pp. 47–67, Ray Jackendoff similarly argues for what he calls 'enriched composition'.

[26] Rumelhart, 'Problems with Literal Meanings', p. 78.

meanings has been selected. My approach suggests that comprehension, like perception, should be likened to Hebb's paleontologist (Hebb 1949) who uses his beliefs and knowledge about dinosaurs in conjunction with the clues provided by the bone fragments available to construct a full-fledged model of the original. In this case the words spoken and the actions taken by the speaker are likened to the clues of the paleontologist, and the dinosaur, to the meaning conveyed through those clues. On this view the processing is much more 'top down' in that internal hypotheses are actively imposed on the observed utterances.[27]

On the third type of view – the Wrong Format view (WF) – modulation is ineliminable for deeper reasons. It's not just semantic composition which requires adjustment and modulation of word meaning. Individual word meanings themselves are such that they *could not* go directly into the interpretation. They don't have the proper format for that. They are either too abstract and schematic, in such a way that elaboration or fleshing out is needed to reach a determinate content;[28] or they are too rich and must undergo 'feature-cancellation',[29] or some other screening process through which some aspects will be backgrounded and others focused on.[30] Note that there are versions of this view which take the meaning of a word to consist both in some abstract schema in need of elaboration *and* a large store of encyclopedic representations most of which must be screened off as irrelevant, on any particular use.[31]

According to WF modulation is mandatory, hence it becomes harder to distinguish it from saturation. This is the point where Indexicalism and Contextualism meet (§6.6). An indexicalist will argue that the schematicity of word meaning invoked by (some versions of) WF just is the presence in that meaning of free variables or parameters. So there is no modulation really, only saturation. A contextualist will reply, as I did in §6.4, that the alleged parameters do not behave like standard indexical variables.[32]

---

[27] *Ibid*. I am not suggesting that Rumelhart himself advocated the Pragmatic Composition view. I think his Contextualism was more radical than that. As the above passage shows, he held that semantic composition is, to a large extent, a top down process. But he would presumably not have accepted the claim that the meaning of a linguistic expression could go directly into the interpretation, without modulation. (The same thing holds for Benveniste, whose conception of word meaning was close to the 'Wrong Format' view I am about to introduce.)

[28] Gustave Guillaume, *Temps et Verbe* (Champion, 1929), pp. 132–4; Ruhl, *On Monosemy*; Victorri and Fuchs, *La Polysémie*.

[29] See Cohen, 'Grice's Views about the Logical Particles' and 'The Semantics of Metaphor', and Franks, 'Sense Generation'.

[30] See for example James Pustejovsky and Branimir Boguraev, 'A Richer Characterization of Dictionary Entries: The Role of Knowledge Representations', in Sue Atkins and Antonio Zampolli (eds.), *Computational Approaches to the Lexicon* (Oxford University Press, 1994), 295–311.

[31] See Langacker, *Foundations of Cognitive Grammar*.

[32] In his contextualist manifesto, 'Is Snow White?', Julius Moravcsik points out that contextual indices of the sort used to deal with indexicals have two important properties. First, they 'simply limit or relativize truth to a frame of application within which variations in extension and truth do not arise'. Second, 'for most of the standard indices we can find individual lexical items to which these are linked'. Neither of these conditions holds in the case of modulation. The phenomenon

The last view of interest to us, Meaning Eliminativism (ME), is a sort of WF pushed to the extremes. According to WF, words have meanings, but those meanings don't have the proper format for being recruited into the interpretation of utterances; they are not determinate senses but overly rich or overly abstract 'semantic potentials' out of which determinate senses can be constructed. ME goes farther in the same direction. It denies that words (*qua* linguistic types) have 'meanings' in anything like the traditional sense – not even abstract or knowledge-rich meanings, as in WF. Meanings for types undergo wholesale elimination, in favour of the senses contextually expressed by particular tokens. ME is implicit in the writings of some of the early contextualists (Austin, Wittgenstein, and others), and before comparing it to WF, it is worth taking a look at their view.

9.4   Truth-conditional unstability: from Waismann's 'open texture' to Searle's 'background'

A good place to start is Waismann's classic paper 'Verifiability', and more specifically the passage where he introduces the notion of 'open texture'.[33] That passage is representative of a view (and a type of example) which Waismann shared with Austin and Wittgenstein, and which has been revived recently by contemporary contextualists such as Travis and Searle. According to this view, truth-conditional content is essentially unstable and context-dependent.

What Waismann says in introducing open texture can be paraphrased as follows. It seems that we have no problem assigning truth-conditions to ordinary sentences. To do so we describe a state of affairs, that is, a type of situation, the obtaining of which is necessary and sufficient for the sentence to be true. That seems easy enough to do. Thus we think we know the truth-conditions of 'There is a cat next door', or 'This is gold' (or 'This is a man'): we can specify a state of affairs s such that the utterance is true if and only if s obtains. But this is an illusion – we can't really. Given an utterance u and the state of affairs s which is its alleged truth-maker, it is always possible to imagine a world in which, although s obtains, yet it is not the case that u is true (with respect to that world).

'is not linked to a specific sub-vocabulary of English. Practically the whole descriptive vocabulary is affected.' Moreover, 'the various practical contexts create rather than restrict extension. It is not as if we could survey all of the possible future extension-creating contexts that our future and possible interactions with the world can create. Thus the intuitive idea that underlies the practice of relativizing truth is missing in our type of case. The expanding ranges of application and contexts cannot be described in a rigorous way, while this is possible in the cases in which the introduction of indices is legitimate.' (All quotations are from Julius Moravcsik, 'Is Snow White?', in Paul Humphreys (ed.), *Patrick Suppes: Scientific Philosopher* (Kluwer, 1994), p. 77. See also Moravcsik's *Meaning, Creativity, and the Partial Inscrutability of the Human Mind* (CSLI Publications, 1998), pp. 39–48.)

[33] Friedrich Waismann, 'Verifiability', in Anthony Flew (ed.), *Logic and Language,* 1st series (Blackwell, 1951), pp. 119–23.

To show that, one has only to *embed* the state of affairs *s* within a larger situation, by providing further details about an imagined world in which *s* obtains. If the world in question is sufficiently unlike our world (for example, if the 'cat' talked about turns out to speak Latin, or grows to a fantastic size, or changes into a fish), we shall be at a loss when it comes to deciding whether the statement 'There is a cat next door' is actually true, with respect to that world, even though the state of affairs we initially specified obtains. Is a world in which there is an animal next door exactly like a cat in all respects except that it speaks Latin a world in which there is a *cat* next door? We don't know, because 'most of our empirical concepts are not delimited in all possible directions'.[34] Or, to take another classic example:

The notion of gold seems to be defined with absolute precision, say by the spectrum of gold with its characteristic lines. Now what would you say if a substance was discovered that looked like gold, satisfied all the chemical tests for gold, whilst it emitted a new sort of radiation? 'But such things do not happen.' Quite so; but they *might* happen, and that is enough to show that we can never exclude altogether the possibility of some unforeseen situation arising in which we shall have to modify our definition. Try as we may, no concept is limited in such a way that there is no room for any doubt. We introduce a concept and limit it in some directions; for instance, we define gold in contrast to some other metals such as alloys. This suffices for our present needs, and we do not probe any farther. We tend to *overlook* the fact that there are always other directions in which the concept has not been defined. And if we did, we could easily imagine conditions which would necessitate new limitations. In short, it is not possible to define a concept like gold with absolute precision, i.e. in such a way that every nook and cranny is blocked against entry of doubt. That is what is meant by the open texture of a concept.[35]

We find something analogous to Waismann's embeddings in Searle's writings on the 'background'. In 'Literal Meaning', Searle enquires into the truth-conditions of 'The cat is on the mat.' It's easy to describe the sort of state of affairs that would make the sentence true (with respect to a particular assignment of values to indexical expressions). But once we have described such a state of affairs, we can embed it within an extraordinary situation:

Suppose that the cat and the mat are in exactly the relations depicted only they are both floating freely in outer space, perhaps outside the Milky Way galaxy altogether . . . Is the cat still on the mat? And was the earth's gravitational field one of the things depicted . . .?

What I think is correct to say as a first approximation in answer to these questions is that the notion of the literal meaning of the sentence 'The cat is on the mat' does not have a clear application, unless we make some further assumptions, in the case of cats and mats floating freely in outer space.[36]

---

[34] *Ibid.*, p. 120.   [35] *Ibid.*
[36] John Searle, 'Literal Meaning', in *Erkenntnis* 13 (1978), p. 211.

Now Waismann has an explanation for the fact that, in extraordinary situations, 'words fail us', as Austin puts it. Here it goes:

If I had to describe the right hand of mine which I am now holding up, I may say different things of it: I may state its size, its shape, its colour, its tissue, the chemical compound of its bones, its cells, and perhaps add some more particulars; but however far I go, I shall never reach a point where my description will be completed: logically speaking, it is always possible to extend the description by adding some detail or other. Every description stretches, as it were, into a horizon of open possibilities: however far I go, I shall always carry this horizon with me. (. . .) [This] has a direct bearing on the open texture of concepts. A term is defined when the sort of situation is described in which it is to be used. Suppose for a moment that we were able to describe situations completely without omitting anything (as in chess), then we could produce an exhaustive list of all the circumstances in which the term is to be used so that nothing is left in doubt; in other words, we could construct a *complete definition*, i.e. a thought model which anticipates and settles once and for all every possible question of usage. As, in fact, we can never eliminate the possibility of some unforeseen factor emerging, we can never be quite sure that we have included in our definition everything that should be included, and thus the process of defining and refining an idea will go on without ever reaching a final stage.[37]

Waismann's point is simple enough. A term is used in, or applies to, situations of a certain type – situations with which we are acquainted. (Or at least: our mastery of the term is somehow connected to our having experienced the type of situation in question.) To define a term is to describe the type of situation in question. The problem is that the situations in question, like Waismann's right hand or any aspect of empirical reality, cannot be completely described: they possess an indefinite number of features, some of which may never have been noticed and perhaps will never be noticed by anyone. When we describe an empirical situation, we make certain features explicit, but an indefinite number of other features remain implicit and constitute a sort of hidden 'background'. (Here I use Searle's term, on purpose.) Now the applicability of a term to novel situations depends on their similarity to the source situations, that is, to the situations by association with which the term has acquired the meaning it has. For the term to be (clearly) applicable, the target situation must be similar to the source situations not only with respect to those features which easily come to mind and constitute the 'explicit' definition of the term (the 'tip', to use the iceberg metaphor), but also with respect to the hidden background. If the two situations considerably diverge with respect to the latter, it's unclear whether or not the term will be applicable, even though the explicit conditions of satisfaction are satisfied.

Other examples can be provided where the divergence between the source situation and the target situation affects not only the hidden background but also the explicit part (the tip of the iceberg). Thus Searle imagines that 'Snow is white' is uttered as a description of the following situation:

---

[37] Waismann, 'Verifiability', pp. 121–3.

Suppose that by some fantastic change in the course of nature the earth is hit by an astronomical shower of radiation that affects all existing and future water molecules in such a way that in their crystalline form they reflect a different wave length when in sunlight from what they did prior to the radiation shower. Suppose also that the same shower affects the human visual apparatus and its genetic basis so that snow crystals look exactly as they did before. Physicists after the shower assure us that if we could see snow the way we did before, it would look chartreuse but because of the change in our retinas, which affects our observation of snow and nothing else, snow looks the same color as ever and will continue to do so to ensuing generations . . . Would we say that snow was still white?[38]

Putnam's twin-earth thought-experiment has the same structure.[39] It's a case of divergence between source situations and target situation, where the divergence affects the tip and not merely the hidden background. For if we are to define water, we shall say that it's a liquid with such and such phenomenal properties, and that its chemical structure is H_2O, in the same way in which the whiteness of snow has to do both with its reflecting a certain wavelength *and* with its looking to us a certain way. We can imagine an extraordinary situation where the two things that go together as part of the tip are actually divorced from one another. In such cases we don't know what to say because there is some measure of similarity between the source situations and the target situation, but we have no contextual clue as to which dimension of similarity matters.

9.5   Ostensive definitions

Waismann's argument for the unstability of application conditions can be objected to on two grounds. First, it presupposes 'descriptivism', that is, the idea that the only way to define words is to do so descriptively. Second, it conflates the semantic and the epistemological.

(First objection) All that Waismann's argument establishes, arguably, is that words cannot be defined *in purely descriptive terms*. But this does not imply that words cannot be defined *at all*, or that they do not possess definite (stable) conditions of application. The reason why words cannot be defined in purely descriptive terms is that they have an irreducibly referential dimension: they, as it were, point to real situations in the world – situations which have an indefinite number of features and cannot be exhaustively described. Why not simply incorporate this referential dimension into our statements of truth- and application-conditions? Why not follow Putnam and define a cat as an animal belonging to the same species as *this specimen* (or those specimens, where the specimens in question are normal cats found in the local environment)? Why

---

[38] Searle, 'The Background of Meaning', p. 230.
[39] Hilary Putnam, 'The Meaning of "Meaning"', in his *Philosophical Papers, vol. 2: Mind, Language and Reality* (Cambridge University Press, 1975), pp. 223–7.

not define gold as *this metal* (while pointing to a piece of gold)? By explicitly incorporating ostensive reference to the actual environment into the definition of predicates like 'gold' and 'cat', it seems that we can overcome the alleged unstability of truth-conditions. 'There is a cat next door' will be true, in the imagined situation (where a cat-like animal next door speaks Latin), provided the cat-like animal belongs to the same species as *our* cats (the cats to be found in ordinary situations).

(Second objection) Of course, we do not *know* whether or not the strange animal we imagine would be considered a cat by the scientists, just as we don't know whether or not a gold-like metal emitting a new sort of radiation would count as gold. But our epistemic limitations do not prevent the word 'gold' (or the word 'cat') from having a definite content and a definite extension: gold is anything that is the same metal as this, and a cat is any animal of the same species as those. Our epistemic limitations, so much emphasized by Waismann, have no bearing on the properly semantic issue.

These objections are well-taken but they are not decisive. In particular, they do not threaten Waismann's conclusion (or at least, *my* conclusion) regarding the unstability of truth- and application-conditions. They would threaten that conclusion if, by appealing to ostensive definitions, we could determine a stable content (that is, stable conditions of application) for the word thus defined. But we cannot. For a stable content to be determined by an ostensive definition à la Putnam, *the dimension of similarity to the demonstrated exemplars must itself be fixed.*[40] But what fixes the dimension of similarity? On Waismann's picture, words are associated with situations of use, that is all. To apply the word to or in a novel situation, that situation must be similar to the source situations; but we cannot survey in advance all the possible dimensions of similarity between the source situations and possible target situations: open texture again.

According to Putnam, the predicate 'water' means something like: 'same-L as the transparent, odourless, thirst-quenching stuff to be found in lakes and rivers in the local environment', or more simply 'same-L as *that*' (pointing to a sample of water). If we change the demonstrated stuff (that is, the liquid which satisfies the stereotype of water in the local environment) we thereby change the extension of 'water'. 'Water', therefore, has an indexical component, Putnam says. Yet there is another form of context-sensitivity in play here, which Putnam's ostensive definitions do not properly capture: *the dimension of similarity itself is not given, but contextually determined.* In some contexts the chemical composition of the demonstrated stuff will be relevant, in other

---

[40] As McKay and Stern point out, 'to determine the extension of the natural kind term, we need, in addition to the sample, at least some indication of the breadth of the term – the respects in which other individuals [in the extension] must be related to the sample' (Thomas McKay and Cindy Stern, 'Natural Kind Terms and Standards of Membership', in *Linguistics and Philosophy* 3 (1979), p. 27).

contexts only functional properties will be relevant.[41] Accordingly XYZ will count as water in some contexts simply because it's that liquid which is odourless, colourless, quenches thirst, and can be found in lakes and rivers. If the conversation bears on the issue of what currently fills a certain bottle, milk or water, then plainly the answer 'It's water' will be true, even if it's XYZ rather than H_2O.[42] Putnam himself expresses awareness of this point:

> x bears the relation same-L to y just in case (1) x and y are both liquids, and (2) x and y agree in important physical properties . . . Importance is an interest-relative notion. Normally the 'important' properties of a liquid or solid, etc., are the ones that are *structurally* important; the ones that specify what the liquid or solid, etc., is ultimately made out of . . . From this point of view the important characteristic of a typical bit of water is consisting of H_2O. But it may or may not be important that there are impurities . . . And structure may sometimes be unimportant; thus one may sometimes refer to XYZ as water if one is *using* it as water . . .
>
> Even senses that are so far out that they have to be regarded as a bit 'deviant' may bear a definite relation to the core sense. For example I might say 'did you see the lemon', meaning the *plastic* lemon. A less deviant case is this: we discover 'tigers' on Mars. That is, they look just like tigers, but they have a silicon-based chemistry instead of a carbon-based chemistry . . . Are Martian 'tigers' tigers? It depends on the context.[43]

We now have in hand all the ingredients necessary to define the theoretical position I want to ascribe to the (radical) contextualist: the irreducibly referential dimension of meaning; the central role of similarity in determining extension (hence truth-conditions); and finally the context-dependence of similarity relations. With those ingredients, we can concoct an extreme view very much in the spirit of Austin and Wittgenstein: Meaning Eliminativism.

9.6   Meaning Eliminativism

According to WF, the sense expressed by an expression must always be contextually constructed on the basis of the (overly rich or overly abstract) meaning, or semantic potential, of the word type. Just as the reference of an indexical expression is not linguistically given but must be contextually determined, the sense of an ordinary expression is not linguistically given but must be

---

[41] A reader of Saul Kripke's *Naming and Necessity* (Blackwell, 1980) might object as follows: We are concerned only with what words mean in our language, not with what they mean in other possible situations; now in our language water is H_2O, and 'This is water' is true iff the demonstrated stuff is H_2O. This pseudo-Kripkean objection is mistaken and easy to rebut. I am talking about *our* language. Our language is such that we can imagine contexts in which it would be true to say 'This is water' of some stuff if the stuff in question had certain phenomenal/functional properties, whether or not the thing in question was H_2O.

[42] Noam Chomsky, *New Horizons in the Study of Language and Mind* (Cambridge University Press, 2000), p. 41.

[43] Putnam, 'The Meaning of "Meaning" ', pp. 238–9.

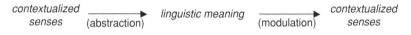

Figure 9.1 Abstraction and modulation

constructed. In that framework there still is a role for the linguistic meaning of word types: it is the input (or one of the inputs) to the construction process.

The difference between Meaning Eliminativism (ME) and WF is that, according to ME, we don't need linguistic meanings even to serve as input to the construction process. The senses that are the words' contributions to contents are constructed, but the construction can proceed without the help of conventional, context-independent word meanings.

Note that, according to a trivial extension of WF, the linguistic meaning of a word is not merely the input to the process of semantic modulation: it is also the output of a process of induction through which the child, or anyone learning the language, abstracts the meaning of the word from the specific senses which it expresses, or seems to express, on the observed occasions of use. It is a truism that the child or language learner starts not with pre-formatted linguistic meanings, but with actual uses of words and the contextualized senses that words assume on such uses. So both contextualized senses and context-independent linguistic meanings are input, and both are output, in some construction process. The linguistic meaning of a word type is the output of an abstraction process; that process takes as input the contextualized senses used as evidence by the language learner. On the other hand, the linguistic meaning of a word type also serves as input to the modulation process which yields as output the contextualized sense of the word on a particular occasion of use (figure 9.1).

ME purports to simplify WF by *suppressing the intermediary step* (linguistic meaning) and computing directly the contextual sense which an expression assumes on a particular occasion of use on the basis of the contextual senses which that expression had on previous occasions of use – without ever abstracting, or needing to abstract, 'the' linguistic meaning of the expression type.[44] This amounts to merging the two construction processes: the abstraction of meaning from use, and the modulation of meaning in use (figure 9.2). According to ME, there is a single process of abstraction-modulation which takes as input previous uses of the expression and yields as output the contextual sense assumed by the expression on the current use.

On the resulting picture, words are not primitively associated with abstract 'conditions of application', constituting their conventional meaning (as on the

---

[44] For a detailed psychological model supporting ME, see Douglas Hintzman, '"Schema Abstraction" in a Multiple-Trace Memory Model', in *Psychological Review* 93 (1986), 411–28, and 'Judgments of Frequency and Recognition Memory in a Multiple-Trace Memory Model', in *Psychological Review* 95 (1988), 528–51.

THE TRADITIONAL PICTURE:

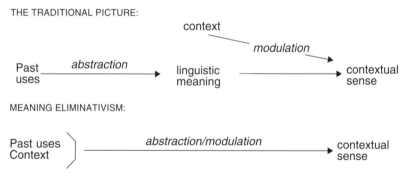

Figure 9.2 A single process of abstraction/ modulation

Fregean picture). The conditions of application for words must be contextually determined, like the reference of indexicals. What words, *qua* linguistic types, are associated with are not abstract conditions of application, but rather *particular applications*.

In the spirit of Wittgenstein, consider what it is for someone to learn a predicate P. The learner, whom I'll call Tom, observes the application of P in a particular situation S; he associates P and S. At this stage, the semantic potential of P for Tom is the fact that P is applicable to S. In a new situation S', Tom will judge that P applies only if he finds that S' sufficiently resembles S. To be sure, it is possible for S' to resemble S in a way that is not pertinent for the application of P. The application of P to S' will then be judged faulty by the community, who will correct Tom. The learning phase for Tom consists in noting a sufficient number of situations which, like S, legitimate the application of P, as opposed to those, like S', which do not legitimate it. The semantic potential of P for Tom at the end of his learning phase can thus be thought of as *a collection of legitimate situations of application*; that is, a collection of situations such that the members of the community agree that P applies in or to those situations. The situations in question are the *source-situations*. The future applications of P will be underpinned, in Tom's usage, by the judgment that the situation of application (or *target-situation*) is similar to the source-situations.

In this theory the semantic potential of P is *a collection of source-situations*, and the conditions of application of P in a given use, involving a given target-situation S'', are *a set of features which S'' must possess to be similar to the source-situations*. The set of features in question, and so the conditions of application for P, will not be the same for all uses; it is going to depend, among other things, on the target-situation. One target-situation can be similar to the source-situations in certain respects and another target-situation can be similar to them in different respects. But the contextual variability of the conditions of application does not end there. Even once the target-situation is fixed, the relevant dimensions for evaluating the similarity between that situation and the source-situations remain underdetermined: those dimensions will vary as a function of the subject of conversation, the concerns of the speech participants, and so on.

One particularly important factor in the contextual variation is the relevant 'contrast set'. As Tversky has pointed out, judgments of similarity are very much affected by variations along that dimension.[45] If we ask which country, Sweden or Hungary, most resembles Austria (without specifying the relevant dimension of similarity), the answer will depend on the set of countries considered. If that set includes not just Sweden, Hungary and Austria but also Poland, then Sweden will be judged more like Austria than Hungary; but if the last of the four countries considered is Norway and not Poland, then it is Hungary which will be judged more like Austria than Sweden. The explanation for that fact is simple. Poland and Hungary have certain salient geopolitical features in common which can serve as basis for the classification: Hungary and Poland are then put together and opposed to Austria and Sweden. If we replace Poland by Norway in the contrast set a new principle of classification emerges, based on the salient features shared by Norway and Sweden: in this new classification Hungary and Austria are put together. Tversky concludes that judgments of similarity appeal to features having a high 'diagnostic value' (or classificatory significance), and that the diagnostic value of features itself depends on the available contrast set.

So the set of similarity features on which sense depends itself depends upon the relevant contrast set, and the relevant contrast set depends upon the current interests of the conversational participants. It follows that one can, by simply shifting the background interests ascribed to the conversational participants, change the truth-conditions of a given utterance, even though the facts (including the target-situation) don't change, and the semantic values of indexicals remain fixed. Charles Travis has produced dozens of examples of this phenomenon of truth-conditional shiftiness over the last thirty years, and his examples often involve manipulating the relevant contrast-set.[46]

---

[45] See Amos Tversky, 'Features of Similarity', in *Psychological Review* 84 (1977), 327–52.

[46] See Charles Travis, *Saying and Understanding* (Blackwell, 1975), *The True and the False* (Benjamins, 1981), *The Uses of Sense* (Clarendon Press, 1989), and *Unshadowed Thought* (Harvard University Press, 2000). The following example, inspired by Austin, is taken at random from a list of Travis-examples compiled by Claudia Bianchi (then a graduate student of mine): 'Fred is walking with his young nephew beside a pond where a decoy duck is floating. Pointing to the decoy, he says, "That's a duck." Again we might ask whether what he said is true or false. But again, the above description is not enough for us to tell. If Fred has just finished laughing at a sportsman who blasted a decoy out of the pond, and if he has been trying to show his nephew how to avoid similar mistakes, then what he said is false. But suppose that Fred and his nephew are attending the annual national decoy exhibition, and the boy has been having

In this framework the background-dependence of truth-conditions emphasized by Searle is accounted for by appealing to the *global* character of the similarity between target-situation and source-situations. As Waismann stresses, the source-situations are concrete situations with an indefinite number of features. Some of these features are ubiquitous and their diagnostic value in a normal situation is vanishing.[47] They belong to the most general and immutable aspects of our experience of the world: gravity, the fact that food is ingested via the mouth, and so on. When we specify the truth-conditions of a sentence (for example the sentence 'The cat is on the mat'), or the conditions of application of a predicate (for example the predicate 'on' in that sentence), we only mention a small number of features – the 'foreground' features – because we take most of the others for granted; so we do not mention gravity, we presuppose it. Nevertheless, gravity is one of the features possessed by the situations which are at the source of the predicate 'on'; and there is an indefinite number of such features. These background features of the source-situations can be ignored inasmuch as they are shared by the situations of which we may wish to speak when we utter the sentence; but if we imagine a target-situation where the normal conditions of experience are suspended, and where certain background features of the source-situations are not present, then we shatter the global similarity between the target-situation and the source-situations. *Even if the target-situation has all the foreground features which seem to enter into the 'definition' of a predicate P, it suffices to suspend a certain number of background features in order to jeopardize the application of P to the target-situation.* That shows that the semantic potential of P is not, as in Fregean semantics, a set of conditions of application determined once and for all, but a collection of source-situations such that P applies to a target-situation if and only if it is relevantly similar to the source-situations.

A caveat: as Searle himself emphasizes, the fact that the target-situation does *not* possess certain background features of the source-situations does not automatically entail the non-applicability of the predicate P. It can be that the background features which the target-situation does not possess (for example gravity) are contextually irrelevant and do not affect the application conditions of the predicate.[48] For the same sort of reason, the possession by the

trouble distinguishing ducks from geese. Then what Fred said may well be true. It would also be true had Fred said what he did in pointing out the fact that all the other ducks were poor copies (perhaps on the order of Donald Duck).' (*Saying and Understanding*, p. 51).

[47] See Tversky, 'Features of similarity', p. 342: 'The feature "real" has no diagnostic value in the set of actual animals since it is shared by all actual animals and hence cannot be used to classify them. This feature, however, acquires considerable diagnostic value if the object set is extended to include legendary animals, such as a centaur, a mermaid or a phoenix.'

[48] It is easy to imagine a context with respect to which it would be definitely true to say 'the cat is on the mat' of the gravitationless situation described by Searle: 'For example, as we are strapped in the seats of our spaceship in outer space we see a series of cat-mat pairs floating past

target-situation of what I have called the foreground features of the source-situations is no more a necessary condition for the application of the predicate than it is a sufficient condition. For a predicate (or a sentence) to apply to a target-situation that situation must resemble the source-situations under the contextually relevant aspects. So a predicate can apply even if the target-situation differs markedly from the source-situations, as long as, in the context and taking into account the contrast set, the similarities are more significant than the differences. Thus, in certain contexts, as Putnam notices, the predicate 'lemon' will apply to plastic lemons, or the word 'water' to XYZ.

9.7   Conclusion

Meaning Eliminativism gets rid of abstract meanings for types, in favour of particular uses. The contextualized sense carried by the word on a particular use depends upon similarity relations between that use of the word (as applied to the 'target-situation') and past uses of the same word (as applied to the 'source-situations'). The features of similarity that are perceived are so context-dependent (and in particular, contrast-dependent) that the truth-conditional sense of the word is susceptible to vary, and to vary more or less indefinitely, even after we have fixed (i) the collection of past situations of use, (ii) the target-situation in which or to which the word is currently applied, and (iii) the reference of indexicals and the semantic values of all expressions in need of saturation.

Meaning Eliminativism is, as I said, the most extreme form of Contextualism. It is probably too extreme, but what strikes me most in that framework is its surprising viability. The knock-down objections such an extreme view is supposed to raise (and does raise in the classroom) do not sound so devastating when explicitly stated. To close this chapter, let me briefly consider two standard objections to the elimination of linguistic meaning.

The first objection (which I may have heard about fifty times) runs like this. Granted, the senses expressed by words are affected by contextual factors; they are 'modulated'. But we *must* treat modulation effects as arising from the interaction of context with context-independent linguistic meanings. If, instead, we go eliminativist and say that the context does everything, while the words themselves contribute nothing, then it does not matter any more whether the word one utters is 'red' or 'rectangle'. But it makes a big difference which word we actually utter. This shows that Meaning Eliminativism goes too far: it throws out the baby with the bathwater.

our window. Oddly, they come in only two attitudes. From our point of view they are either as depicted in figure 1 or as would be depicted if figure 1 were upside down. "Which is it now?", I ask. "The cat is on the mat", you answer. Have you not said exactly and literally what you meant?' (Searle, 'Literal Meaning', p. 212.)

This objection presupposes that, for the eliminativist, 'the words themselves contribute nothing'. But that is not true. There is something which words do contribute, and which is sufficient to account for the difference it makes when we substitute a word for another one. That thing is not a 'meaning' in the traditional sense: it is what I called the 'semantic potential' of words. 'Red' and 'rectangle' have very different semantic potentials. The semantic potential of a word is the collection of past uses on the basis of which similarities can be established between the source situations (that is, the situations such uses concerned) and the target situation (the situation of current concern). So there is, indeed, interaction between the 'context' and what words themselves contribute. Context does not do everything, even on the most extreme form of Contextualism.

According to the second objection, there is actually more stability in semantic content than ME suggests. Not only do words have relatively stable conditions of application, across uses; there is also interpersonal stability: language users converge in their judgments regarding conditions of application or truth-conditions. How will that stability be accounted for?

With regard to the first part of the objection the contextualist pleads guilty: the unstability and shiftiness of truth-conditional content across uses he takes to be an empirical fact, sufficiently established by the wealth of examples and thought-experiments provided by the authors I have mentioned. Still, according to the objection, the contextualist goes too far in that direction. But the contextualist will deny that that is so. The degree of unstability achieved will depend upon details of the model, and can be varied so as to fit experimental data. (See Hintzman's papers for suggestions.) As for the second part of the objection, the contextualist will be happy to grant the interpersonal stability of truth-conditional content. That stability can be accounted for on psychological rather than linguistic grounds. Thus Bolinger notes that

speakers not only share the same code but also share the ability to see the same resemblances between what their code already designates and what they would like it to designate, and so to make the old forms reach out to new meanings. That is how language breaks free of its rigidity.[49]

In any event, there are all sorts of versions of the contextualist position which are intermediate between WF and ME. Like Rumelhart and most lexical semanticists, we may consider that words are associated not so much with (a collection of) particular, episodic situations of use, but with more abstract schemata corresponding to types of situations. Insofar as there still is a referential or quasi-referential dimension in virtue of which, through these schemata, words point to actual situations of use, the basic mechanisms posited by ME remain in play. Or we may favour a model in which both episodic traces of

[49] Bolinger, *Aspects of Language*, p. 230.

situations of use and abstract schemata are stored and exploited in contextually determining truth-conditional content. Whichever option we take the important contextualist idea should not be misconstrued. How much abstraction takes place is not the issue, for the contextualist. The important idea – which forms the core of Austin's theory of truth – is twofold: first, words are associated with worldly situations (at whatever level of abstractness and fine-grainedness), that is, entities at the level of reference rather than the level of sense; second, the content (sense) of words depends upon context-sensitive similarities between those situations and the target-situation in which or to which the word is applied.

Conclusion

At the beginning of chapter 6, I said that the debate between Literalism and Contextualism, which stood at the forefront of attention in the middle of the twentieth century, is widely, and wrongly, believed to have been settled in favour of (an attenuated version of) Literalism. My aim, in this book, has been to revive that debate, and to show that Contextualism is still a live option. By 'Contextualism' I mean the view according to which it is speech acts, not sentences, which have a determinate content and are truth-evaluable: sentences themselves express a determinate content only in the context of a speech act. In this concluding chapter I will summarize the discussion and deal with a few residual issues.

10.1   Alleged arguments against Contextualism

First, I should say something of the philosophical arguments which, in the sixties, led to the demise of Contextualism. Two arguments, in particular, have been so generally taken to constitute a complete and final refutation of Contextualism, that I cannot close this book without saying what is wrong with them. One argument, due to Peter Geach, makes use of what he calls the 'Frege point'. The other, due to Paul Grice, invokes a principle which he calls 'Modified Occam's Razor'.

The Frege Point is the view that 'a thought may have just the same content whether you assent to its truth or not; a proposition may occur in discourse now asserted, now unasserted, and yet be recognizably the same proposition'.[1] Now proponents of Contextualism hold that sentences have determinate contents only in the context of a speech act. This, according to Geach, conflicts with the Frege point. A sentence that is unasserted because, say, it occurs as the antecedent in a conditional or as one of the disjuncts in a disjunction may nevertheless possess a determinate, truth-evaluable content, and must do so in

---

[1] Peter Geach, 'Assertion', in *Logic Matters* (Blackwell, 1972), pp. 254–5. By 'proposition' Geach means 'a form of words in which something is propounded, put forward for consideration' (p. 255).

order for the complex sentence in which it occurs itself to express a determinate, truth-evaluable content:

Oxford-trained philosophers often say nowadays that a sentence can have a truth value assigned to it only in that it is 'used to make a statement' in a given context. If this were literally true, then a truth-functional account of '*p vel q*' or of '*p aut q*' would be impossible: for the disjunct clauses represented by '*p*' and '*q*' would not be being 'used to make statements' in a context in which only the disjunction was asserted, and would thus not have any truth values for the truth value of the whole proposition to be a function of.[2]

But this objection misses its target. What matters, from the contextualist point of view, is not whether or not a sentence is asserted. Sentences are said to carry determinate contents only insofar as they are used to make a statement (or to perform another speech act). The unasserted clauses that occur in conditionals or disjunctions satisfy this constraint no less than the complex sentences in which they occur: the speech act which the *complex* sentence is used to perform is sufficient to endow the *constituent sentences* (as much as the complex sentence itself) with a determinate content. It is not necessary that the constituent sentences be used to perform a speech act of their own. Thus I agree with Aaron Snyder's rebuttal of Geach's argument:

Geach claims that, in a context in which only the disjunction, '*p vel q*' was asserted, the disjunct clauses represented by '*p*' and '*q*' would not be being used to make statements. However, they certainly would be being used to make the statement that *p vel q*. It might be that Geach means that they would not be being used to make the statements that *p* and that *q*, respectively. But if this is what he means, his argument is an *ignoratio elenchi*, for it counts against only such specific theories as would hold that the sentence represented by '*p*' has truth value only in that it is used to make the statement that *p*.[3]

Note that the speech acts (or thought acts) in the context of which sentences are said to carry determinate contents need not be construed too restrictively. The list will include supposing that *p* and making as if to say that *p*, as well as asserting that *p*.

I turn to the Gricean argument, the influence of which was decisive in the downfall of Contextualism. That argument actually is a counterargument: it aims at undermining the standard contextualist argument, which we may call 'the argument from the contextual variability of truth-conditions'. The contextualist argument runs as follows: in an indefinite number of cases, one and the same sentence can be used to make different statements, with different truth-conditions, depending on the context; this shows that the sentence itself does not carry definite truth-conditions. For example, in *Introduction to Logical Theory*,

---

[2] *Ibid.*, p. 258. Geach uses the Latin words 'vel' and 'aut' as connectives corresponding to the inclusive ('vel') and exclusive ('aut') readings of 'or'.

[3] Aaron Snyder, 'On What Has Truth-Value', in *Philosophical Studies* 23 (1972), p. 131.

Strawson claims that there is a difference between the logical formula '$p \wedge q$' and the natural-language sentence 'p and q': while the former is logically equivalent to '$q \wedge p$', the statement made by 'They had a child and got married' is not the same as the statement made by 'They got married and had a child'; in the latter case, Strawson points out, the order of the clauses 'may be relevant . . . to the truth-conditions', while the truth-conditions of '$p \wedge q$' are given by the truth-table for '$\wedge$' and are therefore independent of the order of the clauses.[4] Whether the order of the clauses is actually relevant to the truth-conditions of a given utterance of 'p and q' depends on the context. In Strawson's terminology, there are various 'uses' of 'and' in natural language, corresponding to different truth-conditions for 'p and q'. Sometimes a sentence 'p and q' is used to say that p and then q, and sometimes it is used to say something different (for example the same thing as '$p \wedge q$'). There is no 'rule' fixing definite truth-conditions for 'p and q' independent of the context, contrary to what happens in the case of '$p \wedge q$'.

To counter that argument, in this and other cases, Grice has shown – convincingly, I think – that another explanation of the (apparent) variability of truth-conditions is available, consistent with the claim that the sentence carries definite truth-conditions. Not only is such an alternative explanation available: according to the Gricean argument, it is to be preferred, on methodological grounds. That is what I find dubious and controversial. I think Grice's methodological argument, to the effect that a non-contextualist explanation is superior to a contextualist explanation, rests on a fallacy which I am going to expose.

In 'Contextualism and Anti-Contextualism' I have reconstructed the Gricean argument as resting on two main premises – one explicit and the other implicit. I start with the implicit premiss:

Parallelism Principle
If a (syntactically complete) sentence can be used, in different contexts, to say different things (to express different propositions), this is evidence that the sentence has different linguistic meanings and is therefore ambiguous.

To be sure, another explanation for a contextual variation of content is possible (and actually preferable) when the sentence contains an indexical expression; for indexical sentences express different propositions in different contexts without being semantically ambiguous. But indexicality is taken to be a well-circumscribed phenomenon. Indexicality is the characteristic property of a finite class of expressions, the members of which are well known: personal pronouns, demonstratives, tenses, some adverbs indicating location in space and time, some predicates such as 'come', etc. If a sentence which

---

[4] Strawson, *Logical Theory*, pp. 80–1.

expresses different propositions in different contexts does not contain one of these recognizable expressions, or if the contextual variation in propositional content seems unrelated to the fact that it contains one, then we may safely use the Parallelism Principle to conclude that the sentence is semantically ambiguous.

The second premiss in the Gricean argument is what Grice called Modified Occam's Razor:[5]

Modified Occam's Razor
Senses (linguistic meanings) are not to be multiplied beyond necessity.

By virtue of Modified Occam's Razor, the analyst who observes that a sentence has two different interpretations when uttered in different contexts must refrain from considering that this intuitive difference in interpretation reflects a difference in linguistic meaning, that is, a semantic ambiguity. She must, if possible, ascribe this difference to a property of the context of utterance rather than to an ambiguity in the sentence itself.

Together, Modified Occam's Razor and the Parallelism Principle entail that the analyst must not only refrain from considering that a contextual difference in interpretation reflects a difference in linguistic meaning, but also refrain from considering that it reflects a difference in propositional content, in 'what is said' by the sentence when it is uttered in this or that context. For suppose we take the difference in interpretation to be a difference in propositional content. Then, by virtue of the Parallelism Principle, this difference in content is to be explained in terms of a difference in linguistic meaning (semantic ambiguity); but positing a semantic ambiguity is precisely what Modified Occam's Razor says the analyst should refrain from doing. It follows that the analyst must, if possible, explain the contextual difference in interpretation by a property of the context of utterance, while maintaining that the sentence itself is not ambiguous and that 'what is strictly and literally said' (the propositional content) does not change from one context to the next.

A general solution along these lines has been sketched by Grice, based on the notion of conversational implicature. A conversational implicature is something which is communicated by an utterance and therefore belongs to its overall interpretation, but which belongs neither to the linguistic meaning of the sentence uttered nor to what is said by the utterance of this sentence; it is an aspect of interpretation that is *external* to what is said. (Indeed, working out the implicatures of an utterance presupposes identifying what this utterance 'says'.) Modified Occam's Razor and the Parallelism Principle lead one to favour an analysis that accounts for a contextual difference in interpretation in terms of conversational implicature, over an account in terms of a variation in

---

[5] Grice, *Way of Words*, pp. 47–50.

propositional content. This is, basically, the Gricean argument against Contextualism. In the case of 'and', the argument proceeds as follows:

(i) Instead of saying, with Strawson, that there is a semantic difference between '$p \wedge q$' and 'p and q', we may consider that there is no such difference and that the truth-conditions of 'p and q' are actually the same as those of '$p \wedge q$'. For example, we may consider the temporal implication in 'They got married and had a child' as a conversational implicature, external to what is said, rather than considering it as part of the truth-conditions of the utterance in a certain type of context. In this way, we are able to maintain that the truth-conditions of 'p and q' are determined by the truth-table for '$\wedge$', independently of the context of utterance.

(ii) By virtue of Modified Occam's Razor and the Parallelism Principle, the account in terms of conversational implicature is preferable to the account in terms of a truth-conditional difference between '$p \wedge q$' and 'p and q'.

As I hope the reconstruction makes clear, the argument is fallacious, because it begs the question. It involves a premiss, namely the Parallelism Principle, which a contextualist cannot accept. Certainly, for a contextualist, it is not true, even in general, that a variation of propositional content has to be accounted for in terms of a variation in linguistic meaning. The contextualist holds that the propositional content of an utterance depends on the context and not just on the linguistic meaning of the sentence. It follows that a contextual variation in the propositional content of the utterance does not entail a corresponding variation in the linguistic meaning of the sentence. The Parallelism Principle has therefore to be dropped, but if it is dropped, then Modified Occam's Razor can no longer be used to show that an account in terms of implicature is preferable to an account in terms of a contextual variation in propositional content. Modified Occam's Razor shows that an account in terms of implicature is preferable to an account in terms of *semantic ambiguity*, but an account in terms of contextually variable propositional content can no longer be reduced to an account in terms of semantic ambiguity, once the Parallelism Principle is dropped. I conclude that the Gricean argument succeeds only by begging the question against Contextualism.[6]

---

[6] In actual practice, the Parallelism Principle is not explicitly stated as a premiss of the Gricean argument. However, Modified Occam's Razor (or an equivalent principle of economy) is used to support the conclusion that an account in terms of implicature is preferable to an account in terms of truth-conditional content, and I believe that Modified Occam's Razor can be used to that effect *only if* one accepts the Parallelism Principle. So the latter is actually *presupposed* by the Gricean argument. (In 'Contextualism and Anti-Contextualism', I gave two examples of actual uses of the Gricean argument. The first example is its use by Grice himself, against Strawson's treatment of 'and'. The second example is a classical use of the Gricean argument – by Kripke and many others – against Donnellan's view of the referential/attributive distinction. The Gricean argument against Donnellan is extensively discussed in my 'Referential/Attributive: A Contextualist Proposal', in *Philosophical Studies* 56 (1989), 217–49, and in *Direct Reference*,

10.2   Remnants of Literalism

Literalism minimizes context-sensitivity. It strives at preserving the view that the proposition expressed by a (complete) sentence *is* the linguistic meaning of that sentence – or one of its meanings, if the sentence is ambiguous. The only exception that is provided for is indexicality. But indexicality is not considered as a threat to the general picture, for two reasons. First, as I pointed out in discussing the Parallelism Principle, indexicality is (or was) taken to be a limited, well-circumscribed phenomenon, concerning a restricted class of natural language expressions: 'I', 'here', 'now', 'today', 'this', and so on. Indexicals are 'l'exception qui confirme la règle', as the French say. The proposition expressed by a sentence is its conventional, linguistic meaning – *unless* a recognizable indexical expression occurs in the sentence, forcing us to draw an otherwise useless distinction between linguistic meaning ('character') and propositional 'content'. Second, it was thought that so-called 'pure indexicals' were typical. Now in the case of pure indexicals there is a linguistic rule that determines content in context, quite independently of 'speaker's meaning'.[7] So, even if the linguistic meaning of the sentence cannot be equated to the content it expresses, because of context-sensitivity, still it fully determines that content.

Contextualism makes the opposite claims. First, pure indexicals are not representative of the whole class of context-sensitive expressions. Semantically underdeterminate expressions are such that the content they contextually express depends upon the speaker's meaning, thus blurring the semantics/ pragmatics distinction. Second, the distinction between linguistic meaning and propositional content must be generalized. We don't know in advance which expressions are context-sensitive and which are not. It follows that there are, in principle, three ways of handling examples in which the utterance of the same sentence has different interpretations depending on the context. One may (A) consider the sentence as semantically ambiguous, or (B) consider that the propositional content (the truth-conditions) of the utterance depends on the context, or (C) account for the difference in interpretation by positing a conversational implicature or some other meaning component that is external to what is said and combines with it in some contexts but not others. Modified Occam's Razor may provide a reason for avoiding (A) if possible, but it does not provide an argument against (B), contrary to what is often claimed. By assuming the Parallelism Principle, literalists unjustifiably do *as if* solution (B) was not a genuine possibility; they recognize the possibility of solution (B) only when the

---

pp. 284–8. See also Anne Bezuidenhout, 'Pragmatics, Semantic Underdetermination, and the Referential/Attributive Distinction', in *Mind* 106 (1997), 375–409.)

[7] As Barwise and Perry write, 'even if I am fully convinced that I am Napoleon, my use of "I" designates me, not him. Similarly, I may be fully convinced that it is 1789, but it does not make my use of "now" about a time in 1789' (*Situations and Attitudes*, p. 148).

sentence is a standard (that is, an already familiar type of) indexical sentence. This simply begs the question and hinders research.

I conclude that, even if one is attracted to literalist conclusions, one should not beg the question and take those conclusions for granted. One should at least adhere to a weak form of Contextualism, which I have called 'Methodological Contextualism'.[8] Methodological Contextualism says that there is, in principle, a difference between the linguistic meaning of the sentence and what is said by an utterance of the sentence, and a correlative difference between the linguistic meaning (or semantic potential) of an expression and the contribution the expression makes to the proposition expressed by the sentence where it occurs. Any expression may, upon analysis, turn out to have a context-sensitive semantics, that is, be such that its truth-conditional contribution varies across contexts. Whether or not that is the case, in a particular instance, is a matter for empirical analysis, not for a priori stipulation.

In semantics, over the past twenty years, those lessons have been drawn. The distinction between linguistic meaning and propositional content has been generalized, and a number of new sources of context-sensitivity have been discovered in natural language constructions. The indexicalist position defended by Jason Stanley is typical in this regard. In his framework indexical variables can be found all over the place; and the role of pragmatics and speaker's meaning in contextually assigning values to those variables is fully acknowledged. Does this mean that Literalism has been defeated? No. Literalism survives, in a weaker form, through the minimalist principle, which Stanley formulates as follows:

All effects of extra-linguistic context on the truth-conditions of an assertion are traceable to elements in the actual syntactic structure of the sentence uttered.[9]

This excludes 'top-down' or 'strong' pragmatic effects on truth-conditions. Such an exclusion I find as dogmatic and stipulative as the literalist restriction of context-sensitivity to a short list of familiar indexical expressions. If we give up (strong) Literalism and admit that the content of an utterance is not entirely fixed by linguistic rules, but has to be contextually determined by making sense of the speaker's speech act, is it not obvious that some aspects of content may happen to be contributed entirely by context? Why insist that *all* aspects of content must be traceable to aspects of linguistic form, if not because one is still in the grip of the literalist prejudice? Can we ignore the cases in which the meaning of words is adjusted to the situation talked about, or treat modulation as irrelevant to truth-conditional content, without, once again, taking a stipulative and question-begging stance on empirical matters?

---

[8] Recanati, 'Contextualism and Anti-Contextualism', p. 166.
[9] Stanley, 'Context and Logical Form', p. 391.

Minimalism can be defended, by explicitly going stipulative. One may grant the existence, or at least the possibility, of strong pragmatic effects, while defining 'the proposition literally expressed by an utterance' in such a way that it can only satisfy the minimalist constraint. In other words, one may draw a distinction between what is said in the intuitive sense – the actual content of one's utterance – and the proposition which can be assigned to that utterance as its 'literal' content, that is, the minimal content that results from contextually assigning values to all indexical or free variables. That is the gist of the 'Syncretic View'. In this framework the proposition literally expressed satisfies Minimalism by definition: it does not incorporate the output of pragmatic processes unless they are mandatory and triggered by elements in the syntactic structure of the sentence.

What is the point of positing such a minimal proposition? As I have been at pains to emphasize, the minimal proposition is not computed and does not play a role in the actual process of interpretation. Bach says we need it to account for 'the character of the information available to the hearer'.[10] The minimal proposition, he says, is 'included in the information available to the hearer in understanding an utterance'.[11] What this means, presumably, is that the hearer knows the literal semantic values of the constituents, and knows the appropriate composition rules. He should therefore be credited with the ability to compose those values so as to determine the literal semantic value of the whole – the minimal proposition. In practice, that need not be done. Since primary pragmatic processes, including those that are optional, take place locally, the interpreter does not actually compose the literal semantic values of the constituents to determine the minimal proposition; rather, he directly determines what is said (in the intuitive sense) by composing the pragmatic values resulting from whatever pragmatic processes locally operate on the literal semantic values of the constituents.[12] Be that as it may, the minimal proposition is said to be 'available to the hearer, even if not actually accessed'.[13] The interpreter does not compute it, but he could.

In chapter 9, I have questioned the claim that, independent of modulation, it is possible to determine a minimal proposition by mechanically composing the literal semantic values of the constituents. It is, I think, essential to realize that that literalist assumption, pervasive though it is among philosophers of language, rests on a substantial and highly controversial conception of both word meaning and sentence meaning.

In this concluding chapter, I would like to explore a residual issue, pertaining to the relations between the view I have just ascribed to Bach (according to which the minimal proposition is 'consciously accessible' even if it is not

---

[10] Bach, 'Conversational Impliciture', p. 158.   [11] *Ibid.*, p. 159.
[12] See above, pp. 64–5.   [13] Bach, 'Conversational Impliciture', p. 158.

'consciously accessed')[14] and my own view regarding the availability of what is said. In 'Gricean Rational Reconstructions', Carpintero has argued that, if one accepts the availability of what is said, while giving a dispositional account of availability (as I myself did in §3.6, in response to objections from relevance theorists), then one is led to embrace Minimalism; or at least, one no longer has any reason for rejecting Minimalism, contrary to what I claimed throughout this book.

10.3   Availability, Minimalism, and the dispositional/occurrent contrast

In discussing my Availability Principle, Kent Bach has argued that people's untutored intuitions are 'educable'.[15] Even though what is strictly and literally said by an utterance 'is not what people's intuitive judgments are focused on',[16] still 'it is easy to sensitize people's intuitions about what is said to Grice's cancellability test for what is not said'.[17] One has simply to give them 'the opportunity to make cancellability judgments or comparative judgments about what is said by explicitly qualified utterances as opposed to unqualified ones'.[18] Thus, according to Bach, even if 'I've had breakfast', in the appropriate context, is readily understood as asserting that the speaker has had breakfast on the day of utterance, still it is pretty clear, and should be granted by anybody, that this sentence differs from 'I've had breakfast today' in, precisely, not *saying* explicitly when the breakfast was had. This shows that the minimal proposition – what is strictly and literally said – is available, potentially at least, and can be accessed if necessary. According to Bach, considerations pertaining to what is strictly and literally said 'can play a dispositional role even when they do not play an explicit role. They lurk in the background, so to speak, waiting to be taken into account when there is special reason to do so.'[19]

In 'Gricean Rational Reconstructions', Manuel Carpintero defends Minimalism by arguing against the 'Wittgensteinian' assumption that 'semantic facts are those, and only those, which can easily become objects of conscious, explicit, occurrent judgments made by competent users of the language'.[20] Semantic facts, he claims, are known tacitly rather than explicitly; hence the fact that we are not consciously aware of the minimal proposition expressed by an utterance does not show that that proposition is not 'what is said' by that utterance. Carpintero stresses that he *accepts* my Availability Principle: he accepts that

---

[14] Bach, 'You Don't Say?', p. 25.
[15] Bach, 'Conversational Impliciture', p. 137.   [16] Bach, 'You Don't Say?', p. 26.
[17] *Ibid.*, p. 27, and 'Seemingly Semantic Intuitions', also p. 27.
[18] Bach, 'Seemingly Semantic Intuitions', pp. 26–7.   [19] Bach, 'You Don't Say?', p. 25.
[20] Carpintero, 'Gricean Rational Reconstructions', p. 116. This formulation is too strong. I am one of the alleged 'Wittgensteinians', and I certainly do not want to claim that *all* semantic facts must be available to language users. (See below.)

what is said must be available to the language users.[21] But he construes availability dispositionally rather than occurrently. Carpintero therefore distinguishes three positions. The 'Wittgensteinians', as he calls the contextualists, hold that what is said must be available in the strong sense, that is, can easily become objects of conscious, explicit, occurrent judgments (= 'CEO' judgments) made by competent users of the language. The 'Chomskians' reject the Availability Principle and appeal only to tacit knowledge of the sub-personal variety. Carpintero himself advocates an intermediate, 'Gricean' position, according to which semantic knowledge (including knowledge of what is said) 'is constituted by personal-level psychological states, like those easily accessible in the form of CEO-thoughts, and unlike the Chomskian states of tacit knowledge; but, like the latter, it is only available after reflection heuristically of a scientific character, taking as data intuitions about the evaluation of utterances relative to several circumstances'.[22] This position, Carpintero says, 'tries to navigate a middle course between the Scylla of the subpersonal view, and the Charibdis of the surface-psychological view, defended by Recanati and others'.[23]

I myself have given an analogous interpretation of 'availability' in chapter 3, when responding to objections from relevance theorists. The inference which gives rise to implicatures is available to interpreters, I said, but this availability need not be cashed out as involving on the part of the subject a CEO-inference. A tacit inference is sufficient, provided it is of the 'personal' variety, that is, provided the subject herself has the reflective capacities for making the inference explicit.[24] If we generalize this dispositional interpretation of availability, the Availability Principle can no longer be used to rule out the minimal proposition, on the grounds that it is not 'available' to the language users. On the contrary, it turns out that the pragmatic, Gricean conception of saying which I argued for in chapter 1 *is* compatible with the standard, minimalist conception of what is strictly and literally said.

In arguing against Minimalism in this book, I have taken for granted the strong availability requirement – the requirement that what is said be 'CEO-available'. But that requirement is too strong, according to Carpintero. Weak (that is, dispositional) availability is sufficient:

I share with Recanati and others the view that some form of 'first-personal availability' is required. However, the one attainable through the process of ordinary scientific-semantic theorizing is in my view quite enough. It also involves psychological processes, although not the sort of psychological process on which Recanati et al. focus: it requires us to

---

[21] 'I should say straight away that I sympathize to a certain extent with the attraction to assumptions, such as Recanati's Availability Principle. The Gricean picture of language use emphasizes that it is a rational process. Merely "sub-personal-level" states cannot account for this' (*ibid.*, p. 121).

[22] Carpintero, 'Gricean Rational Reconstructions', p. 123.

[23] *Ibid.*, p. 121.   [24] See above, p. 50.

evaluate our intuitions regarding the satisfaction or otherwise, of hypothesized truth-conditions of utterances, including the relevant expressions under different conceivable situations. I think that, ultimately, this is the source of the trouble. The writers whose views I have been discussing concentrate on, as it were, local psychological matters: the semantic intuitions of competent speakers about concrete utterances. The Gricean picture encourages us to focus on more global issues: semantic intuitions of competent speakers concerning the systematic contribution of semantic units to different utterances in different contexts.[25]

Note, however, that Carpintero himself presupposes that we have first-level intuitions regarding the truth-conditions of situated utterances.[26] By reflecting upon those intuitions, and varying the contexts with respect to which the linguistic material is taken to be interpreted, we are able to uncover the systematic contribution of recurring semantic units, thereby gaining second-level intuitions concerning the systematic contribution of semantic units to different utterances in different contexts. Now the first-level intuitions which Carpintero's account presupposes *are themselves CEO-intuitions*. So it is misleading to say that reflective availability of the sort attainable through the process of ordinary scientific-semantic theorizing 'is quite enough'. For that weak form of availability itself presupposes the stronger form: the minimal proposition (or, more generally, the systematic contribution of semantic units) is weakly or dispositionally available, only to the extent that the actual content of situated utterances is CEO-available. CEO-intuitions regarding individual utterances are the raw material from which a reflective user of the language can abstract the systematic contribution made by recurring units in those utterances.

Viewed in this light the issue becomes: should we, in our descriptions of the personal-level information available to language users, mention the minimal proposition *over and above* what is said in the intuitive sense? According to Carpintero, what justifies mentioning the minimal propositions is that we have (reflective, second level) intuitions regarding them. Now I do not deny that we have or can gain such reflective, metalinguistic intuitions. But I deny that the underlying reflective abilities are constitutive of our conversational competence. Even if we did not have such abilities – if, therefore, the systematic contribution of words and constructions across contexts was not even weakly available at the personal level, but was merely a matter of sub-personal, tacit knowledge – that would not hinder communication, or at least, that would not prevent it from taking place.[27]

---

[25] Carpintero, 'Gricean Rational Reconstructions', pp. 123–4.

[26] Semantic knowledge, Carpintero says, 'is meant to be available (. . .) through a theoretically driven abductive process *whose "empirical" basis lies in semantic intuitions*' (p. 127 n., emphasis mine).

[27] Carpintero thinks we need to be able to access the minimal proposition, when it is absurd or incoherent, in order to start the Gricean derivation of non-literal meaning: 'A good reason to trigger the derivation is that the literal (. . .) interpretation is 'incoherent'; the hypothesis that the

As it turns out, Carpintero demands *more* availability than I do. We both require CEO-availability regarding first-level intuitions. Carpintero takes reflective availability for second-level intuitions to be required also, but I don't. Reflective, dispositional availability is required for implicatures, because implicatures are constitutively reflective and inferential, on my account. Primary pragmatic processes are unreflective, and if we are able, or can be trained, to make explicit the step from linguistic meaning to pragmatic value by reflecting on the senses which the same recurring units can take in different contexts, this ability is not constitutive of the more basic ability to take that step unreflectively in interpreting a concrete utterance in a given context.

Note that, if Carpintero were right, that would rule out an account according to which word meaning is so abstract that it is not representable at the personal level. Now Carpintero himself accepts that there are semantic facts that are not personally available. Thus he writes:

I am not denying the relevance of empirical, subpersonal facts for the determination of the semantics of a given language. On the contrary, I think that many fine-grained semantic facts can only be adjudicated on that basis; I am thinking, for instance, of facts about binding constraints.[28]

Which facts belong to which category certainly is an empirical matter; so there is no reason to rule out, a priori, a contextualist account of word and sentence meaning along the lines of chapter 9, even if such an account entails the non-existence of 'minimal propositions'. I conclude that, here also, we need to embrace a methodological form of Contextualism: getting rid of the last literalist prejudice, we must stop *presupposing* that there is such a thing as the minimal proposition expressed by an utterance.

---

speaker is abiding by the conversational maxims, together with this first blush blatant violation of the first maxim of quality, then takes the audience (as indeed intended by the speaker) to the non-literal (. . .) one. 'Bill is not himself today' (which will be interpreted as non-literally meaning that today Bill lacks some of the attributes that characterize him) is a good example of this.' (p. 119).

But this is precisely what I deny when I insist that primary pragmatic processes take place locally and are not 'inferential'. See above, §2.2 (pp. 27–9). For a review of the psychological literature on how non-literal meaning is actually processed, see Gibbs, *The Poetics of Mind.*

[28] Carpintero, 'Gricean Rational Reconstructions', p. 124.

Bibliography

Ariel, Mira, 'Accessibility Theory: An Overview', in Ted Sanders, Joost Schilperoord and Wilbert Spooren (eds.), *Text Representation: Linguistic and Psycholinguistic Aspects* (John Benjamins, 2001), 29–87.

Atkins, Sue, 'The Contribution of Lexicography', in Madeleine Bates and Ralph Weischedel (eds.), *Challenges in Natural Language Processing* (Cambridge University Press, 1993), 37–75.

Atlas, Jay, *Philosophy without Ambiguity* (Clarendon Press, 1989).

Austin, John, 'Truth', in his *Philosophical Papers* (2nd edition, Oxford University Press, 1970), 119–33.

Bach, Kent, *Thought and Reference* (Oxford University Press, 1987).

'On Communicative Intentions: A Reply to Recanati', in *Mind and Language* 2 (1987), 141–54.

'Semantic Slack', in Savas Tsohatzidis (ed.), *Foundations of Speech Act Theory* (Routledge, 1994), 267–91.

'Conversational Impliciture', in *Mind and Language* 9 (1994), 124–62.

'The Semantics–Pragmatics Distinction: What it is and Why it Matters', in *Linguistische Berichte* 8 (1997), 33–50.

'The Myth of Conventional Implicature', in *Linguistics and Philosophy* 22 (1999), 327–66.

'You Don't Say?', in *Synthèse* 128 (2001), 15–44.

'Seemingly Semantic Intuitions', in Joseph Keim Campbell, Michael O'Rourke and David Schier (eds.), *Meaning and Truth* (Seven Bridges Press, 2002), 21–33.

Bach, Kent and Harnish, Mike, *Linguistic Communication and Speech Acts* (MIT Press, 1979).

Barsalou, Lawrence, 'Ad hoc Categories', in *Memory and Cognition* 11 (1983), 211–27.

Barsalou, Lawrence and Billman, Dorrit, 'Systematicity and Semantic Ambiguity', in D. Gorfein (ed.), *Resolving Semantic Ambiguity* (Springer, 1989), 146–203.

Bartsch, Renate, 'The Structure of Word Meanings: Polysemy, Metaphor, Metonymy', in Fred Landman and Frank Veltman (eds.), *Varieties of Formal Semantics* (Foris, 1984), 25–54.

Barwise, Jon, 'Situations, Facts, and True Propositions', in his collection *The Situation in Logic* (CSLI Publications, 1989), 221–54.

Barwise, Jon and Etchemendy, John, *The Liar: An Essay on Truth and Circularity* (Oxford University Press, 1987).

Barwise, Jon and Perry, John, *Situations and Attitudes* (MIT Press, 1983).

Benveniste, Emile, 'La Forme et le Sens dans le Langage', in his *Problèmes de Linguistique Générale* II (Gallimard, 1974), 215–38.

Berg, Jonathan, 'In Defense of Direct Belief: Substitutivity, Availability, and Iterability', in *Lingua e Stile* 33 (1998), 461–70.

Bezuidenhout, Anne, 'Pragmatics, Semantic Underdetermination, and the Referential/ Attributive Distinction', in *Mind* 106 (1997), 375–409.

Bianchi, Claudia, *La Dipendenza Contestuale: Per una Teoria Pragmatica del Significato* (Edizioni Scientifiche Italiane, 2001).

Blackburn, Patrick, 'Tense, Temporal Reference and Tense Logic', in *Journal of Semantics* 11 (1994), 83–101.

Blackburn, Patrick, de Rijke, Maarten and Venema, Yde, *Modal Logic* (Cambridge University Press, 2001).

Blakemore, Diane, *Understanding Utterances: An Introduction to Pragmatics* (Blackwell, 1992).

Bolinger, Dwight, *Aspects of Language* (Harcourt, Brace and World, 1968).

Borg, Emma, 'Saying What You Mean: Unarticulated Constituents and Communication' (typescript).

Braun, David, 'Demonstratives and Their Linguistic Meaning', in *Noûs* 30 (1996), 145–73.

Burge, Tyler, 'Content Preservation', in *Philosophical Review* 102 (1993), 457–88.

Campbell, Robin, 'Language Acquisition, Psychological Dualism and the Definition of Pragmatics', in Herman Parret, Marina Sbisà and Jeff Verschueren (eds.), *Possibilities and Limitations of Pragmatics* (Benjamins, 1981), 93–103.

Cappelen, Herman and Lepore, Ernie, 'On an Alleged Connection Between Indirect Speech and the Theory of Meaning', in *Mind and Language* 12 (1997), 278–96.

'Radical and Moderate Pragmatics: Does Meaning Determine Truth-Conditions?' (typescript).

Caramazza, Alfonso and Grober, Ellen, 'Polysemy and the Structure of the Subjective Lexicon', in Clea Rameh (ed.), *Semantics: Theory and Application* (Georgetown University Press, 1976), 181–207.

Carston, Robyn, 'Implicature, Explicature, and Truth-Theoretic Semantics', in Ruth Kempson (ed.), *Mental Representations: The Interface between Language and Reality* (Cambridge University Press, 1988), 155–81.

'Enrichment and Loosening: Complementary Processes in Deriving the Proposition Expressed?', in *Linguistische Berichte* 8 (1997), 103–27.

'Explicature and Semantics', in *UCL Working Papers in Linguistics* 12 (2000), 1–44.

'Linguistic Meaning, Communicated Meaning, and Cognitive Pragmatics', in *Mind and Language* 17 (2002), 127–48.

Thoughts and Utterances: The Pragmatics of Explicit Communication (Blackwell, 2002).

'Semantics and Conversational Implicature', forthcoming in the Proceedings of the Genoa conference *WOC 2002: The Semantics/Pragmatics Distinction*, to be published by CSLI Publications.

'Report on typescript by François Recanati called *Literal Meaning*' (typescript).

Chierchia, Gennaro, 'Scalar Implicatures, Polarity Phenomena, and the Syntax/ Pragmatics Interface' (forthcoming).

Chomsky, Noam, 'Changing Perspectives on Knowledge and Use of Language', in Myles Brand and Mike Harnish (eds.), *The Representation of Knowledge and Belief* (University of Arizona Press, 1986), 1–58.

New Horizons in the Study of Language and Mind (Cambridge University Press, 2000).

Clark, Herb, 'Bridging', in Peter Johnson-Laird and John Wason (eds.), *Thinking: Readings in Cognitive Science* (Cambridge University Press, 1977), 411–20.

Arenas of Language Use (University of Chicago Press, 1992).

Using Language (Cambridge University Press, 1996).

Cohen, Jonathan, 'Some Remarks on Grice's Views About the Logical Particles of Natural Language', in Yehoshua Bar-Hillel (ed.), *Pragmatics of Natural Languages* (Reidel, 1971), 50–68.

'A Problem About Ambiguity in Truth-Conditional Semantics', in *Analysis* 45 (1985), 129–35.

'How is Conceptual Innovation Possible?', in *Erkenntnis* 25 (1986), 221–38.

'The Semantics of Metaphor', in Andrew Ortony (ed.), *Metaphor and Thought* (2nd edn, Cambridge University Press, 1993), 58–70.

Crane, Tim (ed.), *The Contents of Experience* (Cambridge University Press, 1990).

Cresswell, Max, *Semantic Indexicality* (Kluwer, 1996).

Cruse, Alan, *Lexical Semantics* (Cambridge University Press, 1986).

Meaning in Language: An Introduction to Semantics and Pragmatics (Oxford University Press, 2000).

Dahl, Östen, 'On Points of Reference', in *Semantikos* 1 (1975), 45–61.

Dascal, Marcelo, 'Contextualism', in Herman Parret, Marina Sbisà and Jeff Verschueren (eds.), *Possibilities and Limitations of Pragmatics* (Benjamins, 1981), 153–77.

Davidson, Donald, *Inquiries into Truth and Interpretation* (Clarendon Press, 1984).

'Truth and Meaning', in his *Inquiries into Truth and Interpretation* (Clarendon Press, 1984), 17–36.

Dennett, Daniel, *Content and Consciousness* (Routledge and Kegan Paul, 1969).

'Toward a Cognitive Theory of Consciousness', in his *Brainstorms: Philosophical Essays on Mind and Psychology* (MIT Press, 1981), 149–73.

Dokic, Jérôme, 'Steps Toward a Theory of Situated Representations' (typescript).

Ducrot, Oswald, *Le Dire et le Dit*, Editions de Minuit, 1984.

Dummett, Michael 'Existence, Possibility, and Time' (typescript).

Evans, Gareth, 'Does Tense Logic Rest on a Mistake?', in his *Collected Papers* (Clarendon Press, 1995), 343–63.

Evans, Gareth and McDowell, John (eds.), *Truth and Meaning: Essays in Semantics* (Clarendon Press, 1976).

Fauconnier, Gilles and Turner, Mark, *The Way We Think: Conceptual Blending and the Mind's Hidden Complexities* (Basic Books, 2002).

Fillmore, Charles, 'Frame Semantics and the Nature of Language', in *Annals of the New York Academy of Sciences* 280 (1976), 20–32.

'Frame Semantics', in The Linguistic Society of Korea (ed.), *Linguistics in the Morning Calm* (Hanshin, 1982), 111–38.

'Frames and the Semantics of Understanding', in *Quaderni di Semantica* 6 (1985), 222–54.

'Pragmatically Controlled Zero Anaphora', in *Proceedings of the Annual Meeting of the Berkeley Linguistics Society* 12 (1986), 95–107.

Fillmore, Charles and Atkins, Sue, 'Toward a Frame-Based Lexicon: The Semantics of RISK and its Neighbors', in Adrienne Lehrer and Eva Kittay (eds.), *Frames, Fields and Contrasts: New Essays in Semantic and Lexical Organization* (Lawrence Erlbaum Associates, 1992), 75–102.

Fillmore, Charles and Kay, Paul, *Construction Grammar Coursebook* (typescript).

Fodor, Jerry, *The Modularity of Mind* (MIT Press, 1983).

Franks, Bradley, 'Sense Generation: A "Quasi-Classical" Approach to Concepts and Concept Combination', in *Cognitive Science* 19 (1995), 441–505.

Frege, Gottlob, 'Thought', in Michael Beaney (ed.), *The Frege Reader* (Blackwell, 1997), 325–45.

Kleine Schriften (Georg Olms, 1967).

Fuchs, Catherine, 'Polysémie, Interprétation et Typicalité', in Danièle Dubois (ed.), *Sémantique et Cognition: Catégories, Prototypes, Typicalité* (Editions du CNRS, 1991), 161–70.

Garcia-Carpintero, Manuel, 'Gricean Rational Reconstructions and the Semantics/Pragmatics Distinction', in *Synthèse* 128 (2001), 93–131.

Geach, Peter, 'Assertion', in his *Logic Matters* (Blackwell, 1972), 254–69.

Gerrig, Richard and Murphy, Gregory, 'Contextual Influences on the Comprehension of Complex Concepts', in *Language and Cognitive Processes* 7 (1992), 205–30.

Geurts, Bart, 'Donkey Business', in *Linguistics and Philosophy* 25 (2002), 129–156.

Gibbs, Raymond, *The Poetics of Mind: Figurative Thought, Language, and Understanding* (Cambridge University Press, 1994).

Gibbs, Raymond, and Moise, Jessica, 'Pragmatics in Understanding What is Said', in *Cognition* 62 (1997), 51–74.

Giora, Rachel, *On Our Mind: Salience, Context, and Figurative Language* (Oxford University Press, 2003).

Goschke, Thomas and Koppelberg, Dirk, 'Connectionist Representations, Semantic Compositionality, and the Instability of Concept Structure', in *Psychological Research* 52 (1990), 253–70.

Grandy, Richard, 'Understanding and the Principle of Compositionality', in *Philosophical Perspectives* 4 (1990), 557–572.

Grice, Paul, 'The Causal Theory of Perception', in *Proceedings of the Aristotelian Society*, Supplementary Volume 35 (1961), 121–52.

'Retrospective Epilogue', in his *Studies in the Way of Words* (Harvard University Press, 1989), 339–85.

Studies in the Way of Words (Harvard University Press, 1989).

Groefsema, Marjolein, 'Understood Arguments: A Semantic/Pragmatic Approach', in *Lingua* 96 (1995), 139–61.

Guillaume, Gustave, *Temps et Verbe* (Champion, 1929).

Hampton, James, 'Inheritance of Attributes in Natural Concept Conjunctions', in *Memory and Cognition* 15 (1987), 55–71.

Harman, Gilbert, 'Meaning and Semantics', in his *Reasoning, Meaning, and Mind* (Clarendon Press, 1999), 192–205.

Hintikka, Jaakko, 'Semantics for Propositional Attitudes', in his *Models for Modalities* (Reidel, 1969), 87–111.

Hintzman, Douglas, '"Schema Abstraction" in a Multiple-Trace Memory Model', in *Psychological Review* 93 (1986), 411–28.

'Judgments of Frequency and Recognition Memory in a Multiple-Trace Memory Model', in *Psychological Review* 95 (1988), 528–51.

Horn, Larry, *The Natural History of Negation* (Chicago University Press, 1989).

'The Said and the Unsaid', in Chris Barker and David Dowty (eds.), *SALT 2: Proceedings of the Second Conference on Semantics and Linguistic Theory* (Ohio State University Working Papers in Linguistics 40, 1992), 163–92.

Jackendoff, Ray, *The Architecture of the Language Faculty* (MIT Press, 1997).

Kaplan, David, 'Demonstratives', in Joseph Almog, Howard Wettstein and John Perry (eds.), *Themes from Kaplan* (Oxford University Press, 1989), 481–563.

King, Jeffrey and Stanley, Jason, 'Semantics, Pragmatics, and the Role of Semantic Content' (typescript).

Kotthoff, Helga, 'Irony, Quotation, and Other Forms of Staged Intertextuality', in Carl Graumann and Werner Kallmeyer (eds.), *Perspective and Perspectivation in Discourse* (Benjamins, 2002), 201–29.

Kripke, Saul, *Naming and Necessity* (Blackwell, 1980).

Kuroda, Yuki, 'Indexed Predicate Calculus', in *Journal of Semantics* 1 (1982), 43–59.

Lahav, Ron, 'Against Compositionality: The Case of Adjectives', in *Philosophical Studies* 57 (1989), 261–79.

Langacker, Ronald, 'Active Zones', in *Proceedings of the Annual Meeting of the Berkeley Linguistics Society* 10 (1984), 172–88.

Foundations of Cognitive Grammar, vol. 1 (Stanford University Press, 1987).

Levin, Beth, *English Verb Classes and Alternations* (University of Chicago Press, 1993).

Levinson, Stephen, *Pragmatics* (Cambridge University Press, 1983).

Presumptive Meanings: The Theory of Generalized Conversational Implicature (MIT Press, 2000).

Lewis, David, 'General Semantics', in *Synthèse* 22 (1970), 18–67.

'Attitudes *de dicto* and *de se*', reprinted (with a postscript) in his *Philosophical Papers* vol. 1 (Oxford University Press, 1983), 133–59.

Marr, David, *Vision: A Computational Investigation into the Human Representation and Processing of Visual Information* (Freeman, 1968).

Martin Jr, Edwin, 'Truth and Translation', in *Philosophical Studies* 23 (1972), 125–30.

Matsui, Tomoko, 'Experimental Pragmatics: Towards Testing Relevance-Based Predictions about Anaphoric Bridging Inferences', in Varol Akman, Paolo Bouquet, Richmond Thomason and Roger Young (eds.), *Modeling and Using Context* (Springer, 2001), 248–60.

McConnell-Ginet, Sally, 'Adverbs and Logical Form', in *Language* 58 (1982), 144–84.

McKay, Thomas and Stern, Cindy, 'Natural Kind Terms and Standards of Membership', in *Linguistics and Philosophy* 3 (1979), 27–34.

Medin, Douglas and Shoben, Edward, 'Context and Structure in Conceptual Combination', in *Cognitive Psychology* 20 (1988), 158–90.

Millikan, Ruth, *Language, Thought, and Other Biological Categories* (MIT Press, 1984).

Mitchell, Jonathan, *The Formal Semantics of Point of View*, PhD dissertation, University of Massachusetts, Amherst, 1986.

Montague, Richard, *Formal Philosophy: Selected Papers* (Richmond Thomason ed., Yale University Press, 1974).

Moravcsik, Julius, 'Is Snow White?', in Paul Humphreys (ed.), *Patrick Suppes: Scientific Philosopher* (Kluwer, 1994), 71–85.

Meaning, Creativity, and the Partial Inscrutability of the Human Mind (CSLI Publications, 1998).

Murphy, Gregory 'Noun Phrase Interpretation and Conceptual Combination', in *Journal of Memory and Language* 29 (1990), 259–88.

'The Comprehension of Complex Concepts', in *Cognitive Science* 12 (1988), 529–62.

Neale, Stephen, *This, That and the Other*, chapter 1 (typescript).

Nunberg, Geoffrey, 'The Non-Uniqueness of Semantic Solutions: Polysemy', in *Linguistics and Philosophy* 3 (1979), 143–84.

'Indexicality and Deixis', in *Linguistics and Philosophy* 16 (1993), 1–43.

'Transfers of Meaning', in *Journal of Semantics* 12 (1995), 109–32.

Nunberg, Geoff and Zaenen, Annie, 'Systematic Polysemy in Lexicology and Lexicography', in Hannu Tommola, Krista Varantola, Tarja Tolonen and Jürgen Schopp (eds.), *Proceedings of Euralex 2* (University of Tampere, 1992), Part II, 387–98.

Partee, Barbara, 'Some Structural Analogies Between Tenses and Pronouns in English', in *Journal of Philosophy* 70 (1973), 601–9.

'Compositionality', in Fred Landman and Frank Veltman (eds.), *Varieties of Formal Semantics* (Foris, 1984), 281–312.

'Binding Implicit Variables in Quantified Contexts', in *CLS* 25 (1989), 342–65.

Pelczar, Michael, 'Wittgensteinian Semantics', in *Noûs* 34 (2000), 483–516.

Perry, John, 'Thought Without Representation', reprinted (with a postscript) in his collection *The Problem of the Essential Indexical and Other Essays* (Oxford University Press, 1993), 205–25.

The Problem of the Essential Indexical and Other Essays (Oxford University Press, 1993).

Reference and Reflexivity (CSLI Publications, 2001).

Prandi, Michele, *Grammaire Philosophique des Tropes* (Editions de Minuit, 1992).

Prior, Arthur, *Past, Present, and Future* (Clarendon Press, 1967).

'Egocentric Logic', in Arthur Prior and Kit Fine, *Worlds, Times and Selves* (Duckworth, 1977), 28–45.

'Now', in *Noûs* 1 (1968), 101–19.

Pustejovsky, James, 'The Generative Lexicon', in *Computational Linguistics* 17 (1991), 409–41.

The Generative Lexicon (MIT Press, 1995).

Pustejovsky, James and Boguraev, Branimir, 'A Richer Characterization of Dictionary Entries: The Role of Knowledge Representations', in Sue Atkins and Antonio Zampolli (eds.), *Computational Approaches to the Lexicon* (Oxford University Press, 1994), 295–311.

Putnam, Hilary, 'The Meaning of "Meaning" ', in his *Philosophical Papers, vol. 2: Mind, Language and Reality* (Cambridge University Press, 1975), 215–71.

Quine, Willard van Orman, 'Variables Explained Away', in his *Selected Logic Papers* (Harvard University Press, 1995), 227–35.

Recanati, François, *La Transparence et l'Enonciation* (Editions du Seuil, 1979).

'Insinuation et Sous-Entendu', in *Communications* 30 (1979), 95–106.

'On Defining Communicative Intentions', in *Mind and Language* 1 (1986), 213–42.

'Contextual Dependence and Definite Descriptions', in *Proceedings of the Aristotelian Society* 87 (1987), 57–73.

Meaning and Force: The Pragmatics of Performative Utterances (Cambridge University Press, 1987).

'Rigidity and Direct Reference', in *Philosophical Studies* 53 (1988), 103–17.

'Referential/Attributive: A Contextualist Proposal', in *Philosophical Studies* 56 (1989), 217–49.

'The Pragmatics of What is Said', in *Mind and Language* 4 (1989), 295–329.

Direct Reference: From Language to Thought (Blackwell, 1993).

'Contextualism and Anti-Contextualism in the Philosophy of Language', in Savas Tsohatzidis (ed.), *Foundations of Speech Act Theory: Philosophical and Linguistic Perspectives* (Routledge, 1994), 156–66.

'Processing Models for Non-Literal Discourse', in Roberto Casati, Barry Smith and Graham White (eds.), *Philosophy and the Cognitive Sciences: Proceedings of the 16th International Wittgenstein Symposium* (Hölder-Pichler-Tempsky, 1994), 277–90.

'The Alleged Priority of Literal Interpretation', in *Cognitive Science* 19 (1995), 207–32.

'Domains of Discourse', in *Linguistics and Philosophy* 19 (1996), 445–75.

'La Polysémie Contre le Fixisme', in *Langue Française* 113 (1997), 107–23.

'The Dynamics of Situations', in *European Review of Philosophy* 2 (1997), 41–75.

'Pragmatics', in *The Routledge Encyclopedia of Philosophy* (Routledge, 1998), vol. 7, 620–33.

'Situations and the Structure of Content', in Kumiko Murasugi and Rob Stainton (eds.), *Philosophy and Linguistics* (Westview Press, 1999), 113–65.

Oratio Obliqua, Oratio Recta. An Essay on Metarepresentation (MIT Press, 2000).

'Déstabiliser le sens', in *Revue Internationale de Philosophie* 216 (2001), 197–208.

'What is Said', in *Synthèse* 128 (2001), 75–91.

'Literal/Nonliteral', in *Midwest Studies in Philosophy* 25 (2001), 264–74.

'Unarticulated Constituents', in *Linguistics and Philosophy* 25 (2002), 299–345.

'Does Linguistic Communication Rest on Inference?', in *Mind and Language* 17 (2002), 105–26.

'The Limits of Expressibility', in Barry Smith (ed.), *John Searle* (Cambridge University Press, forthcoming).

'Pragmatics and Semantics', in Larry Horn and Gregory Ward (eds.), *Handbook of Pragmatics* (Blackwell, forthcoming).

'Descriptions and Situations', in Marga Reimer and Anne Bezuidenhout (eds.), *Descriptions and Beyond: An Interdisciplinary Collection of Essays on Definite and Indefinite Descriptions and Other Related Phenomena* (Oxford University Press, forthcoming).

'Relativized Propositions', in Michael O'Rourke and Corey Washington (eds.), *Situating Semantics: Essays on the Philosophy of John Perry* (MIT Press, forthcoming).

Reichenbach, Hans, *Elements of Symbolic Logic* (Macmillan, 1947).

Reid, Thomas, *Essays on the Intellectual Powers of Man* (MIT Press, 1969).

Ross, James, *Portraying Analogy* (Cambridge University Press, 1981).

Ruhl, Charles, *On Monosemy: A Study in Linguistic Semantics* (State University of New York Press, 1989).

Rumelhart, David, 'Schemata: the Building Blocks of Cognition', in R. Spiro, B. Bruce and W. Brewer (eds.), *Theoretical Issues in Reading Comprehension* (Lawrence Erlbaum, 1980), 33–58.

'Some Problems with the Notion of Literal Meanings', in Andrew Ortony (ed.), *Metaphor and Thought* (2nd edn, Cambridge University Press, 1993), 71–82.

Rumelhart, David, Smolensky, Paul, McClelland, James, and Hinton, Geoffrey, 'Schemata and Sequential Thought Processes in PDP Models', in James McClelland and David Rumelhart (eds.), *Parallel Distributed Processing: Explorations in the Microstructure of Cognition*, vol. 2 (MIT Press, 1986), 7–57.

Rumfitt, Ian, 'Content and Context: The Paratactic Theory Revisited and Revised', in *Mind* 102 (1993), 429–53.

Sag, Ivan, 'Formal Semantics and Extralinguistic Context', in Peter Cole (ed.), *Radical Pragmatics* (Academic Press, 1981), 273–94.

Salmon, Nathan, 'The Pragmatic Fallacy', in *Philosophical Studies* 63 (1991), 83–97.

Sandford, Anthony and Garrod, Simon, 'The Role of Scenario Mapping in Text Comprehension', in *Discourse Processes* 26 (1998), 159–90.

Santambrogio, Marco, 'Translational Semantics', forthcoming.

Schwanenflugel, Paula (ed.), *The Psychology of Word Meanings* (Lawrence Erlbaum Associates, 1991).

Searle, John, *Speech Acts* (Cambridge University Press, 1969).

'Literal Meaning', in *Erkenntnis* 13 (1978), 207–24.

'The Background of Meaning', in John Searle, Ferenc Kiefer and Manfred Bierwisch (eds.), *Speech Act Theory and Pragmatics* (Reidel, 1980), 221–32.

Intentionality (Cambridge University Press, 1983).

The Rediscovery of the Mind (MIT Press, 1992).

Snyder, Aaron, 'On What Has Truth-Value', in *Philosophical Studies* 23 (1972), 131–4.

Soames, Scott, 'Incomplete Definite Descriptions', in *Notre Dame Journal of Formal Logic* 27 (1986), 349–75.

Beyond Rigidity: The Unfinished Semantic Agenda of 'Naming and Necessity' (Oxford University Press, 2002).

'Naming and Asserting', in Zoltán Szabó (ed.), *Semantics and Pragmatics* (Oxford University Press, forthcoming).

Sperber, Dan, 'How Do We Communicate?', in J. Brockman and K. Matson (eds.), *How Things Are: A Science Toolkit to the Mind* (Morrow, 1995), 191–9.

'Intuitive and Reflective Beliefs', in *Mind and Language* 12 (1997), 67–83.

Sperber, Dan and Wilson, Deirdre, *Relevance: Communication and Cognition* (Blackwell, 1986).

'Loose Talk', in *Proceedings of the Aristotelian Society* 86 (1986), 153–71.

'Précis of *Relevance: Communication and Cognition*', in *Behavioral and Brain Sciences* 10 (1987), 697–754.

'The Mapping Between the Mental and the Public Lexicon', in Peter Carruthers and Jill Boucher (eds.), *Language and Thought: Interdisciplinary Themes* (Cambridge University Press, 1998), 184–200.

Stalnaker, Robert, *Context and Content* (Oxford University Press, 1999).

Stanley, Jason, 'Context and Logical Form', in *Linguistics and Philosophy* 23 (2000), 391–434.

'Making it Articulated', in *Mind and Language* 17 (2002), 149–68.

'Modality and What is Said', forthcoming in *Philosophical Perspectives* 16.

Stanley, Jason and Szabó, Zoltán, 'On Quantifier Domain Restriction', in *Mind and Language* 15 (2000), 219–61.

Stanley, Jason and Williamson, Tim, 'Quantifiers and Context-Dependence', in *Analysis* 55 (1995), 291–5.

Strawson, Peter, *Introduction to Logical Theory* (Methuen, 1952).

Taylor, Ken, 'Sex, Breakfast, and Descriptus Interruptus', in *Synthèse* 128 (2001), 45–61.

Tesnière, Lucien, *Eléments de Syntaxe Structurale* (2nd edn, Klincksieck, 1969).

Thau, Michael, *Consciousness and Cognition* (Oxford University Press, 2002).

Travis, Charles, *Saying and Understanding* (Blackwell, 1975).

The True and the False: the Domain of the Pragmatic (Benjamins, 1981).

The Uses of Sense: Wittgenstein's Philosophy of Language (Clarendon Press, 1989).

Unshadowed Thought (Harvard University Press, 2000).

Tversky, Amos, 'Features of Similarity', in *Psychological Review* 84 (1977), 327–52.

Victorri, Bernard and Fuchs, Catherine, *La Polysémie* (Hermès, 1996).

Waismann, Friedrich, 'Verifiability', in Anthony Flew (ed.), *Logic and Language*, 1st series (Blackwell, 1951), 117–44.

Walton, Kendall, *Mimesis as Make-Believe* (Harvard University Press, 1990).

Wilson, Deirdre and Sperber, Dan, 'Truthfulness and Relevance', in *Mind* 111 (2002), 583–632.

Ziff, Paul, 'What is Said', in Donald Davidson and Gilbert Harman (eds.), *Semantics of Natural Language* (Reidel, 1972), 709–21.

Index

7296   57